2001: A Faith O

Jack Shaw

2001 a faith odyssey

Jack Shaw

The Hallamshire Press
2000

For our grandchildren — hope for the future

©2000 Jack Shaw

Published by The Hallamshire Press Limited
Broom Hall
Sheffield S10 2DR
England

Typeset by The Hallamshire Press Limited
Printed in Great Britain by Cromwell Press, Wiltshire

All rights reserved. No part of this publication may be reproduced, stored in a retrieval system, or transmitted, in any form or by any means, electronic, mechanical, photocopying, recording or otherwise, without the prior permission in writing of the publishers.

British Library Cataloguing in Publication Data:
   A catalogue record for this book is available from the British Library.

ISBN 1 874718 39 3

Contents

	Foreword	7
	Acknowledgements	8
	Introduction	9
1	Persecution and Apologies	13
2	Royal Approval	37
3	Monastics	51
4	Shaking the Foundations	69
5	Christianity in Britain	77
6	The Rise of Islam	85
7	Worlds Collide	95
8	Teachers, Preachers and Builders	107
9	Crusades	119
10	Dramas in Europe	135
11	Renaissance and Reformation	145
12	Counter Reformation	179

13	Royals and Puritans	187
14	Awakening	207
15	Social Gospel	217
16	Seeds of Doubt	239
17	Sects	253
18	The World at War	261
19	Postscript	299
	Appendix	301
	Index	303

Foreword

Jack Shaw needs no introduction to the people of South Yorkshire, least of all by a Lancastrian import, albeit of the same name! Yet, he does deserve a wider audience. This book proves what many of us know already, that in Jack Shaw there is more than meets the eye. Beneath the friendly, yet perceptive, radio presenter and interviewer is a treasury of accumulated knowledge covering two thousand years. In this book Jack shares with us the story of a vast living tradition of witnesses to what the millennium celebrations are all about—Jesus Christ. Here is a Christian book of memories produced at a time when the World needs desperately to be reminded of that which it has forgotten. Here is the story out of which we Christians come and if we do not know our story then we are in grave danger of forgetting who we are.

As one would expect, the book is eminently readable, it is simple yet profound, with not a few smiles to help us on our journey. This book is fascinating, a real treasure. Jack, you have done us proud—thank you.

The Bishop of Sheffield
The Rt Reverend Jack Nicholls

Acknowledgements

I have always believed that people understand the greatness of biblical characters when their lives are described in context and considered in the light and milieu of their own times. Hence the reason for the overview of the Bible contained in my book, *Through the Bible in Eighty Days*. In this book I have gone for an overview again, this time looking back at 2000 years of the Christian era. I hope it will prove to be a useful tool for those seeking to make some sense of past millennia.

Once again the Hallamshire Press have helped me enormously with the project and I am very grateful to them for their skill. I would like to thank Pauline Climpson especially who encouraged me through the 'Dark Ages'. Paul Rowland has again livened a few pages with his drawings for which I warmly thank him, while my wife has been very understanding when I disappeared into the study for long periods. Bishop Jack could not have been kinder in his Foreword and I thank him sincerely for that.

Introduction

That fine Methodist preacher William Sangster told a story of a missionary who discovered moon worshippers living on an island in the South Seas. He thought moon worshippers had disappeared in the time of Abraham. He found out that these islanders worshipped the moon because it shed light in the darkness when it was needed, unlike the silly sun, which shone during the daytime when there was plenty of daylight! Sangster used that story to point out that there are people living today who live in the light of Christianity without ever realising where that light comes from. Even Christians, who believe in the Bible as the word of God, can be very sketchy about secondary chapters of God's story written within the Church. For, make no mistake about it, the faith Christians accept in modern times has been greatly shaped by decisions and experiences of Christians over the past 2000 years. Faith has not reached us ready packed. There is a definite ancestry in Christianity, which we should know something about, just like any good citizen would want to know something about the origins and history of his own nation. The life of Jesus may have been short, his people politically unimportant, he may never have written a book or worked out a systematic body of teaching, yet no other life lived on this planet has affected the affairs of the world so profoundly. Over the years that life has been talked about, argued about and fought about so much, that it must be very doubtful if Jesus would recognise himself in the rituals and practices that have grown up to celebrate his life. So I invite you to join me on a journey through two millennia, where we will trace how a few years lived out in Galilee and Judah led to a powerful set of convictions, which changed the shape of the world *and still does*.

We will be dealing with the lives of people who lived and died for their beliefs because they mattered to them more than anything else in the world. We will also consider how those beliefs were arrived at. Today belief in a God of Trinity is commonplace in Christian churches, as is the belief that Jesus had something divine about him as well as human. Yet all the early heresies in Christianity were disputes about these things and were of vital importance to believers. In the fourth century, Gregory of Nyssa, one of the church fathers, complained that he could not go anywhere in Constantinople without tradespeople engaging him in debates about the Trinity. He wrote, 'If you ask for change, someone philosophises to you on the Begotten and the Unbegotten. If you ask the price of bread, you are told, "The Father is Greater, and the Son is inferior". If you ask, "Is the bath ready?" someone answers, "The Son was created from nothing".' When people die for a faith it is clearly important to know what that faith was.

The New Testament ends abruptly. Paul, the intrepid Jewish missionary, is imprisoned in Rome and the hostility of the Roman Empire is building up against both Jews and Christians. A truce between Jews and the sect of Christianity is weakening and some Gentile Christians have broken with the mother faith completely, despite earlier compromises worked out by Paul and Jesus' brother James. The hub of Christianity quickly moved away from Jerusalem to influential areas of Greek culture like Antioch, Ephesus and Rome, leaving the distinctive Jewishness of the new faith to fade. The Jewish Messiah was gradually weaned away from his Jewish womb. Most of the early apostles, the eye witnesses and contemporaries of Jesus were dead and only a few ageing patriarchs remained. The end of the age, which some had expected, had not come, the Messiah had not returned and the Roman Empire continued to hold complete control of the Mediterranean region and beyond.

In this 'new age', Jews and Christians began to reorganise. Jews had endured the destruction of Jerusalem, their capital city, yet again, and the sacrificial system had been abolished. This time it would never be restored. Some Jews were sent to the mines of Egypt and others to Rome, where they worked on building the Colosseum. Emperor Vespasian and his son Titus led a great procession through the streets of Rome, parading Jewish loot stripped from the Temple. The great Arch of Titus clearly shows the golden seven-branched candlestick being pillaged by soldiers. For Jews the destruction of the Temple was sheer catastrophe. The cessation of sacrifices meant Jewish people had lost the spiritual focus they had previously maintained even in the dark days of Babylonian exile. The Sadducees, the hereditary priests, were out of a job. There were further attempts to win back political independence, notably in AD 132 when Simeon bar Kokhba, aided by Rabbi Akiva, resisted Emperor

Hadrian's Greek liberalisation programme (Hellenization) but after three years Simeon was killed in battle and Rabbi Akiva was captured and flayed alive. Jews were forbidden to set foot inside the ruins of Jerusalem and the new Roman city of Aeolia Capitolina was built on the site. In Judea, for three years, even the practice of Judaism was outlawed as part of terrifying Roman vengeance. 985 towns and villages were destroyed and the Roman historian Dio Cassius reported that 580,000 Jews died in the fighting and others from starvation and fire. A Bethlehem tradition said there were so many Jewish slaves on the market the price dropped to less than that of a horse.

But Christianity thrived and soon groups of believers were on every shore of the Eastern Mediterranean. Soon converted soldiers were taking the story of Jesus to the misty island of Britain where, as W.H. Auden suggests in his poem *Over The Heather the Wet Wind Blows*, the secret fish sign was being discussed by troops on Hadrian's Wall:

> *Piso's a Christian he worships a fish;*
> *There'd be no kissing if he had his wish.*

Torn away from the mother faith of Judaism, bereft of the charismatic leadership of the early apostles, the Christian believers were cast adrift in a hostile world. How they organised themselves, regulated their beliefs, struggled against tyrants, dissension and the rise of new faiths, is the history of the Christian era. It is both tremendously inspiring and dreadfully disappointing, with stories of incredible achievement and stories that chill the heart, for, like the Bible story itself, it is the saga of the sons and daughters of Adam, always aspiring to heaven and yet firmly rooted to earth.

This book is a sequel to *Through the Bible in Eighty Days* and uses the same format. Selecting prominent people from various historical periods it seeks to show how the flame of faith was passed on from generation to generation. Sometimes the flame burned brightly and New Jerusalem seemed but a whisker away. At other times faith was engulfed in monstrous tyranny and unspeakable crime when the streets ran red with the blood of martyrs and the skies were black with the despair of unanswered prayers. Like all history, *2001: A Faith Odyssey* is selective and other people might have chosen other subjects. This selection charts us through a bewildering 2000 years. Years shaped by the suffering of the Jews, the rise of Islam, the scepticism of the modern age and, most of all, by the haunting legacy of Jesus of Nazareth, for something amazing happened years ago, which released incredible power into the world. The tremors are still very much with us today.

Main Christian Streams

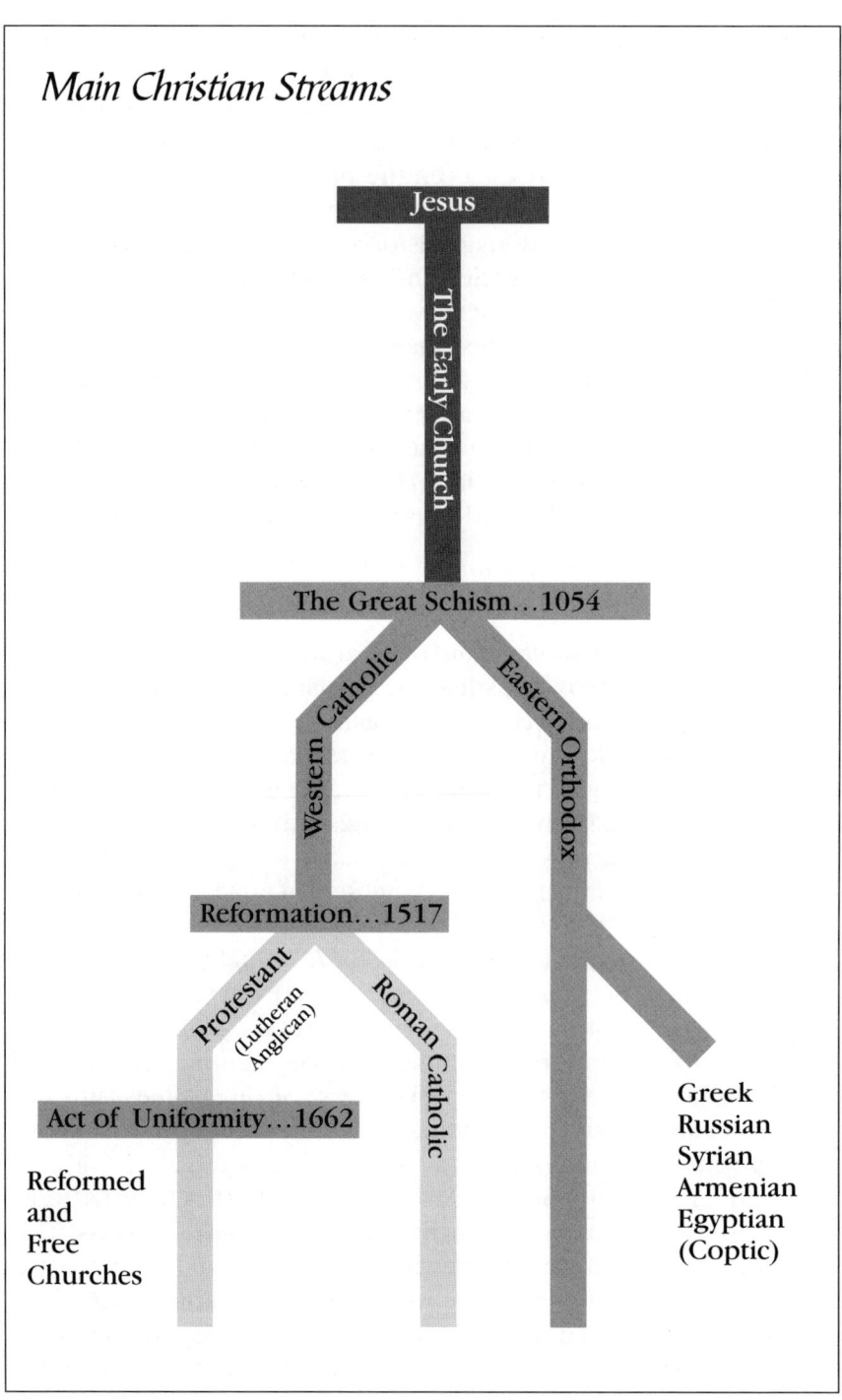

1 Persecution and Apologies

Ignatius of Antioch	17
Polycarp	18
Justin Martyr	19
Martyrs of Gaul	21
Irenaeus	22
Martyrs of Africa	23
Tertullian	25
Canons and Creeds	27
Cyprian and the Decian Persecution	27
Origen of Alexandria	30
The Great Persecution	33
Effects of Persecution	35

The beginnings of Christianity corresponded with great changes in the Roman Empire. All semblance of Roman democracy disappeared as power steadily moved into the hands of fewer people. After the assassination of Julius Caesar and the ensuing civil war, it rested almost solely with the emperor who was given all the attributes of divinity. An inscription from the Forum at Ephesus speaks of Octavius as 'divine Augustus'.

Jewish sages, banished from Jerusalem after the Bar Kokhba revolt, moved to Javneh on the coast and later to Galilee where they wrestled with plans for the future of Judaism. Scholars and students from near and far joined in the gatherings which organised regular Jewish prayer and regulated rabbinical ordination. They also made historic decisions about the Old Testament books, which were to be defined as holy writ.

Meanwhile, the Jewish sect of Christianity spread its wings claiming to be the true Israel fulfilling all Jewish hopes. Once Jesus had said of the Jewish Pharisees 'they cross land and sea to make one convert' and now Christians were doing the same but making thousands of converts. The fledgling faith was on a collision course with Judaism despite the fact that all the first Christians were died in the wool Jews. Occasional dialogue was conducted without rancour but by the end of the first century Christians had firmly placed the blame for the death of Jesus at the door of the Jews and a split became a chasm. The seeds of anti-Semitism were sown.

At this juncture, as far as Rome was concerned, there was no difference between Jews and Christians and both were persecuted with vigour. *Revelation*, the last and most abused book of the New Testament, makes it clear that Christians were soon subjects treated with suspicion and cruelty by the authorities. The book addresses, in cryptic language, the break out of persecution amongst the new churches of Asia where deification of the emperor expressed itself in the most extreme form. Sporadic outbursts against the Christians could break out anywhere, and the Roman historian Tacitus suggests that Emperor Nero, in Hitler-like style, blamed them for a disastrous fire which swept through Rome in AD 64:

> *To kill the rumours, Nero charged and tortured some people hated for their evil practices—the group popularly known as Christians… hundreds were convicted, more for their antisocial beliefs than for fire raising. In their deaths they were made a mockery. They were covered in the skins of wild animals, torn to death by dogs, crucified or set on fire…although they were guilty of being Christians and*

deserved death, people began to feel sorry for them. They realised that they were being massacred, not for the public good, but to satisfy one man's mania.
(Tacitus, *Annals*, 15.44)

Films like *Quo Vardis* have depicted Nero as the terrorising megalomaniac who threw Christians to the lions in the Colosseum, but in fact that great amphitheatre was not opened until AD 80. This theatre, one of the great sights of Rome to this day, took eight years to build, stands 165 feet high and rises in magnificent tiers capable of accommodating 50,000 spectators. On special occasions an immense awning was stretched over the vast oval to protect spectators from the sun. Such consideration did not extend to the gladiators who put their lives on the line every time they battled in the arena. The fate of combatants was determined by thumbs from the crowd. Up was life, down was death! Gladiators greeted the emperor with the cry, 'Hail Caesar! Those about to die salute you'. Christians were usually

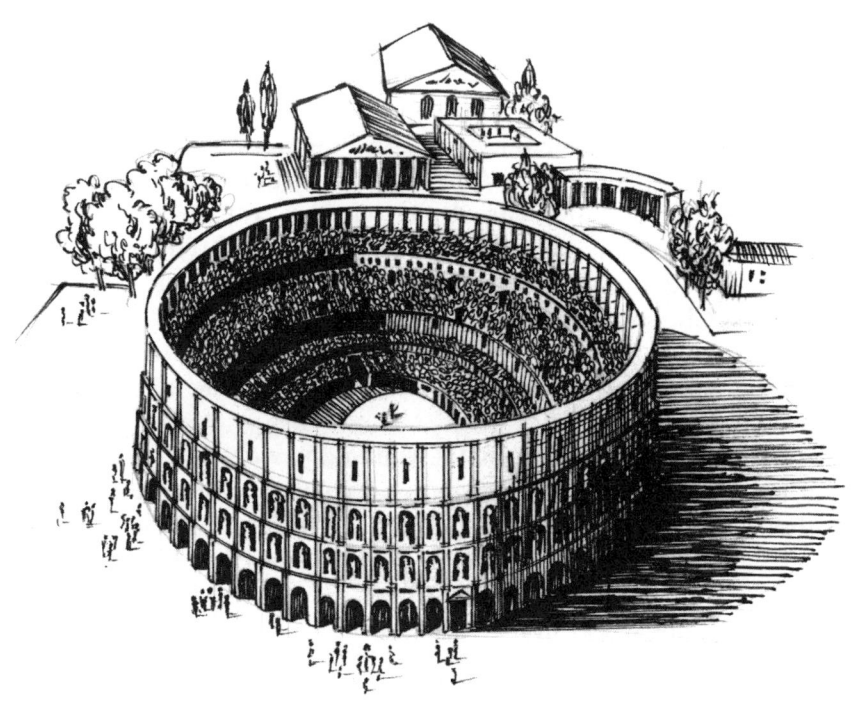

The Colosseum…one of the great sights of Rome to this day.

involved in *venationes*—fights against wild beasts. These beasts entered the arena from cages below ground and were hoisted on lifts and goaded into action. Other spectacles included mock naval battles when the huge oval was flooded for the event. Close by was the Circus Maximus used for the chariot races and capable of holding 250,000 spectators as depicted memorably in the film *Ben Hur*.

In the circus atmosphere early Christians paid for faith with their lives. Some emperors, desperate to hold on to power, provided ever more extravagant shows to satisfy the increasing lust for blood. Theatres all over the empire, from Jerash in Jordan to El Djem in Tunisia, were built to accommodate the mixture of drama, music, athletics and the deadly mayhem of blood-sports. Yet the faster the blood flowed the faster Christianity grew. 'The blood of the martyrs is the seed of the church', wrote Tertullian in his *Apology*, and so it seemed.

Trajan (AD 98–117) was one of the more enlightened emperors and the first after Augustus to extend the empire when he conquered Dacia (modern Romania). He was respected and acknowledged as 'a good man'. It was during his reign that a young governor of Bithynia called Pliny wrote to the emperor for advice on how to deal with people accused of being Christians, who were widely spread and attracting great numbers of adherents of all ages and ranks. The temples of the gods were virtually deserted and there was no demand for sacrificial animals. His practice was to ask those accused to deny such belief, warning them of dire consequences if they refused. He asked them three times and if they would not deny the new faith they were executed or, if they were Roman citizens, as Paul had been, they were sent to Rome to be judged. Pliny was perturbed that some were being accused anonymously. He also added that he had discovered that these Christians met on a fixed day of the week and sang hymns to Christ as though to a god and then pledged themselves to abstain from theft, robbery, adultery and vowed not to break faith. They also shared a simple meal.

Trajan's reply was diplomatic. Christians were not to be sought out and anonymous accusations were to be ignored. Nevertheless, if they were accused and convicted then they had to be punished. So, clearly, Christianity was a crime in itself even though Trajan discouraged systematic persecution. What it did do, of course, was leave Christians susceptible to accusations from people with a grudge and that probably included priests of the old religions and all those whose livelihoods were being threatened.

Ignatius of Antioch

Ignatius was one Christian leader to die in this period—sometime between AD 110–115. His problems began when he was accused by some citizens of Antioch of having caused an earthquake! The Emperor Trajan was in Antioch and when Ignatius boldly confessed his faith Trajan sentenced him to be thrown to the lions in the Colosseum at Rome.

The journey to Rome exposed Ignatius to full view and overnight he was transformed from a local leader to a full-blown Christian hero. His journey, part by land and part by sea, demonstrated the remarkable communication system developed by the early Jesus communities. Seven letters written by Ignatius on his way to martyrdom are now widely accepted as authentic. These were to the churches in Ephesus, Magnesia, Tralles, Rome, Philadelphia and Smyrna, with a personal one to Polycarp, the bishop of Smyrna, whose name was destined to pass into posterity later. The letters do show signs of hurry and perhaps the stress of being chained but they are full of vigour and zeal for the faith. They are thrilling documents which portray a man taking on the vast machinery of imperial power armed only with faith but they also tell of the way in which centres of the church, not only communicated with each other but, when the chips were down, risked their own lives to encourage their brother.

The stress in the letters of Ignatius is for Christian unity and, as bishop of one of the most influential churches of these earliest days and acquainted with the apostles, his influence was probably considerable. He talks of bishops, presbyters and deacons not as offices, which need explaining, but as established positions already in the church. It is in his letters that the expression 'catholic church' is first used. He emphasises church officers and practices like the Eucharist because he is anxious for the believers to be united in faith. His letters are shot through with allusions to Paul's letters and to John's Gospel but the style is all his own and in his letter to Rome he pleads with the church not to attempt to save his life. He is on fire for martyrdom and like God's wheat he is about to be 'ground by the teeth of wild beasts that I may be found pure bread'.

Along his route to death Christians travelled to meet him until finally he reached Rome and embraced the martyrdom he desired. Little else is known about the life of Ignatius but there is enough in these letters to reveal a man of enormous courage, a generous heart and remarkable faith. His life reminds us of all those others who died and have no known memorial.

Polycarp (c. 70–156)

One of the seven letters of Ignatius was a personal letter to Polycarp the bishop of Smyrna (present day Izmir). He was a respected, even venerated leader, whose Christian roots stretched back to the apostles and it is quite likely that he had known John, the beloved disciple of Jesus. On his way to martyrdom Ignatius was concerned for the church he had been snatched away from and exhorted Polycarp to organise envoys to be sent to Antioch to encourage the fellowship there and he also encouraged Polycarp himself to be strong and courageous in the faith. In his old age it was a courage which would be tested to the full.

Copies of the letters of Ignatius were sent around the churches and accompanying those sent to Philippi was a personal letter from Polycarp. It is full of references and quotes from the New Testament and while encouraging the Philippians to faithfulness, he reminds them of the special love the Apostle Paul had for them. He specifically warns the church of the sin of covetousness and laments the fall of a presbyter called Valens who, along with his wife, had succumbed to that particular vice. Polycarp was keen to settle a difference between the churches of East and West who celebrated Easter on different dates. He travelled to Rome to meet bishop Anicetus and though they failed to agree (indeed to this day there is no agreement) they parted good friends and Polycarp was invited to celebrate the Lord's Supper with the Roman church before he departed for home.

About AD 155 persecution broke out in Smyrna and eleven Christians were tortured and thrown to wild beasts. The Procurator, Stratus Quadratus, seems to have invited those accused of being Christians to save their lives by renouncing their faith in Christ and offering incense to the emperor. One man, a Phrygian called Quintus, did renounce the faith and soon the mob were clamouring that this man's place should be taken by the aged Polycarp. He had been persuaded to hide but he was soon found and taken to the arena. The Proconsul sought ways to release the old man but the eye-witness account says he was shouted down by the vehemence of heathens and Jews, who demanded that he should be executed. Clearly the animosity between Jews and Christians had not abated and when he was asked to revile Christ his answer sealed his fate—'Eighty and six years have I served Him and He has never wronged me, so how can I blaspheme my King and Saviour'.

Polycarp had confessed his faith and was tied to a stake to be burnt alive. The record says the fire was slow to kindle and he was eventually stabbed to death and his body burnt. When all was over, friends gathered his charred bones and buried them, celebrating the day of his martyrdom as his true birthday.

Justin Martyr (c. 100–165)

Sporadic persecution continued throughout the reigns of Hadrian and Antoninus Pius, who were both enlightened men in their own way. Hadrian was one of the most cultured scholars of his day with knowledge from every branch of learning. He travelled widely and no part of the empire was unknown to him. His greatest memorials are in Britain, where he built the great wall from Carlisle to Newcastle in an attempt to keep the Scots in Scotland, and in Rome, where his great mausoleum was converted into a fortress in the Middle Ages and is now known as the Castle of San Angelo. We know little of Antoninus Pius apart from his virtues for he was widely respected as a leader who studied peace, was charitable and lived a quiet life, free from ostentation in his country home in Etruria. He was the kind of man Christians felt they could do business with and appeals were made to him on behalf of the Christians. Some of these appeals, or Apologies as they were known, are still extant and are fascinating insights into the way Christian leaders were articulating their faith and how the early Christians met to conduct their worship. Apologists turned to the hostile world outside the church and tried to explain to the powerful within the empire what the Christian belief was. They were intelligent men who took on the pagan world and out thought the sophisticated and learned men of the day and, in the process, prevented Christianity from becoming just another mystery religion amongst many others. They carved out a unique position quite distinct from Judaism and related their belief to the wider world of Greek philosophy.

One Apology addressed to Antoninus was from a man called Justin. He was Greek, though born in Palestine, and from early years pursued a study of philosophy. He was familiar with the philosophical schools of his day and read Aristotle, the Stoics, Pythagoras and Plato but he was won for Christianity when an old man directed him towards the Hebrew prophets and to Jesus Christ. It was as a Christian teacher that he travelled as a mature man and ultimately made his way to Rome where he addressed his Apology to the emperor and his family. He wrote on behalf of those 'who are unjustly hated'.

Justin is at pains to deny charges of atheism, immorality and disloyalty to the emperor and stressed the strong morality of Christians in contrast to that of others. He also explains Christian beliefs and worship, which were being grossly misinterpreted by an ignorant populace. He even stresses that the Word or Spirit, which came to life in Christ, had previously been at work in people like Socrates who could be described as a Christian before Christ. His description of early Christian gatherings is most interesting. On the so-called day of the Sun (because it was the first day of creation, the day of light and because on it the Saviour rose from the dead) the Christians assemble:

> *At the end of the prayers, we greet one another with a kiss. Then the president of the bretheren is brought bread and a cup of wine mixed with water; and he takes them and offers up praise and glory to the Father of the universe, through the name of the Son and the Holy Spirit... When he has concluded the prayers and thanksgivings all the people express their joyful assent by saying Amen. ('Amen' means 'so be it' in Hebrew). Then those whom we call deacons give to each of those present the bread and wine and carry away a portion to those who are absent.*

Justin's Apology doesn't seem to have had much effect because he later directed another shorter Apology to the Roman Senate. In this letter he speaks of plots made against him personally by a Cynic philosopher called Crescens who was a bitter enemy of the Christians. There is also an account of a dialogue he had with a Jewish rabbi called Trypho, that indicates clearly the way Christians were using the Old Testament to show how it had been fulfilled in the life of Jesus. Understandably, the two of them disagreed but the debate was conducted with courtesy by both men. Obviously, hostility between Christians and Jews was not inevitable.

Despite the reasoned faith of Justin, sometime between AD 163–167 his ministry was dramatically cut short by a prefect called Rusticus, who ordered that Justin and six others should be put to death by beheading. Justin was added to the growing list of those who made the ultimate sacrifice for their faith. The word 'Martyr' became his surname.

Martyrs of Gaul

The great philosopher Plato once said, 'The world will not be right until philosophers are kings and kings philosophers'. That belief was about to be put on trial when the adopted son of Antoninus Pius put on the purple. His name was Marcus Aurelius and in him all the wisdom and virtue of the ancient world seemed to converge. He was a Stoic, disciplined and yet benevolent, ascetic in life-style and diligent in his pursuit of truth. His book of *Meditations*, written down like a diary, often from within his tent during his travels and campaigns, reveals high and noble thoughts but also the kind of high brow snobbishness one might associate with a public school boy incapable of seeing the world through any eyes other than those of the very privileged. His few references to Christianity only indicate contempt. There were Christians with a philosophical flair who sought the sympathy of Marcus Aurelius, notably Mileto, bishop of Sardis, Apollinarius, bishop of Hieropolis and an Athenian called Athenagoras who argued that the good lives of the Christians should strike a chord with the noble emperor and 'make you bend your royal head in approval'.

The royal head did not bend in approval and later events in Southern Gaul were so dreadful that the name of Marcus Aurelius has been forever tarnished by the blood-letting that took place in the prosperous French towns of Lyons and Vienne. The year 177 saw a number of Christians abused by thugs. Rather than offer support, the chief magistrate turned his venom on the Christians and soon the church was enduring full scale persecution. Many were tortured in attempts to make them renounce their faith and while some succumbed, most stubbornly resisted the trials. Slaves of the Christians were also tortured and made accusations against their masters, which was quite illegal, but which roused the mobs to greater fury.

Letters written by the churches of Lyons and Vienne to churches in Asia and Phrygia, recount how many died in prison through ill treatment. Among them was a venerated old bishop called Pothinus who was ninety years of age. Like Polycarp before him, 'his life was preserved that Christ might triumph through it'. Those that survived the prison ordeal were finally offered as sport in the amphitheatre in a carnival of violence where they were burned or torn apart by wild animals. Some of those who perished are known by name; Sanctus a deacon, Attalus an eminent Roman citizen, Alexander a physician and Ponticus a boy of fifteen. Most notably, there was a slave-girl called Blandina who was tortured so severely that even her tormentors were amazed by her resilience and her constant response to their cruelty with the words, 'I am a Christian, and there is nothing vile done by us'. After unspeakable suffering she was finally enclosed in a net and gored to death by a bull.

Even after death the martyrs were not left alone, for their bodies were burned and their ashes thrown into the Rhone lest their bodies should attain the resurrection they longed for. Perhaps no persecution in the earliest days of the church illustrated more clearly the incredible courage, forbearance and self-sacrifice than those of the Christians from Lyons and Vienne.

Irenaeus (c. 140–211)

The man to succeed the venerable Pothinus as bishop of Lyons was Irenaeus. He had studied under Polycarp of Smyrna, another venerated old man of the church, and he proved to be a strong link between the churches of East and West, which were tending to develop separately. Outlines of Christian belief were being included in the Apologies, many directed to the emperor himself. Irenaeus is one of the first writers to spell out a definite Rule of Faith, passed on, it was claimed, via the apostles. It was belief in one God, the Father Almighty, who had created all things, and in Jesus Christ, the Son of God, who became man for our salvation; and in the Holy Spirit who had made known through prophets of old the plan of salvation and foretold the coming of Christ and his birth from a virgin, his death and resurrection and ascension into heaven. Such statements were not established creeds in the sense that they were fixed and immutable. They were rather beliefs expressed to counteract claims, which strayed from things held in common since apostolic days. The Rule of Irenaeus was probably the first attempt at systematic Christian doctrine and it was forged not in the academics study but in hot disputes with heretics. His concepts of salvation go beyond anything mentioned specifically in Scripture but they are presented as interpretations of Scripture.

Much of Irenaeus' energy went into arguing against a rising heresy called *gnosticism*, which claimed a specially revealed knowledge given to a few. There were different branches of Gnosticism but all of them regarded the material creation as evil and inferior and this to Irenaeus, was a fundamental misunderstanding of Christianity. We will return to Gnosticism later but two major works of Irenaeus directed to this heresy survive. They are *Against Heresies* and *Proof of the Apostolic Preaching*. He is at pains to point out that Christianity is a fulfilment of the Old Testament, which knows nothing of special knowledge reserved for a few. Nor does it know anything of an inferior god who created the world. The world was created by Almighty God and the incarnation of Jesus was necessary to offer a new beginning to the human race. The church was scattered throughout the world, but the faith was still that received from the apostles, namely faith in One God, the Creator, in one Jesus Christ who died for our salvation, and in the Holy Spirit who has always been at work in the world.

Irenaeus maintained that truth in the church had been passed down from the apostles and the key to interpreting Scripture had to be in the church. It was not a lifeless tradition but a precious deposit in an excellent vessel, which constantly replenished itself, changing and forever new. He also thought that the Eucharist or Communion contained an earthly and a divine reality, which lifted it above the merely symbolic. His theology developed the idea of Jesus being like a second Adam who sanctified the whole of life previously tainted by Adam's sin. In this explanation the Virgin Mary becomes a new kind of Eve. Irenaeus' idea of Christ's work reversing the disobedience of Adam became standard Christian theology in the Eastern and Western Churches for ages to come. He set the base line for all subsequent orthodox theology and not until the Reformation was his work considered to be at all controversial. It can also be claimed that Irenaeus gave Christianity a distinct Greek colouring as the influence of Jews inside the church disappeared.

Irenaeus lived until the beginning of the third century before he too was added to the growing list of martyrs.

Martyrs of Africa

It often comes as a surprise to learn that in the early days of the church some of the most inspiring Christian lives and the greatest Christian thinkers came from Africa. The Roman Empire extended into present day Tunisia, Algeria and Morocco and Africa was a rich province blessed with great cities like Carthage which, after the devastation of the Punic Wars, had been restored by Julius Caesar. The fields of North Africa supplied Rome with most of its corn and in turn Africa received all the benefits of Rome's organised civilisation. But Roman religion had never won the hearts of Africans and when the seeds of Christianity were sown there in the first century by persons unknown, the harvest was rich and plentiful. It was a brand of Christianity unlike any other, passionate, emotional and uncompromising. It flowered briefly in the heady days of early growth producing some remarkable figures and adding many to the list of martyrs.

In 181, during the reign of Commodus, the son of Marcus Aurelius, there were several attacks on the African church. Twelve martyrs from the town of Scilla included three women who were all taken to Carthage and beheaded. Their testimony was preserved—'We render honour to Caesar as Caesar but worship and prayer to God alone'. Twenty years later, the Emperor Severus turned his wrath in their direction and forbade all conversions to Christianity and Judaism. From then on the church was subject to more outbursts of violence, Irenaeus was murdered as was Leonides, the father of the great scholar Origen who was only saved from following his father by his distraught mother. But it was Africa which suffered most. On March 7th 202, several Carthaginians were arrested, including two young women called Perpetua and Felicitas. They were locked in a dark, fetid cell and the suffering of Perpetua was particularly poignant because she had only recently given birth to a son and for a period fed the child in the prison. Her father begged her to obey the authorities and renounce her Christianity if only for the sake of the child but she told him she could not be called anything other than what she was—a Christian. Her testimony reads:

> *Hilarianus the governor said to me, 'Have pity on your father's grey head, have pity on your infant son. Offer the sacrifice for the welfare of the emperors'.*
> *'I will not', I retorted.*
> *'Are you a Christian?' asked Hilarianus.*
> *'Yes I am', I replied.*
> *Then sentence was passed on all of us, we were condemned to the beasts and we returned to the prison in high spirits.*

Perpetua was killed in the arena, dispatched with a sword after being tossed by a wild cow. Much of our information for the African martyrs we owe to Tertullian, to whom we now turn.

Tertullian (c. 160–215)

Tertullian was born in Carthage about the year 160. The son of a Roman centurion, he studied law and for a while practised his profession in Rome. In the capital he was converted to Christianity and shortly afterwards, about 192, he returned to Carthage, married and became a presbyter in the church there.

He was an original thinker and a quite brilliant writer, the first important Christian to use Latin, his work bristled with wit, satire and enormous vigour. He loved a fight and was called 'the fierce Tertullian'. He used his writing skills to defend the Christians and an Apology, addressed to the Proconsul of Africa, pleaded passionately for justice to be given them because they were people of high morals who were also loyal citizens who prayed regularly for the emperor and for the empire. Tertullian no doubt felt obliged to emphasise the loyalty of Christians to the emperor because the church was spreading so rapidly it could have been seen as an empire within an empire. Even so, he could not resist a jibe and pointed out that the reason for their success was because the soul is by nature Christian and cannot be repressed. 'We are but of yesterday', he claims, 'and we have filled all that you possess. Only the temples we have left you'. Attempting to stop the onward rush of faith is like trying to stop the sea, 'the more you mow us down the fuller is the harvest; the blood of the martyrs is seed'. Tertullian used his preaching gifts to express his belief in imaginative ways:

> *When a ray is projected from the sun it is a portion of the whole sun; so from the spirit comes spirit and God from God as light is kindled from light…This ray of God glided down into a virgin…is born as a man mixed with God. The flesh was built up by the spirit, was nourished, grew up, spoke, taught, worked, and was Christ.*
> **(Apology, XXI)**

In his work *On the Claims of Heretics*, Tertullian is at pains to take on those who distort Scripture to support heresy. Scripture belongs to the church he says because it has come from God and been passed down through the apostles. 'Is it likely', he asks, 'that all the churches worldwide would have gone astray into the same faith?' Error produces diversity not unity. Tertullian's argument has validity even today for, despite church divisions, the fundamentals of Christianity remain remarkably constant through the ages.

However, there were differences of thought within the church and Tertullian was not happy with the way some Apologists were stressing the philosophy of Greece at the expense of Jewish ideas in the Old Testament. In Alexandria a man called Clement (c. 150–211) was teaching Christianity in such a way that it wove Christianity into the Greek culture of the day. He was a master of ancient literature, which he quoted profusely in his writing. Clement was a prototype of the liberally minded Christian who wants to present the faith in such a way that it accommodates fellow academics. Truth was God's truth wherever it came from. He saw the best of Greek philosophy in Socrates and Plato and thought of them as schoolmasters bringing Greeks to Christ. He calls Plato, 'Moses talking Greek'. He was continuing the example of Irenaeus and there is no doubt such writing did much to help in the fight for acceptability. Tertullian was not always happy with this approach and asked on one occasion, 'What has Athens to do with Jerusalem?' He could speak on occasion as if he believed that philosophy was the *cause* of heresy in the church. If Clement and his followers in the East (especially his pupil Origen) looked for correlation between speculation and revelation, Tertullian needed little more than biblical revelation to guide him into saving truth.

Thirty-six of Tertullian's treatises have survived to reveal his profound knowledge of Greek and Latin and of pagan and Christian writers. One of the first to take on the challenge of confronting the pagan thinkers of the day, he did much to establish Christianity as a rational religion quite able to satisfy academics and confound cynics. His later work tends to be more censorious and he criticises the baptising of infants, which was becoming popular. He is also concerned about lax discipline, remarriage and the desire to flee from persecution. His own mercurial temperament led him latterly into the arms of the ascetic Montanist sect, whose meetings were highly charged with emotion and contained visions and speaking in tongues. The sect was named after an enthusiastic young Asian from Phrygia called Montanus, who proclaimed the imminent return of Christ and encouraged believers to welcome martyrdom. The fanatical aspects of Montanism appealed to the passionate nature of the fierce Tertullian who was well aware of his own frailties, 'Most wretched I am, ever sick with the heat of impatience'.

It is an irony that this great advocate of Christian orthodoxy, who pleaded so eloquently for church unity, should himself be led into a sectarian cul de sac. Nevertheless, this zealous champion of Christianity deeply influenced all later Christian thinkers, not least when he picked up on the teaching of Irenaeus, that mankind is by nature sinful, in a state of hereditary corruption dating back to Adam. This condition could only be overcome by divine grace, a force so potent it seeps into a person bringing spiritual conversion. Tertullian's exposition of the Trinity and of the humanity and deity of Christ is so precise that it is not an exaggeration to say that he had the doctrines worked out years before the rest of the church settled them at the Council of Nicaea in 325.

Canons and Creeds

At this juncture it is wise to remind ourselves that during the second and third centuries *exact belief and a definitive Bible* were still unfixed. There was an Apostles' Creed underlining belief in God as creator, outlining the salient features of Christ's life, death and resurrection and affirming belief in the Holy Spirit, the Church, communion of saints, forgiveness of sins and everlasting life. There was also a collection of favourite gospels, letters and homilies providing an appendix to the Hebrew Scriptures. But the final form of the New Testament was not fixed and some writings like *Shepherd of Hermas*, *Didache* and the *Epistle of Barnabus* were probably more read than say, *Hebrews* or *Revelation*. Creed and Bible both developed out of thought and experience and neither came to the church ready made or set on tablets of stone.

Cyprian *(c. 200–258) and the Decian Persecution*

Persecution was not a consistent policy of Rome but the threat of it was always in the wings and Christians had to live with uncertainty. This uncertainty was exacerbated during the third century by a succession of unpredictable military adventurers who clawed their way to the throne. One emperor called Heliogabulus (218–222) was a priest of a Syrian sun god who had a morbid obsession with suicide and collected an array of implements for self-destruction. He never had time to put any of them to the test because he was murdered without ceremony by a member of his own guard. His successor was Alexander Severus

(222–235) whose mother was reputed to have received Christian instruction from the great Christian scholar Origen. Severus was another to be murdered by the army. Philip the Arabian (244–249) was believed to have studied Christianity and accepted the faith secretly.

By the year 251 the church in Rome had become a substantial organisation. There were forty-six priests in the church supported by seven deacons. At least 1,500 widows and orphans were being supported by the church and special buildings had been erected for worship and meetings. The catacombs, named after burial chambers at a place called Kata Kumbas, were established as Christian burial sites, and administered by the church. In Rome at least, Christianity was becoming acceptable and as a consequence the early rigour of the faith diminished. Then, during the brief reign of Decius (249–251), this changed with the suddenness of a thunderbolt. Seeking to restore Roman discipline, he reintroduced compulsory obedience to the traditional Roman gods and attempted to suppress Christianity. He issued an edict that everybody should sacrifice to the ancient gods. Those who complied with the edict were given certificates (libelli). Those who refused had their goods confiscated and faced exile, torture and death. Some Christians, clergy and laity, complied with the edict and denied their faith. Others obtained libelli by devious means including bribery. Yet despite defections, the prisons were thronged with 'confessors' ready to die for the faith. In this reign of terror the death toll included Fabian, the bishop of Rome, Babylas, bishop of Antioch and Alexander, bishop of Jerusalem. The scholar Origen survived but suffered dreadful torture which marked him for the rest of his life.

This Decian persecution was curtailed when the emperor was killed in a battle with Gothic invaders on the banks of the Danube but the ramifications of his reign of terror were far-reaching. When the storm subsided many of the Christians who had weakened in the heat of persecution, repented and sought a way back into the fellowship of the church. Not all were welcomed. Some felt the denial of Christ was apostasy, the worst of all possible sins and nothing could restore these 'lapsed'. Others believed concessions to human weakness should be made and ways found to welcome back prodigals. The issue was complicated still further when martyrs about to die appealed for clemency on behalf of the lapsed. Martyrs were deeply venerated and it was hard to resist their pleas making the dilemma more acute.

The dispute went on throughout the church but had two main focal points at Rome and Carthage. The bishop of Carthage was a remarkable man called Cyprian (c. 200–258). He advocated that penitents should be received back into fellowship, though clergy who had apostatised were not to resume office. A Carthaginian priest, called Novatus, disagreed with this judgement and he was supported by a minority in the church at Rome. Together they sought to elect an alternative bishop of Rome who was hostile to Cyprian. Oddly, he was called Novatian and he and Novatus were responsible for the first great schism in the church, ever after called Novatianism. They had a large following. Calling themselves 'Cathori' (Puritans) they advocated a strong disciplinary edge to the faith and, while the views of Cyprian did prevail, the Novatian schism lasted for hundreds of years producing its own bishops, saints and monks.

During this dispute, Cyprian faced strong personal attacks because he himself avoided martyrdom. Following the advice of Jesus himself, 'When they persecute you in one city, flee to another', he had led the church from hiding and was accused by some of cowardice. It was criticism he did not deserve for he had shown great personal courage and charity during a dreadful plague in Carthage during 252. Then, when persecution flared up again under Emperor Valerian (257–258), Cyprian did not go into hiding. Christian clergy perished, senators were exiled and Christians within the imperial household were sentenced to penal servitude. Called before a tribunal by the Proconsul of Africa, Cyprian made a calm and courteous defence of his faith before being beheaded on September 14th, 258. This litany of the dead included Xystus, the bishop of Rome, the bishop of Tarragona and several other deacons. Leadership in the church did not offer much chance of a long life.

The life of Cyprian pours light onto the life and development of the Christian church during the third century. He had been born into a wealthy African family and by middle age had a reputation in Carthage for learning and eloquence. Then in 246 he was converted and baptised. Three years later he was the bishop of Carthage. Influenced greatly by Tertullian, whom he called 'the master', he had the same incisive thought and passion as Tertullian, to which he added wise statesmanship and practical ability. It was largely due to Cyprian that the Novatian schism did not turn the church into an austere unforgiving community, unwilling to forgive the weakness of Christians under the fire of persecution.

An important aspect of Cyprian's life concerns his relationship with the bishop of Rome. Did he regard the bishop of Rome as a pope or as an equal? A council of Carthage held in 255 provides the clue. This council discussed whether or not people who had been baptised by the Novatian schism needed to be rebaptised if they sought to come back to orthodox Christianity. The African church did rebaptise but Rome did not. The council followed Cyprian and eighty-seven bishops held firm in this view despite a threat from Rome to withdraw from communion with them. Obviously Cyprian and these bishops regarded their decision as valid even though the Roman church disagreed.

In a short work, *The Unity of the Church*, Cyprian pleads for oneness in the Church of Christ. He accepts that the fullness of apostolic power was bestowed on Peter *but he does not identify the primacy of Peter with that of the bishops of Rome*. His claim is that the bishop's office is one but each individual bishop is equal as successor to the apostles. Keeping the unity of the church intact is binding upon all bishops. Cyprian did not deny the unique position of the bishop of Rome but did not accept 'papal claims' or any attempt to exercise universal supremacy. He held his views firmly but when he died his martyr's death he was still at peace with the Roman church, which later canonised him as a saint.

Origen of Alexandria (185–254)

Alexandria in Egypt was one of the world's great cities. It boasted in its port the famous lighthouse, one of the Seven Wonders of the Ancient World. It was home to some 300,000 free citizens made up chiefly of Greeks, Egyptians and Jews. The city library contained nearly 500,000 volumes, the largest library in the world and a magnet for the world's greatest scholars. It was also the centre of many troubles like the Jewish uprising of 215, when Emperor Caracalla massacred Jewish males and decimated the Jewish population for reasons that remain obscure.

It was here that Origen, the most gifted scholar the church had produced since the Apostle Paul, was born and raised. His tutor was Clement, the distinguished Christian scholar we have already referred to, who taught in Alexandria for over twenty years, until the persecutions of the year 202 scattered the school and sent Christians into hiding or to the blood letting of the arenas. Origen was a teenager at this time and witnessed his father Leonides dragged away to execution. Only the restraining influence of his mother prevented him from following his father when she hid his clothes. Young as he was, Bishop Demetrius appointed him successor to Clement as head of the school. For 28 years he instructed Christians and pagans alike. His teaching methods were broad and included instruction in mathematics, science and philosophy before going onto theology, the queen of the sciences. The cosmopolitan nature of Alexandria led to a great cross-pollination of ideas and Origen effectively combined the philosophy of Greece with Hebrew Scriptures and Christian revelation. Hebrew Scriptures had already been translated into Greek by this time and Philo, a Jewish philosopher living in Alexandria, had tried to interpret Judaism in terms of Greek philosophy. Origen's tutor, Clement, had continued the process. Origen was one of the few scholars before the Reformation to master Hebrew, allowing him to study the Scriptures in their original tongue. As a Platonist philosopher himself, Origen fused the greatness of Greek and Hebrew thought and bathed it in Christianity. He developed the idea from John's Gospel that Christ was the Logos, the incarnate Word of God who existed from the beginning but became flesh amongst us.

> *God must not be thought of as a physical being, or as having any kind of body. He is pure mind. He moves and acts without needing any corporeal space, or size, or form, or colour, or any other property of matter.*
> **(De principiis i, c. 254)**

Origen also pioneered the critical study of the Biblical text and produced a magnificent version of the Old Testament called the *Hexapla* which consisted of six parallel columns of text in Hebrew, a Greek transliteration, the *Septuagint*, and three other early Greek versions. He also produced commentaries on all the books of the Bible. Another task he set himself was to answer, in minute detail, an attack on the church from a man called Celsus who several years before had lampooned Christianity in a work called *True Word*. This work has never been found but Origen answered the criticisms so precisely it is possible to reconstruct Celsus' arguments from his replies. In a style similar to that used today by the humanist publication *The Freethinker*, Celsus sneers at Christian belief, scorning the idea that humans should consider themselves superior to animals. To Celsus, the fact that Jesus was executed as a criminal and had an appeal to the down-and-outs of society disqualified him as someone to be taken seriously. He ignores the moral force of Christianity and regards the cross as mere foolishness. The tirade of *True Word* certainly shows that the fledgling faith was being taken seriously and spreading fear amongst those with a vested interest in suppressing the vigorous belief now reshaping the Roman world. Confronting Celsus with such panache Origen soundly defeated a Goliath of opposition and added still more credence to the expanding faith.

The intellectual output of Origen was phenomenal but his great learning was more than matched by the goodness of his own life. It was said he took too literally the command of Jesus, 'If your eye is your undoing, tear it out and fling it away' (Matt. 5:29), and this led to self castration. Certainly this was a hammer critics used to beat him with, but by then the reputation of Origen was secure. He was invited to preach and teach in places away from Alexandria. Whilst visiting Palestine in 216, he was invited by the bishops of Jerusalem and Caesarea to expound the Scriptures for them. Some years later these bishops ordained him as a presbyter without informing Demetrius, his own bishop in Alexandria. Demetrius objected and sought to deprive him of his priesthood. Origen settled in Caesarea and began a new school of literature, philosophy and theology and it was here that he was severely weakened by torture during the Decian persecution of 251. He died a few years later.

Origen was no stranger to suffering but his work, scholarly and methodical, is shot through with the sure hope that what we glimpse of truth in this life we will see clearly in the hereafter. In *De principiis*, he writes:

> *Those who devote themselves with great labour to the pursuit of piety and religion are made fitter for receiving the instruction that is to come.*

Sketches we may attempt now are but the outline of a perfect painting yet to be.

Origen and Clement before him, achieved a great deal in the crucial task of making the gospel understandable to people raised in the Greek culture. The intellectual respectability of Christianity was firmly established when Origen answered the criticisms of Celsus line by line and pointed out that disciples would scarcely have been likely to die for something they knew to be a lie. Then again, would Christians have recorded the betrayal of Judas and the denial of Peter if they were trying to win the approval of a pagan world? Deceived they could possibly have been. Deceivers, never. A century later Athanasius, a bishop of Alexandria, took this argument further by asking if it was likely that a dead Christ would be revolutionising the lives of men in the present.

The Great Persecution

In the year 284 Diocletian became emperor. The son of slave parents, he was elected by the army and immediately began to reconstruct the imperial system. He appointed a colleague called Maximian as a support emperor, giving him the title 'Augustus' and then chose two subordinate 'caesars', Galerius and Constantius, with rights of succession. Maximian was a warrior who had distinguished himself on every frontier of the Empire and he acted as the hatchet man for the more aloof Diocletian. The two caesars had the job of keeping Rome's borders secure from the Barbarians who threatened the peace from every side. Central government was moved from Rome to the provinces and Milan and Nicomedia became the emperor's favourite residences. Almost overnight Nicomedia became a magnificent city inferior only to Rome, Alexandria and Antioch in size and population. Only rarely did Diocletian set foot in Rome. Gibbon says of the new system and shared power, 'The happiness of their union has been compared to a chorus of music, whose harmony was regulated and maintained by the skilful hand of the first artist'. (*Decline and Fall of the Roman Empire*, Ch. XIII.) Unfortunately for Christians, this harmony did not leave room for them in the orchestra.

On the surface the church had grown into a strong position. Diocletian's wife and daughter were inclined towards Christianity, as was Constantius, and large, specially built churches bore witness to the confidence of the faith, which had grown despite hardships. Churches were crowded with worshippers and the name of Jesus was known throughout the empire. Old suspicions however were slow to die, especially in the army where allegiance to the emperor was difficult for Christians to demonstrate when it meant doing obeisance to an effigy or Roman eagle. Martyrdoms in the army were not unusual and St Albans in Hertfordshire, is named after a soldier martyr of this period. Along with doubts about the loyalty of Christians was a jealousy about their growing wealth and influence. The hostility of pagan priests may have contributed to a growing inflammatory situation but it was almost certainly Galerius who lit the fire. On the 23rd February 303, during the festival of Terminalia, the central church in Nicomedia was broken open and ransacked. All copies of the Scriptures were burnt and the church was razed to the ground by soldiers. An edict was posted on the palace gate announcing the suppression of Christianity. This was immediately torn down by an enthusiastic young soldier (some identify him as George, the patron saint of England).

He was arrested, tortured and killed. Further edicts prevented meetings for worship, more church closures and the destruction of all Christian literature. People who were known to have surrendered books to the authorities were branded by the church as 'traditors' (traitor stems from this word). Hundreds of early manuscripts were lost in this purge on the written word, a purge repeated many times in history, right down to the present day.

The number of Christians who perished during Diocletian's persecution is impossible to calculate. In the West the worst excesses subsided after some three years due to the influence of Constantius but, in the East, persecution raged for all of ten years. Eusebius, a contemporary historian, writes of 'thousands who died', hundreds in single incidents and multitudes throughout the eastern churches. From personal knowledge Eusebius describes dreadful atrocities committed by a Himmler-type character called Maxys, who refused to bury victims and dispersed their fragments through the city. During the carnage, rain fell which led some to say the heavens were weeping over the dreadful scene. The historian Gibbon is restrained in his descriptions of Diocletian's horrors but he leaves us in no doubt about the severity of the fate which met the man who tore up the first edict in Nicomedia:

> *He was burnt, or rather roasted, by a slow fire and his executioners exhausted every refinement of cruelty without being able to subdue his patience, or to alter the steady and insulting smile, which in his dying agonies, he still preserved on his countenance.*
> **(Decline and Fall, Ch. XVI)**

Then suddenly, in 305, Diocletian took the unprecedented step of resigning the throne. Attempts were made to get him to change his mind but he responded by showing off the cabbages he had grown with his own hands in Salona and adamantly refused to trade in this happiness for a throne.

> *What infinite hearts-ease must kings neglect*
> *That private men enjoy!*
> *And what have kings that privates have not too*
> *Save ceremony.*
> **(Henry V, Act IV Sc 1)**

Diocletian's unexpected move sparked off a terrific struggle for power amongst his protégés. For a time East and West each had three emperors and in the battle for the ultimate prize the killings began. Contenders fell one by one until a new star began to rise. He was the son of Constantius to his Christian wife Helena—his name was Constantine. He had been summoned by his father to join him in York and he arrived to witness his father's death in 306. Here at York he was acclaimed emperor by the legions and from that moment his rise was irresistible. The truly decisive battle for power was at Milvian Bridge near Rome in 312, where Constantine's vision of 'a cross of light' inspired his victory. It was a moment destined to shape his future life and the pattern of subsequent history. There was still much for Constantine to do before he was the unchallenged emperor but change was now dramatic and far reaching. Christianity, for so long the forbidden religion, became the protected faith of the emperor himself. Official persecution was over. For good and ill state and church climbed into the same bed.

Effects of Persecution

The Christian Church was affected positively and negatively by persecution. Every outbreak produced martyrs and no part of the Roman Empire remained untouched by the violence. Bishops were often amongst the first to suffer and the Great Persecution produced its usual crop of martyrs with the deaths of bishops in Nicomedia, Thruis, Egypt, Gaza and elsewhere. Every Christian community had its heroes and heroines and stories of resistance and fortitude.

This courage under fire did win great admiration for Christians from people who witnessed their amazing constancy. Men, women and children all withstood torture and death with surprisingly few demands for reprisals or vengeance. It was as if a new power had come into the world, overcoming the seemingly natural instinct for survival or even natural justice. Thus, even as the martyrs died they were replaced in the ranks by those won over by their witness. One African philosopher called Annobius, who had long disputed with Christians, was won over not by argument but by the way the martyrs died. When he presented himself for baptism to a church at Sicca, the congregation were so suspicious of him that he was not accepted until he had written a book in defence of Christianity. It is a story which reminds one of the initial reluctance of the church to accept the conversion of St Paul. Annobius later became a priest. A tutor in Diocletian's court, called Lactantius, was also converted by the witness of martyrs. He stood to lose his livelihood but he preferred to use his talents to defend the faith rather than serve the emperor. Constantine did appoint him tutor to his son Crispus in later years.

However, the legacy of the martyrs was not without a negative side. We have already seen, in the Decian persecution, that the influence of the martyrs was a factor in the dispute about how the lapsed should be treated. Once persecution subsided and the battered church had time to reflect, a cult of saints and martyrs sprang up, which tended to confuse the faith handed down through the apostles. Churches were built over the tombs of martyrs and reverence for them provided pagans with substitutes for their gods as Christianity blended with old paganism. Church communities launched into an unhealthy search for relics of the saints to be exhibited in their shrines. Claims often followed that the power of these saints lay in the relics and could be used to overcome illness or barrenness. For some superstitious believers it was a short step from admiration to worship and while the church never sanctioned such belief it was difficult not to be coloured by the tendency. During this period, the veneration of Mary the mother of Jesus struck root when the pagan belief in Isis the Egyptian goddess was blended with Mary as a universal mother image. Gibbon writes:

> *...the worship of saints and relics corrupted the pure and perfect simplicity of the Christian model...The satisfactory experience that the relics of saints were more valuable than gold or precious stones stimulated the clergy to multiply the treasures of the church, without much regard for truth or probability...*
>
> *If Tertullian or Lactantius, had suddenly raised from the dead...they would have gazed with astonishment and indignation on the profane spectacle which had succeeded to the pure and spiritual worship of a Christian congregation.*
> **(Gibbon, *Decline and Fall*, XXVIII)**

Christianity had succeeded in winning the heart of the Roman Empire but the battle to keep the gospel of Jesus free from corruption was only just beginning. The church was about to discover that every generation needed a reformation.

2 Royal Approval

Constantine	38
Heresy and Schism	40
Donatism	41
Gnosticism	42
Arianism and the Battle of the Iota	44
Athanasius	45
Doctrine and Trinity	47
Helena and Pilgrimage	48

Constantine (c. 274–337)

The conversion of Constantine was a decisive moment in the history of Christianity and is well recorded. No doubt his mind had been made receptive by the sympathy shown to the new faith by his parents and by the influences of Christians in Nicomedia during his adolescence. But the turning point of his life came with a Paul like conversion and vision before the historic battle of Milvian Bridge in 312. Constantine's friend, Eusebius, recounts that the emperor saw a cross of light in the sky and was convinced that Christ was commanding him to go into battle under a new ensign, which included the cross. His defeat of the pagan Maxentius was accomplished and the cross became a sign on the official standard of the armies, a sign that Christ had liberated the empire and restored to Rome its former dignity.

Constantine's conversion has been much discussed and its sincerity has been called into question. Certainly, by modern standards, he did some strange things and the execution of his wife and son in 326 and deferred baptism until in death's waiting-room in 337, take some understanding. So does the slow progress in overcoming the persecution of Christians in the East during his early years on the throne. Martyrdom continued in the army for several years, most notably the forty soldiers of Sebaste in Armenia who were immersed all night in a freezing pond before execution. At this time Constantine was sharing power with Licinius who was not a Christian and once that threat to his position was eradicated at the battles of Adrianople and Chrysopolis, his pro Christian legislation did grow apace. From this time it is possible to detect more humane regulations like the abolition of crucifixion, the emancipation of Christian slaves, the building of churches, the granting of equal privileges to believers and unbelievers alike, the banning of emperor worship and, most significantly of all, the declaration that Sunday was to be a weekly holiday throughout the empire.

It was during these Constantine years that sacred places in Palestine were sought out and honoured and Helena, the emperor's mother, played a significant part in this development. She built three basilicas in the 'Holy Land' the first over the traditional place of Jesus' tomb in Jerusalem, the second on the Mount of Olives and the third over the cave of the nativity in Bethlehem. All three were decorated with frescoes, mosaics and marble. Even more significantly Constantine decided to establish a new Christian capital on the crossroad of Europe and Asia at Byzantium, henceforth to be known as Constantinople.

New churches were built there including *Sophia* dedicated to Christ the true wisdom, a church which later served the Muslims of Istanbul as a mosque. In this new city pagan temples were forbidden as were gladiatorial games.

In effect, the world of the early fourth century had been turned upside down. In the twinkling of an eye the impossible had happened and Christianity had become the dominating religious influence of the Roman Empire. Obviously not everybody embraced the new faith with alacrity and the country districts were slower to accept the changes transforming the cities. The word for a rural rustic was *pagan* and this rustic word was eventually applied to those who did not believe. In the cities however, the change from semi-outlawed state to recognised state religion was sudden and just as dramatic for Christians as the collapse of Russian communism was to the world of the 1980s. Christianity was now acceptable and respectable. Blessed by the emperor, sponsored by the state, it became fashionable and, as a result, lost something of its purity and passion. Some church leaders, dazzled by sudden temptations of wealth and power, became time-serving and greedy.

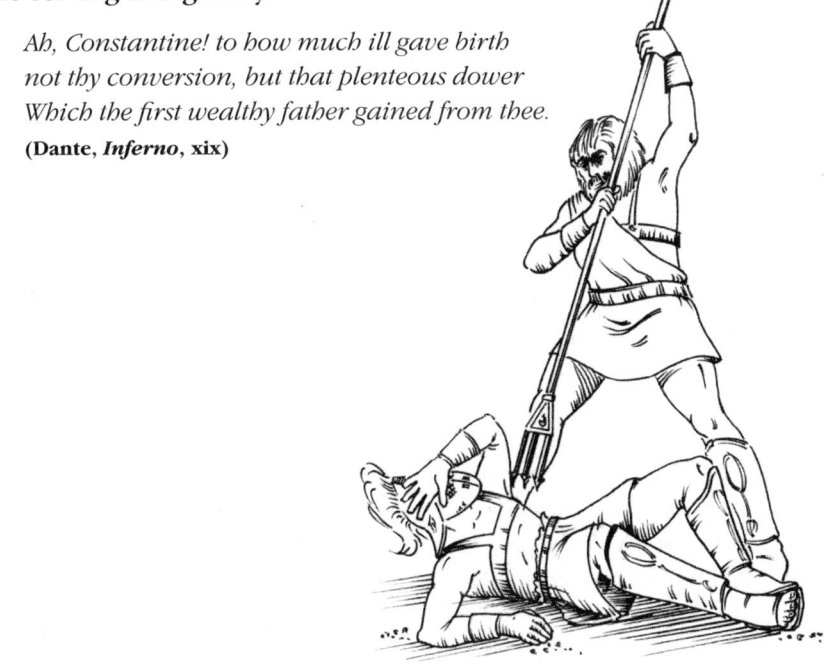

> *Ah, Constantine! to how much ill gave birth*
> *not thy conversion, but that plenteous dower*
> *Which the first wealthy father gained from thee.*
> **(Dante, *Inferno*, xix)**

In Constantinople gladiatorial games were forbidden

The state was now so much tied up with church affairs that clergy called upon the emperor to intervene in ecclesiastical disputes, even though he was still not baptised as a Christian. On the whole, Constantine's touch was light in these affairs, though in Africa where the Donatist schism was tearing the African church apart, he did try to wield the big stick. We will look at these schisms later but suffice to say now that the problems of 'established' religion were firmly with us and the spiritual liberty of Jesus was compromised and sometimes utterly fettered. *Furthermore, in moving to Constantinople, his new capital city in the East, he had given the empire two distinct centres of influence. It was a source of division in the future for both empire and Church, which would ultimately lead to the first great division of the church, that between East and West, between Catholic and Orthodox. After Constantine the two wings of the church developed in different ways with the eastern block much more dependent on the state. That dependency has been a feature of its history ever since.*

Heresy and Schism

Persecution had buffeted the growing church from without but within there were other struggles taking place. Different ways of interpreting the life of Jesus were apparent from the beginnings of the church and have continued ever since.

The core of Christianity is contained in symbols, creeds, worship and sacraments. Yet the church has also been able to go back to primitive declarations of faith for its bench marks. But it must not be forgotten that all creeds and statements of belief are explanations of an experience and not the faith itself. Faith is a living thing in danger of becoming fossilised once it is written down in credal shape. 'Jesus is Lord', has always been a rallying cry for believers but it is a slogan crying out for definition. Jesus, 'Word made flesh', goes deeper but involves philosophical as well as theological explanation. The Eucharist relived the life of Jesus, poured out like wine, broken apart like bread and Baptism declared the need for rebirth, which included the drowning of old ways of living to make possible a life now 'in Christ'. But if the life and death of Jesus were indisputable, how did his sacrifice affect my relationship with God? If a new power entered believers when they declared their faith, how were they to be treated if they fell below the morality expected of them and what happened to them, if, in moments of weakness, they renounced their faith to save their skins? Could they be forgiven for that?

So the growth of Christianity was accompanied by a continuing dialogue about the nature of faith and Christian living. It was a dialogue to exercise nimble minds of the day, often profound but sometimes bigoted and aggressive. It provoked original thought and expression but orthodox belief always held an overriding assumption that the Church was trustee to a body of truth emanating from Jesus and passed on by the apostles. The dialogue begins within the New Testament and has gone on to the present-day. It only takes a provocative remark from a bishop or a new book claiming that Jesus did not die but married Mary Magdala and raised children in France, to breath new life into the debate which started on the streets of Jerusalem two thousand years ago.

Donatism

As people settled into the new life under Constantine, the question of what to do with those people wanting to return to the fold after denying their belief under persecution arose again. In North Africa, many followed a man called Donatus who wanted nothing to do with *traditors* or backsliders. They declared that all those who had denied Christ should be re-baptised and any such clergy who practised their ministry should be shunned. They made themselves into a church for the perfect and drew great support from the poorer classes who had no stake in Roman imperialism. Some lawless bands of Donatists, called Circumcellions, terrorised some regions with their uncompromising attitude and violence, which included blinding victims with lime. Constantine attempted to put down the Donatists but this led to dissension and gave them martyrs of their own. The schism lasted for many years and was a thorn in the side of Augustine of Hippo and a cause of weakness that made the church in Africa less able to withstand the rising tide of Islam in later days.

The heresy did make the church consider the validity of its sacraments. Does the value of Eucharist for instance, depend on the integrity of the priest celebrating the Eucharist or has it got a validity of its own irrespective of the celebrant? It soon became clear that the unworthiness of a minister could not invalidate an act taking place in the name of the church.

Gnosticism

The word *agnostic* is well known to us today. It describes a person who remains ambiguous about belief, he just does not know what he believes. Such people are the opposite of those the church contended with from the second century. These people claimed categorically that they *did* know, they claimed secret knowledge (*gnosis*) not only about themselves but about creation and destiny. This secret knowledge was incorporated into aspects of the Christian gospel, confusing those maintaining the faith handed down from the apostles. Often Gnostics showed a great respect for Jesus himself and imitated Christian meetings and quoted Christian literature. However, there was no need for penitence or forgiveness because these 'chosen few' had the secrets of life. Gnostic writings have survived, some discovered in the twentieth century, but by and large our understanding of their system of belief comes from the writings of Christians who opposed them.

To understand Gnosticism imagine walking in the countryside at midnight. It is a beautiful clear night and as you look into the sky the stars seem brighter than you can ever remember. It starts you thinking. These stars are millions of miles away and beyond them, stretching far beyond where human eye can see, are other stars and other suns and galaxies. You are entranced by the mystery of it all . How can that vast universe come into being by chance? Yet how can the One who created it be concerned about the minuscule life walking in the countryside? The Gnostics answered this ancient mystery by saying that the world was not created by the Supreme God but by a lesser god. They then went on to claim that the way to the Supreme God was by learning secret knowledge passed on to the initiated. Thus the Immortal, Invisible was separated from the life of the here and now, the life of evil and pain. Some Gnostics thought that the lesser god was the god of the Old Testament who had really botched the job and allowed suffering to spoil creation.

Christian belief was therefore reinterpreted by the Gnostics. The Supreme God could not have become a man and suffered all the slings and arrows that man is prone to so, if He did come down to earth he must have been a phantom. When Jesus suffered he only *seemed* to suffer. His life was an illusion and consequently there was no real death and no resurrection. Furthermore, because the physical world was of secondary importance moral codes regulating physical life were also of secondary importance. Salvation came to a person because of intellectual illumination and not through morality or redemption. Such teaching led to a conclusion that if morality was not important then everything was fair game and the devil take the hindmost. Perhaps it was to answer this 'wisdom' that Paul had written to the Corinthians:

> *God has made the wisdom of this world look foolish. As God in his wisdom ordained, the world failed to find him by its wisdom and he chose to save those who have faith by the folly of the Gospel.*
> **(1 Cor. 1:20–21)**

Another branch of Gnosticism went the opposite way to that of blatant immorality. Their reasoning concluded that if this physical life was shot through with evil then this evil must be avoided by a severe asceticism. This led to celibacy, vegetarianism and abstinence from alcohol. Paul had an answer to this misunderstanding of Christianity as well:

> *Why let people dictate to you: Do not handle this, do not taste that, do not touch the other—all of them things that must perish as soon as they are used? That is to follow merely human injunctions and teaching. True, it has an air of wisdom, with its forced piety, its self-mortification and its severity to the body, but it is of no use at all in combating sensuality.*
> **(Colossians 2:21–23)**

The traditional founder of Gnosticism has always been regarded as Simon Magus who is mentioned in chapter 8 of Acts of the Apostles. The church historian Eusebius, who lived in the fourth century, says that the teaching of Magus continued to his own day where people lived immoral lives and still worshipped Simon and his consort Helen, honouring them with sacrifices.

Other Gnostics had their day like Cerinthus in Ephesus who, it is said, caused the apostle John to run from the bath-house there when he put in an appearance, and Basilides whose explanation of creation consisted of downward emanations from the Supreme God, the 365th of which created the world. Such teachings caused fluttering from time to time but never seriously damaged the structure of the Christian faith. Sure, the Gnostics were often ingenious and maybe most Christians found it difficult to dispute with them, but when it came to the crunch Christian life was too vigorous to be weakened by the infection of Gnosticism. Christian orthodoxy held fast to the belief in a God of creation who had also moved positively into human experience in the person of Jesus of Nazareth.

Arianism and the Battle of the Iota

A far more serious problem for the church came with a controversy, which went on acutely for fifty years. It was a titanic struggle to preserve the essentials of belief and became known as the Arian Controversy.

Arius was a presbyter from the church of Alexandria in Egypt. He was a somewhat grave and ascetic man, a persuasive preacher with a following of clergy and disciples who circulated his teaching in verse and song. His method was to pen his views in rollicking metre that lent themselves to popularised 'pop songs' in the streets and the docks—fourth century salvationism! In 319 Arius accused his bishop Alexander of heresy, an accusation the bishop played down with great courtesy. He was soon obliged to take it more seriously however, and a council of Egyptian bishops was called to consider the claims Arius was making. Arius was heard, then overruled, relieved of his priesthood and excommunicated along with his followers. This group left Alexandria and found a welcome with the church at Caesarea where the historian Eusebius was bishop. Just to confuse matters the bishop of Nicomedia, also called Eusebius, added support to Arius. Suddenly the church found itself embroiled in theological conflict of the severest kind. The Emperor Constantine, now supreme East and West, was dismayed to find himself acting as mediator in a conflict he described as a 'theological trifle'. He summoned an assembly of bishops to meet at Nicaea, in Bithynia (modern Turkey) to thrash out this trifle.

It was June 325, when two hundred and twenty gathered at the assembly, initially presided over by the emperor himself. Only a handful of bishops attended from the West and most felt the dispute could be resolved quickly and amicably. It was a sombre gathering with many of those present showing the marks of recent persecutions in scarred bodies and blinded eyes. They must have marvelled at the spectacle of Constantine, the successor to the throne of Diocletian, Marcus Aurelius and Nero, as he opened the assembly with the words:

> *Delay not, you ministers of God and faithful servants of our common Lord and Saviour and begin from this moment to remove the causes of disunion which exist among you...*

Essentially the dispute hinged around the relationship between God and Jesus. What do we mean when we call Jesus 'Son of God'? Was he created? Did he exist before creation? Was he equal with God?

Arius himself was examined twice and clearly stated his belief that the son of God was ***a created being, made out of nothing, and*** *might have sinned*. The council condemned this as heresy almost unanimously. This quickly dispatched the negative side of the proceedings. The creative aspects were to take much longer and involved hammering out a universal or catholic creed acceptable to all the delegates.

Athanasius (c. 300–373)

Cometh the hour, cometh the man. The man was called Athanasius, a mere deacon from the church in Alexandria, who had not even got a vote at council. But it was he, with his learning and eloquence, who dominated the proceedings from now on and led the council to its decisions. He also established himself as the leading ecclesiastical statesman in the church for the next fifty years and the greatest theologian of his time—'royal hearted Athanasi, with Paul's own mantle blest'. Like Martin Luther of the sixteenth century, he faced into the wind of doctrinal conflict and stood firm for the truth he saw clearly. Luther's axiom, 'Peace if possible, but truth at any cost!' could just as well be applied to Athanasius. As emperors attempted to buy unity within the church at any cost, Athanasius maintained that to accept the teaching of Arius was to lose the gospel of Jesus.

Baptismal creeds already existed in the church and these were consulted as 'blue prints' for a universal creed. One offered by Eusebius of Caesarea provided a good framework to start with but it was not specific about the relationship between Father God and Son. Eventually a new phrase was conjured up, which expressed Athanasius' view precisely, though it was not a phrase taken from Scripture. It stated that Jesus the Son is '*of one substance*' (*homoousion*) with the Father. Arius on the other hand, was contending that Jesus was '*of like substance*' (*homoiousion*) to the Father. If you scrutinise these two Greek words you will notice that the only difference between them is a small iota, the smallest letter in the Greek alphabet. That iota became the difference between orthodox belief and heresy. On the surface it may seem like a quibble over nothing but in this case a letter means a great deal for, as has been often pointed out, a cat is not a rat! The final Creed of Nicaea said:

> *We believe in one God, the Father, Almighty,*
> *maker of all things visible and invisible;*
> *And in one Lord Jesus Christ, the Son of God,*

> *begotten of the Father, only-begotten,*
> *that is from the substance* (ousia) *of the Father;*
> *God from God, Light from Light,*
> *Very God from Very God,*
> *Begotten not made,*
> *Of one substance* (homoousios) *consubstantial*
> *with the Father, through whom all things were made,*
> *both in heaven and on earth; who for us men and*
> *for our salvation came down and was incarnate,*
> *was made man, suffered and rose again on the third day*
> *ascended into heaven, and is coming to judge the living and dead;*
> *And in the Holy Spirit.*
>
> *And those who say; 'There was a time when he was not...'*
> *the Catholic and Apostolic Church places under a curse.*

Athanasius insisted on the *homoousios* rather than the *homoiousios* because he maintained that if Jesus Christ was not truly God as the Father is God, then human beings cannot be saved by him and he cannot reveal God to us. Furthermore, the Father would have undergone change in begetting a Son, which is improper to the divine nature. Arius, therefore, was proclaiming a different gospel to that handed on by the apostles. So this creed was circulated around the churches as a true statement of the Universal faith and the crux of the deliberations of the Council of Nicaea. Other issues of less importance were dealt with, like the position of married clergy and a fixed date for Easter, viz—the Sunday after the full moon which occurs after 21st March, Egyptian skills in astronomy were probably responsible for this conclusion!

So the Council of Nicaea ended with statements and a Creed. It did not finish the matter however, and Athanasius, who later became bishop of Alexandria, spent a life time restating the 'orthodox' position arrived at in Nicaea. His life was really a long struggle against Arianism and after personal attacks he was five times banished from Alexandria. The western church, not prominent at the Council, nevertheless supported the conclusions arrived at, whereas most of the eastern churches, which had been present, worked to get them changed. Eusebius of Caesarea and Eusebius of Nicomedia leaned towards Arianism and eventually the emperor was pleased to reinstate many Arians and it was Eusebius of Nicomedia who baptised him on his death-bed in 337. Thus the emperor was born a pagan and died an Arian.

Sadly, the Arian controversy was never fully settled and rumbled on during the years after Constantine when the empire was divided between his sons, Constantius, in the East (an Arian) and Constans in the West (Orthodox). Constans was supported by the pope. Athanasius had to undergo many attacks by his enemies and at various times was exiled for being a troublemaker and was even accused, albeit absurdly, of murder. While in exile he received enthusiastic support from the pope and from monks in the Egyptian desert where he spent many years and wrote a biography of the monk Antony. Athanasius wrote much about the nature of the Trinity and was uncompromising in his contention that Jesus had to be God if he was to be our saviour. The initiative had to come from God because only he had the power to restore man into communion with himself. Athanasius, more than any other person at the Council of Nicaea, seems to have been aware of what was at stake during the protracted disputes over doctrine and it has been said of him that he pulled off the incredible feat of being right when everybody else of importance was wrong. John Henry Newman wrote of him, 'a principal instrument after the apostles by which the sacred truths of Christianity have been conveyed and secured to the world'. Others have not been so complimentary to Athanasius and Robert Funk, founder of the Jesus Seminar, has pointed out that the mark of a Christian should be how he behaves (orthopraxis) rather than orthodoxy.

Doctrine and Trinity

For a man like Constantine, with an empire to oversee, theological dispute may have seemed like a trifle but to thousands of scholars who have tried to plumb the depths of the Arian controversy ever since, it is no mere trifle. Christianity began with experience. It was something believers entered into with the emotion. All things after that are explanations and that includes doctrine and Creeds. Creeds become in effect part of the process of recalling, reliving and rethinking the experience that transformed people's lives. That in turn involves words and wonderful though language is and persuasive though words may be, they can never truly explain life-changing experience. When one person speaks a word or writes down a word, there can never be an absolute guarantee that the meanings of words are transmitted from one mind to the next precisely as intended. Later, when words are translated from one language to another the problems of communication are exacerbated.

On the surface, doctrines involving a God of Trinity may seem to be mere casuistry or even mumbo jumbo. To Christians however, experience of God led them to the conclusion that Trinity was the only form of words they could use to explain their experience in any consistent way. The faith had sprung from Judaism with its belief in a God of creation. They recognised the order present in laws of nature and found no difficulty in believing in a God *above them* who had set things in order, a God who had been present in the origins of the world, a God who, in the beginning, created. But, the apostles had experienced something more. They had shared their life with Jesus and that relationship had changed not only their lives but their understanding of God. They were convinced that in Jesus they had seen God in history. He had been *amongst them* sharing their lives, painting for them incredible vistas and opening possibilities haunting and inspiring. Their belief in a God of creation continued, but now they could claim that they also knew God had walked the streets of Galilee and Jerusalem because they had known it in their own experience. Then Jesus had died. Yet remarkably, He was still with them in their experience, still *within them*, still directing their path, still instructing and inspiring them. They knew God above them, amongst them and within them. He was a God in origins, in history and in experience. He was a God of Father, Son and Holy Spirit. This Triune God was not a vague theological concept but a way of describing experience. Subsequent ages sometimes placed the explanation before the experience and demanded conformity to a creed before any experience could be acknowledged. It was a turnabout leading to inquisition and persecution.

Helena and Pilgrimage

With the toleration of Christianity the character of Sunday and public holidays changed. Sunday was a *holyday* with worship an important part of it. At first it was informal and public preaching was received with cheers and sometimes boos. Fixed formulas of worship with the use of incense, candles and curtains round the altar all came later but greater respect and increasing leisure meant that Christian festivals increased, especially at important periods in the church calendar like Christmas, Easter and Pentecost.

Queen Mother Helena's pilgrimage to the Holy Land started a trend as well and as early as 333 a pamphlet appeared giving a route to Jerusalem from Bordeaux. Jerusalem was Christianised as churches and monasteries were established. A pilgrim called Etheria at the end of the 4th century described services being conducted at Jerusalem in Greek, Latin and Syriac. She also mentioned holy monks who lived near chapels and in isolated places. Clearly the monastic life started very early in Christendom. She describes how monks took them to the edge of Mount Nebo and pointed out places of interest beneath them, part of the panoramic view Moses had seen as he surveyed the Promised Land. It is a view modern pilgrims enjoy in package tours of Jordan in this very day.

Jewish tribulation continued throughout this time and by the fifth century pogroms against Jews in Palestine (sometimes led by Syrian monks) led to synagogues and villages being burnt down.

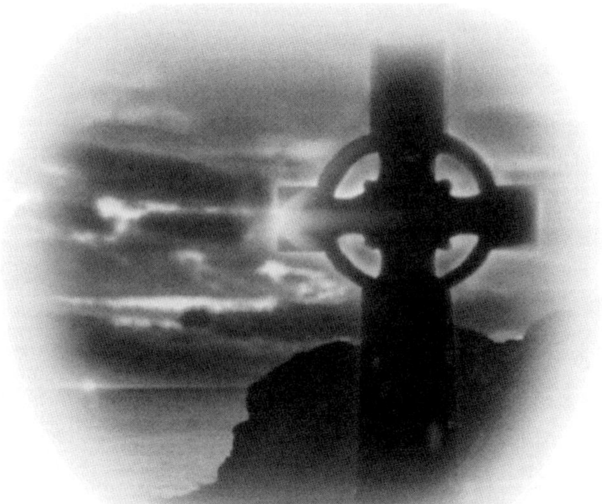

3 Monastics

Antony	52
Pachomius	53
Basil the Great	54
Martin of Tours	55
Ambrose	55
Jerome	57
Augustine	59
John Chrysostom	62
Benedict of Nursia	64
Effects of Monasticism	65

There was a serious attempt to restore paganism to the empire in 362 when the Emperor Julian got as far as withdrawing privileges to the clergy and re-introducing Greek divinities for worship. He paid a backhanded compliment to the Christians ('Galileans' he called them) by advocating that all pagan priests should behave like them:

> *Why do we not notice that it is their kindness to strangers, their care for the graves of the dead and the pretended holiness of their lives that have done most to increase atheism (Christianity)? I believe that we ought really to practice every one of these virtues.*

Julian's attempt to put back the clock came to an abrupt halt when he was killed fighting the Persians the following year. By the end of the fourth century, Christians were moving in high places and some of the 'holiness' Julian had admired was being diluted by proximity to political power.

An attempt to reclaim that purity led some people to withdraw from the world and all its compromises by becoming ascetics and monks. The origins of monasticism go back to the biblical times. There were ascetic features about the lives of Elijah in the Old Testament and John the Baptist in the New. The Essenes of Qumran were also ascetic though by the Christian era Jews had turned their backs on hermitry, advocating temperance rather than abstinence. A central pillar of Christianity is incarnation—the belief that God Himself entered a sinful world and redeemed it from within. Logically, therefore, monasticism would seem to be a denial of that. However, the appeal of a pure, unsullied faith, free of compromise held an attraction for many. Withdrawal from the world was sometimes for short periods but others saw it as a life-long commitment and the lives of some monks became legendary.

Antony (256–356)

Antony was an Egyptian, a Coptic peasant and the first well-known Christian hermit. He spent eighty years of his long life in prayer and physical labour. Prolonged periods of fasting and trances led to hallucinations, which would have psychological explanations today. Athanasius tells the story of Antony's life and his experience of fighting off evil spirits. So much of a hermit's life is lived internally it is difficult to separate fact from fantasy but what is clear is that even holy hermits can never escape from demons within themselves. The story is told of a hermit who was renowned for his piety. When the devil tempted him with images of beautiful women the holy man did not bat an eyelid. Next came images of power, dreams of what he could achieve and the wealth and luxury he could enjoy in places like Alexandria. Again, the holy man shunned all temptation. Finally, the devil became very subtle and whispered into the hermit's ear, 'Have you heard? Your brother has just been made bishop of Alexandria'. The story concludes—'A scowl of malignant jealousy crossed the face of the holy man!'

On two occasions at least, Antony visited Alexandria, once during 311 when his appearance comforted the confessors and martyrs during the Great Persecution of Diocletian. Athanasius also relied on the hermit's support for the 'orthodox' belief hammered out at the Council of Nicaea. Against his will, Antony attracted disciples but he always shunned fame or exhibitionism and withdrew quickly to solitude. Athanasius wrote a hagiography of Antony that made its way to Europe during his exile and this became very influential in the rise of western monasticism for many years to come.

Pachomius (287–346)

Pachomius was a good illustration of Julian's belief that kindness was responsible for winning people to Christianity. He was bowled over by the kindness of Christians in Thebes while he was a military conscript there and when he was released from the army he was immediately baptised. He was probably the first to set up a communal monastery when he took over an abandoned village on the banks of the Nile about the year 320. He wasn't an extremist and insisted on regular patterns for meals, work and prayer. They aimed for self-support through gardening and weaving, with everything communally owned according to his vision of an ascetic fellowship based on primitive Jerusalem communities. Learning was a feature of life there, especially memorising biblical passages. Family life was abandoned and celibacy was the rule. It was a disciplined order as befits a military man, soon it caught on and by the time of his death thousands of monks were living in eleven monasteries within a sixty mile radius of Pachomius' monastery, two of which were for women. These early communities provided a blueprint for all succeeding monasteries.

Basil the Great (330–379)

Basil was another influential monk, though he was less successful at remaining locked from the world than Antony. He was a scholar, educated in Constantinople and Athens before returning in his mid twenties to his home in Cappadocia. Today, tourists can marvel at Cappadocia's other-worldly landscape weathered by time and hollowed by ancient peoples into monastic homes and churches complete with domes, naves and aisles. Helped by friends, Basil was determined to dedicate his life to Bible study and the works of early Christian scholars like Origen. Education featured prominently in monastery life but in Cappadocia the monastery was also the hub of medical enterprise, providing aid for the sick and relief for the poor. Because Basil was not a hole-in-the-corner monk his influence was wide and in 370 he was elected Bishop of Caesarea.

His episcopate only lasted nine years but in that time he accomplished a great deal and made sure that the monasteries did not develop separately from the church but as an integral part of it. He built hospitals, refuge houses for the poor, workshops and an asylum for lepers, completely surrounding the cathedral and bishop's house. It was building on the grand scale, big enough to be called a 'new town'. For Basil worship and service were two sides of the same coin. He was a prolific writer with a lucid mind and waspish sense of humour, used to good effect in the battle against Arianism in the East. But he was concerned that in the debate about the relationship of God the Son and God the Father, the Holy Spirit had been ignored. He wrote much, therefore, about the Holy Spirit as a third distinct person in the Trinity and as a result of his work became known as the 'theologian of the Holy Spirit'. He was not universally liked and was virtually ignored by Rome and the western churches. His monastic rules are those still followed by churches in the East, rules he followed himself with great discipline. His friend, Gregory of Nazianzus, said of him: 'He is without wife, without property, without flesh and almost without blood', yet for sheer industry there were few could touch him. It was an industry, which gained for him the title 'Basil the Great'. Basil's letters reveal him as a warm-hearted pastor genuinely concerned for the well being of his people. Along with his brother Gregory and friend Gregory of Nazianzus, he was revered as one of the 'Cappadocean Fathers'.

Martin of Tours (died 397)

Monasticism in the West grew independently to that in the East and owed much to the life of a man called Martin of Tours who took up the hermit's life after military service. His father had enlisted him at fifteen and three years later Martin shocked everybody by dividing his military cloak with a knife and giving half to a beggar at Amiens. He obtained his discharge and was baptised. He lived in a solitary cell at Liguge, later the basis of the first monastery in Gaul for soon disciples joined him and formed a community following no rules other than the traditions of the ascetic life. He then moved his monastery to Marmoutier and in 372, by popular acclaim, he was reluctantly persuaded to become bishop of Tours. He continued a hermit life outside the town travelling the pagan countryside on foot. He was a merciful man who tried to save heretics from the death penalty and persecution. His burial place was a main pilgrimage centre for over a thousand years.

Ambrose (339–397)

Further encouragement to monasticism in the West came from Ambrose, a man who dominated church life in the West during the last years of the fourth century. He came from a noble Roman Christian family but the story of his elevation to the office of bishop is bizarre.

Auxentius, the bishop of Milan, had died and the great cathedral there was packed with Christians who had gathered to elect a successor. It was a noisy affair and many contentious arguments were taking place between those who desired an Arian successor to Auxentius on the one hand and those who supported the orthodox group on the other. Ambrose was trying to keep order and was shouting at the crowd when a child's voice cried out, 'Ambrose for bishop'. It was a call instantly taken up like a mantra by others all over the cathedral and became difficult to resist. Ambrose was thirty-four years old, had not been baptised and had no ambition to be a bishop. But the incident started off a ground swell, which gathered momentum and soon he was baptised and applied himself to theological study. It was not long before his powerful personality was dominating the Western church, where he became the acknowledged leader of the Catholic tradition.

His influence was enormous. Rome was still officially the centre of Christianity, a man called Sircius occupied the papal chair and felt powerful enough to issue a decree to the Spanish church asserting that all clergy should be celibate. But it was to Milan that emperors came when they journeyed West and therefore they came into direct contact with him. Ambrose's authority resided in himself rather than his office and he was successful in persuading Emperor Gratian to suppress pagan religion. He then resisted Justina, the Queen Mother, when she demanded that Arians be allowed to use the churches of Milan. Soldiers seized one church and they hung up imperial banners. Ambrose organised the populace in a sit-in where they remained all day singing hymns, many of them written by him. He was preaching a sermon to the crowd when news came that the banners had been taken down. During the life of Ambrose, Arianism declined in the western regions and this was largely due to the orthodox position being staunchly proclaimed by the bishop himself as this hymn of his reveals:

Maker of all things, God most high,
Great ruler of the starry sky,
Who, robing day with beauteous light,
Hast clothed in soft repose the night.

That sleep may wearied limbs restore,
And fit for toil and use once more,
May gently soothe the careworn breast
And lull our anxious griefs to rest.

We thank thee for the day that's gone,
We pray thee for the night come on,
O help us sinners as we raise
To thee our votive hymn of praise.

Christ with the father ever one,
Spirit! The Father and the Son,
God over all, the mighty sway,
Shield us, great trinity, we pray.

Towards the end of his life Ambrose was involved in a struggle for power with Emperor Theodosuis. The struggle illustrates well the relationship between church and state in the West. In 391, a heathen general had assassinated Valentinian II who had placed a puppet emperor called Eugenuis on the throne. Theodosuis, a devout Christian, attacked him and once again heathen banners confronted the cross. In a blinding storm when 'the stars in their courses' seemed to fight for him, Theodosuis achieved a victory and in so doing became the last sole ruler of the total Empire, East and West. When the all powerful emperor visited Milan he attended worship in the cathedral and was made to take his place with the laity rather than with the clergy as was customary in Constantinople. On another occasion Ambrose withheld communion from the emperor for eight months, until he had repented for slaughtering seven thousand citizens in Thessalonica following the murder of a military commander. When the doors were shut on him, Theodosuis lay on the floor in sackcloth and promised Ambrose that in future no capital sentence would be carried out until thirty days had passed. They crossed swords again when Theodosuis ordered bishops to rebuild a Gnostic meeting house and synagogue destroyed by over zealous monks. The emperor ordered the monks to be punished but Ambrose imposed his will and persuaded Theodosuis to change his mind. It was a great battle of wills. In the Eastern Church the emperor's will usually prevailed but in the West Ambrose made it plain that 'the emperor is within the church, not above it'.

Months after their last confrontation, Theodosuis was dead, followed two years later, by Ambrose who died on Good Friday, 397. Vast crowds attended his funeral in Milan on Easter Day amid scenes of great mourning. His biographer Paulinus said of him:

For fear of God Ambrose never feared to speak the truth to Kings.

Jerome (345–420)

Eusebius Hieronymus was another outstanding 'Latin Father' of the West. In English we call him Jerome.

He was born in Dalmatia and spent his youth in Rome where he gained a reputation for being a lively, somewhat uncontrollable, spirit. His conversion to Christianity however, soon brought out his gifts for study especially for classical literature and the Bible. There were two distinct sides to Jerome's character, on the one hand he was a winsome teacher who attracted dedicated students, on the other he was an impatient disputer with a vitriolic turn of phrase, which could turn the air blue. He also hankered after the ascetic life and when he left Rome he journeyed to France and then East to Antioch, where he plunged into the life of a hermit in the Syrian Desert. He lived sparsely, working with his hands but keeping his studies going as well. He mastered Hebrew with the help of a converted Jew, perhaps the first of the early Christian scholars of the West to do so. When he returned to Antioch he was ordained as a somewhat reluctant priest but he didn't settle and visited Constantinople where he listened with approval to the teaching of Gregory of Nazianzus, the Cappadocian Father. By 382, he was back in Rome working as a secretary to Pope Damascus and translating the New Testament and Psalms into Latin. He still found time to launch a bitter attack on the pride and luxury of the clergy and act as a spiritual guide to a number of Christian ladies. He eventually left Rome with two of these ladies, Paula and her daughter Eustochium, and settled for the monastic life in Bethlehem where he spent the remaining thirty-four years of his life engrossed in literary labours.

Prodigious in his output, Jerome translated the Bible into Latin from original Hebrew manuscripts rather than use the Greek *Septuagint*. His desire was to 'give my Latin readers the hidden treasures of Hebrew erudition'. The work took twenty-three years and became known as the *Vulgate Bible*, the authorised Latin version for the western church. He always aimed to write a thousand lines per day and when he wrote a commentary on Matthew's Gospel, he finished it in two weeks! His work is a monument to a scholar's industry and tenacity and it was work, which served the church well in dark days about to follow.

Jerome was a hard man to cross (a tirade against a man called Vigilantius, who had warned against venerating the relics of the saints, makes the toes curl) but he could attract devoted friends and the respect of opponents. Fortunately for historians Jerome wrote hundreds of letters, which reveal clearly his own intemperate character and some of the issues concerning the church during his life time. Well aware of his own shortcomings he wrote to Paula and Eustochium, 'I beseech you to pour out your prayers for me to the Lord, that as long as I remain in this feeble body, I may write something pleasing to you, useful to the church and worthy of posterity'. There can be no doubt he achieved that in spectacular fashion and the committee translating the Bible into English in 1611 (the King James version) said Jerome was 'moved to undertake the translating of the Old Testament out of the very fountains themselves; which he performed with that evidence of great learning, judgement, industry and faithfulness, that he hath for ever bound the Church unto him in a debt of special remembrance and thankfulness'.

Augustine (354–430)

A contemporary of Jerome, Augustine owed much to the influence of Ambrose, the bishop of Milan, and to Monica his mother. Augustine said, 'It was because my salvation was at stake that my mother loved Ambrose greatly and he loved her because of her fervent life of devotion, which took the form of good works and frequent church going. Sometimes when Ambrose saw me he would break out in praise of her and congratulate me on having such a mother—not knowing what a son she had'.

He was born in Tagaste in what is now Algeria and his parents were African. Monica's devotion ensured that her son had Christianity in his milk but Augustine had wild oats to sow and he wasn't baptised until he was thirty-three. His *Confessions* reveal in some detail his sharp intellect and an accompanying restlessness, which stayed with him through adolescence, a restlessness summed up in his famous phrase, 'Lord make me chaste, but not yet'. He lived with a mistress for twelve years, perhaps not unusual for an upwardly mobile young man of his day but probably unusual for a man who was enrolled as a catechumen, a candidate for baptism.

Augustine's family was not wealthy but when his father died a generous neighbour ensured that he could progress from school to the University at Carthage (modern Tunisia). He studied rhetoric and mastered Latin, though his Greek was always indifferent. He became a teacher himself and held chairs in Carthage, Rome and finally Milan. His first independent religious inclinations followed the reading of Cicero but he found the Bible uninteresting and some Old Testament passages repulsive. For nine years he followed a semi-Christian sect called the Manichees, which held strict codes of conduct and advocated a sexual renunciation new to Augustine because monasticism had not yet reached Africa. He followed the Manichees as a kind of card-carrying member who admired their devotion without imitating them. Thus he kept his mistress.

His Manicheeism waned when he moved to Milan and fell under the spell of Ambrose. Through the bishop's influence he gained a great respect for Christianity and the Bible. It was the beginning of an internal struggle that reached a conclusion in a Milan garden. He was sitting under a fig tree when he heard a child's voice crying 'Tolle lege' (take up and read). He reached for his Bible and started to read Paul's letter to the Romans, 'Not in rioting and drunkenness...but put you on the Lord Jesus Christ'. It was a moment to change the direction of his life. A year later on Easter Eve, 387, he was baptised by Ambrose in Milan. A few weeks afterwards his mother Monica, who had prayed ceaselessly for her son, died.

After his mother's burial, Augustine returned to Africa and was ordained priest. He gave away his possessions and formed a monastic community for study and contemplation and intended to make study his life's work. Then, in 395, he was elected bishop of Hippo (modern Annaba in Algeria). He developed into a great preacher, theologian and statesman and a staunch defender of orthodox Christianity. He was a shepherd to the people of Hippo and instructed them regularly in his sermons and addresses. He presided over thousands of cases involving litigation and sometimes was so overwhelmed that he had to persuade them to go to the magistrates. He was compassionate with sinners and tireless in reconciling them back into the church.

We learn much about Augustine's view of the church from his battles with the Donatists to whom we have already referred. Donatists dated back to the year 250 and the Decian Persecution and to Bishop Cyprian of Carthage. During these times of persecution some Christians had denied their faith under duress. As we have already seen, this led to a spiritual elitism, a separation between those who stood firm under persecution and those who wilted. The notion of the church as a 'community of saints' took a knock and while this was not abandoned, there was a tendency to look to the clergy for greater holiness than amongst laity. The 'holy clergy' position had been taken by Bishop Cyprian and the Donatists pushed it to the limit. A flash point occurred in 312. A man called Caecilian was consecrated Bishop of Carthage but he was not *persona grata* with everybody because he had played down the adoration being paid to martyrs. His enemies weakened his authority by claiming that one of the bishops taking part in his consecration was a *traditor*, that is, somebody who had handed Scriptures over to pagan authorities in order to obtain a certificate and thereby avoid persecution. Donatists condemned churches that supported Caecilian, saying that they shared the guilt of *traditors*. There was a woman involved as well. She was Lucilla who complained that Caecilian had forbidden her to kiss the bones of a martyr before taking communion. Donatists were strong in Hippo, probably outnumbering the orthodox but Augustine opposed them. There were many issues at stake but essentially Augustine's position was that the whole church needed to pray, 'forgive us our trespasses' because as long as the church was in the world she is imperfect and needs to be cleansed by confession. The church he saw was a mixture of saints and sinners, called to holiness maybe but imperfect nevertheless. Simply, the church was true to Christ when it tolerated sinful members because Christ had done the same himself. The Donatist schism in Africa left wounds that severely weakened African Christianity leaving it vulnerable.

Another problem Augustine dealt with was the British born Palagian heresy. Palagius appeared in Rome about 395 and later moved on to Africa. He declared that man is capable of living without sin and does not therefore require divine grace. This led Jerome to say of him—'his wits are addled with scotch porridge'. He rejected the view that man's fall, his tendency towards sin, had left us with a corrupt nature. Augustine on the other hand saw the full force of Paul's letter to the Romans:

> *I discover this principle then; that when I want to do right, only the wrong is within my reach.*
> **(Rom. 7:21)**

In his *Confessions* Augustine put it this way:

> *You turned your gaze on me, sunk in death, and with your right hand drew out the pit of corruption at the bottom of my heart. As a result I ceased to want what I had wanted before and came to want what you wanted.*
> **(Confessions 9:1)**

Justo Gonzalez, in his book, *A History of Christian Thought, vol. 2*, writes of Augustine, 'The main currents of ancient theology converge in him, and from him flow the rivers, not only of medieval scholasticism, but also of sixteenth century Protestant theology'. Paramount in that theology is a belief in the absolute supremacy of God. There is evil in the world because man has misused freedom given to him and created the gulf which exists between Creator and created. Evil comes to man in his milk because he is a fallen creature with a weakness stretching back to Adam. It is original sin because it involves a seminal identity. Augustine's main theological themes deal with the reality of that separation and the means whereby that gulf can be bridged. Man is a fallen being needing someone to atone for his sin. Jesus did this in his death by restoring man's original relationship with God. He also needs Divine Grace, which only comes as a gift from God. He introduces the idea of Predestination and irresistible grace, calling on his own conversion experience to underline his thinking. He had not chosen God but God had chosen him. He wrote, '*my whole hope is in thy exceeding great mercy and that alone. Give what Thou commandest and command what Thou wilt'*.

Augustine's *City of God* is his major literary achievement. It took thirteen years to write and runs to over a thousand pages. It was written when the Roman Empire was in crisis and people were beginning to think the unthinkable—could Rome one day collapse? Even Jerome had cried, 'If Rome can perish, what can be safe?' Augustine's answer was to say that within the empire two cities existed, one was the pagan city struggling to achieve material well being and riddled with deceit and duplicity. Alongside it lived citizens of the City of God whose hearts were filled with intimations of heaven. The two cities coexist yet one is purely temporal, the second eternal. This interpretation of history was a great inspiration to people going through the direst of troubles and a new hope for those who had come to associate the Christianised Empire with the kingdom of God. Augustine was the last bishop of Hippo. He died in 430, by which time the Roman Empire in the West was in its death throes. Vandals attacked Africa and soon Hippo was under their control. Many bishops were shipped to Corsica and forced to cut timber for Vandal fleets. It was a period of tumult and change not to be seen by the great bishop. He died with a copy of the penitential psalms beside him.

Judged by any standards Augustine was an incredible figure. The Protestant theologian Harnack said of him, 'In the fifth century, the hour that the Church inherited the Roman Empire, she had within her a man of extraordinary deep and powerful genius: from him she took her ideas, and to this present hour she has been unable to break away from them'. On the debit side, the notion of sin transmitted through male sperm from Adam can be viewed as one of the great tragedies of theological history and the reason for the unhealthy view of sexuality contained in Roman Catholicism to the present day.

John Chrysostom (350–407)

The monasticism of people like Basil and Jerome indicated a desire some had to restore to Christianity something of its crusading purity. But the religion of Jesus of Nazareth had been so 'successful' it had attained power and influence and was no longer the faith of the underdog. This success undermined its moral strength. It was a classic paradox. Secret worshippers in homes and catacombs now worshipped in elaborate churches and cathedrals and worshippers included emperors and politicians. An uneasy alliance of church and state ensued. How could Christianity retain its integrity and zeal and remain the recognised religion of the high, mighty and privileged? It was a dilemma, which has never been resolved.

John Chrysostom's life illustrates the dilemma very well. He was raised as a Christian by his widowed mother Anthusa, a woman of such exemplary character that John's pagan professor Libanius said of her, 'God, what women these Christians have'. Libanius wanted John to succeed him in his job but bewailed the fact that the Christians had stolen him. John was nicknamed Chrysostomos (golden mouthed) an indication of his power with words. In 370 he gave up ideas of the legal career he had toyed with and was baptised. Immediately, he began to practice a life of strict self-discipline and when his mother died he spent four years in a monastery and a further two years as a hermit. His privations impaired his health but when he moved to Antioch he was ordained priest and his preaching was so powerful and persuasive that crowds flocked to hear him. Word of his preaching reached Constantinople, where the lackeys of the eastern Emperor Arcadius plotted a kidnap and took him to the capital as a virtual prisoner. Theophilus, bishop of Alexandria, consecrated him as bishop of Constantinople, in a curious example of the way the church of the East was dominated by the state. However, the royal household was in for a shock. Chrysostom may have lacked the statesmanship of Ambrose in the West, but he was no sycophant and soon he was preaching in John the Baptist style about the pompous luxury surrounding the royal household:

> *The emperor wears on his head a crown of gold decorated with precious stones of inestimable value. These ornaments and his purple garments are reserved for his sacred person alone; and his robes of silk are embroidered with the figures of golden dragons. His throne is of massy gold. Whenever he appears in public he is surrounded by his courtiers, his guards and his attendants.*
> (***Decline & Fall***, Ch. XXXVIII)

John's predecessors had spent vast sums of money on hospitality but he gave all the money away to charity and followed that by sacking time-serving clergy and preaching a sermon likening the empress to Jezebel. The Empress Eudoxia, once a devotee, now turned against him in fury. She persuaded her husband to banish the troublesome preacher but no sooner was this done than the people demanded his return. He was triumphantly reinstated in his cathedral and Chrysostom publicly denounced Eudoxia from the pulpit:

> *Again Herodias raves, again she dances, again she demands John's head on a charger.*

Like John the Baptist before him, he was a doomed man. After riot and bloodshed inside the cathedral Chrysostom was arrested and banished to the Taurus Mountains. Even in exile his influence continued until eventually, under instructions, his guards harried him to death.

The work of John Chrysostom lives on through his sermons, letters and missions, especially amongst Goths and Scythians. His life held up a mirror to the uneasy alliance between church and state, to the parlous state of 'professional' faith and the moral weakness in the divided empire. His ill treatment also led Pope Innocent I to break off communion with eastern churches for a period until John had been posthumously vindicated.

Benedict of Nursia (480–547)

By the close of the fifth century monasticism was firmly entrenched as a recognised and admired way of Christian living. Asceticism was a feature of this life but study and scholarship were also important. Cassiodorus (490–583) was another great name in western monasticism and he put stress on the copying of manuscripts and the study of old texts. This became a feature of a monk's life, similar to that lived by the occupants of Qumran who copied out the texts we now know as the Dead Sea Scrolls (see *Through the Bible in Eighty Days*, page 226).

Benedict eventually provided a definitive rule for western monasteries. Information about his life comes from the *Dialogues of Gregory the Great*, which is not so much a biography as snippets from a life. From these snippets we glean that Benedict had a twin sister called Scholastica. They were born in northern Italy but studied in Rome until Benedict, appalled by the licentiousness of his companions, decided to escape. He became a solitary in a village called Enfide, thirty miles from Rome. His success was limited until he moved to the monastery at Monte Cassino, where he worked out his '*rule*' for monastics.

Central to the '*rule*', is the supreme authority of the abbot. A monk is expected to be learned, pious, and beyond reproach. Brothers were to be obedient, subordinate, humble and content. Those breaking rules were warned and could be physically punished. Continuous offending led to excommunication. Brothers took turns to serve others and everybody was expected to do stints in the kitchen and do the less popular tasks of community living. The reward of servers was an extra piece of bread and cup of wine, these were sweeteners to keep them happy and prevent fatigue. Mealtimes were silent except for the reading of Scripture, whispering was forbidden and food was passed round tables in rote so nobody needed to ask for anything. An important rule concerned the sick; they were allowed to eat meat and bathe regularly until they were well again. Prayers were called seven times a day as sanctioned by Psalm 119 and between these times manual labour and study filled in the day.

Personal possessions were meagre: a mattress, two woollen blankets, a pillow, a hood, tunic, shoes, knife, belt, needle and handkerchief. These were necessities of life and were provided by the abbot. Private possessions, other than these, were confiscated. Monasteries themselves were situated near water. Mills, bakeries and gardens provided work within the fellowship, dissuading any dependency on outside facilities. Life in a Benedictine monastery was not the Ritz but it was less harsh then other possible lives and in the context of the fifth and sixth centuries, when life was often short and cheap, it provided security and fulfilment.

As far as is known, Benedict never became a priest himself but people visited him from far and wide until his death in 547, when he was buried beside his sister Scholastica. Shortly after his death the monastery at Monte Cassino was destroyed by the Lombards. Monks fled to Rome taking Benedict's *rule* with them, thus bringing it to the notice of Gregory the Great.

Effects of Monasticism

The desire for spiritual purity, which drove people into monastic life, was laudable enough but it produced fruit good and bad. The monks who lived under regular discipline, submissive to an abbot (Coenibites) were quite different to those who were isolated, extreme and sometimes weirdly bizarre (Anachorets). Occasionally monasteries in Egypt, Palestine and Syria were a mixture of coenibites and anachorets with a main dwelling surrounded by a more distant circle of solitary cells where hermits exhibited extravagant penance, applauded by 'ordinary' Christians. An extreme example of an anachorets was Simon Stylite who became famous for living out much of his life within a circle of stones, where, attached to a chain, he ascended a column, which he raised ever higher from nine feet to sixty feet. In those confines he stayed for thirty years. When he died a church was erected over the pillar, the ruins of which can still be seen in Syria. Such fanaticism is an interesting psychological study of mind over matter but it seems far removed from the life of Jesus of Nazareth.

Other monks were known to take up cudgels in 'spiritual' warfare. Armed gangs of them espousing theological causes were known to overawe some church councils with threats of violence. One abbot called Schnoudi supported Cyril of Alexandria in an 'ecclesiastical protection racket' to ensure a heretic called Nestorius was condemned for heresy at the Council of Ephesus in 431. Sadly, monks were responsible for destroying pagan temples and even murdering pagans. Their conduct was lamentable and led to the unfortunate 'piety' that vandalised many of the reliefs and obelisks of ancient Egypt. Interestingly though, at Karnak, a beautiful hypostile hall with two rows of ten columns and one row of thirty-two rectangular pillars, was converted into a church by Christian monks of the sixth century.

The monastery was their one hope of survival, refuge and succour.

On the credit side, monastic learning undoubtedly ensured that the glories of Greco-Roman culture lived on after those civilisations had crumbled to dust. Even in the darkest days of the Dark Ages, dedicated monks copied and translated the wisdom of the ancient world. Cassiodorus, whose long life bridged the fifth and sixth centuries, had a great enthusiasm for secular learning as well as that of early Christian writers like Clement of Alexandria. He also took on the challenge of translating the work of Josephus, the Jewish historian.

Also on the credit side was the remarkable medical work done by monks. It is difficult for people used to a National Health Service to imagine what life was like for ancient people who were ill or fell on hard times. For such the monastery was their one hope of survival, refuge and succour. Even in our sophisticated times, we should remind ourselves that the oldest of our hospitals date back to the monasteries.

The main centres of spirituality were also to be found in monasteries and the best bishops were commonly called from them to lead the flock. This, in practice, meant that many bishops were celibate and so celibacy grew into something like an ideal to follow. Jerome was especially enthusiastic about celibacy and often seemed to denigrate marriage. Some monks deserted their wives to take up the celibate life and a Roman law had to be passed in 420 to forbid the practice.

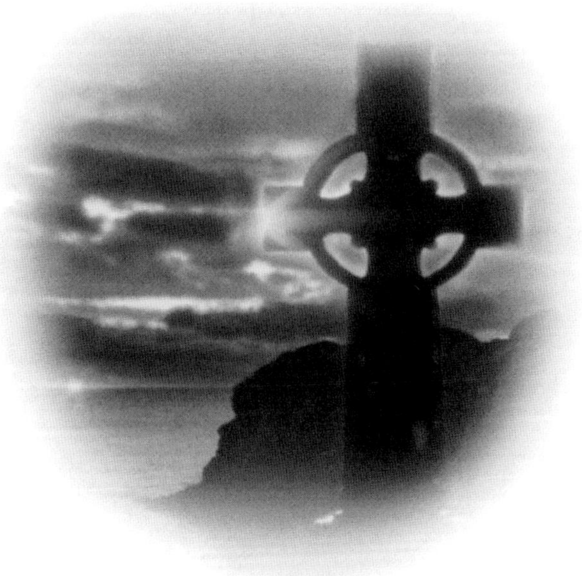

4 Shaking the Foundations

Leo the Great	71
Councils at Ephesus and Chalcedon	72
Clovis	74
Gregory I	74

The fall of Rome was not a single spectacular siege which changed the balance of power overnight. Germanic tribes had been eating away at Roman boundaries since the third century. Goths, Visigoths, Vandals, Lombards and others all made inroads at various times only to be eased back eventually. Visigoths were Christians who had accepted the Arian brand of Christianity having broken with mainstream Christianity after the Council of Nicaea. On the night of 24th August, 410, Alaric, king of the Visigoths, stormed Rome's defences in a surprise attack and for three days the city was sacked and pillaged. Then Alaric withdrew and on the surface no permanent physical damage had been done but the damage to the confidence of the inhabitants of Rome was considerable. After all, Rome had not been under the heel of an aggressor for 800 years and now she looked vulnerable indeed. 'The city which has taken the whole world has itself been taken', cried Jerome. Some felt the shaking of the foundations so much they thought the end of the world had come and the invaders were likened to the Horsemen of the Apocalypse. In 452 Attila the Hun also invaded Italy but he was persuaded to withdraw by a delegation led by Pope Leo I. But then came the Vandals and they were not so ready to withdraw.

The loss of Africa to the Vandals had been a serious blow to the Roman Empire. The wealthy estates of senators were ravaged by them and their wealth ceased to flow across the Mediterranean. Worse was to follow. Genseric, king of the Vandals, now controlled fertile land from Tangier to Tripoli and he was looking for more. Looking seaward from the port of Carthage (like Hannibal had once done before him) he coveted land on the mainland and started to build ships and train sailors who were soon skilled enough to cross the sea and cast anchor at the mouth of the Tiber. Rome was within his grasp. Maximus the Emperor witnessed the landing of Genseric with a supine indifference and only seems to have been roused from lethargy by the fear and exasperation of the populace. When he did venture onto the streets the emperor was greeted with a volley of stones which killed him. His body was mangled and ignominiously cast into the Tiber. The great city of Rome was defenceless.

Expecting to be met by a phalanx of Roman soldiers the Vandals faced instead an unarmed bishop. That bishop was Leo the Great.

Leo the Great *(Pope 440–461)*

The fearless Leo armed with ecclesiastical authority sought mitigation from Genseric for the people of Rome. Since the sack of Rome by Alaric in 410, the mantle of Roman authority had been assumed by Constantinople and there was an imperial court at Ravenna on the Adriatic, but Leo guessed correctly that there was to be no 'cavalry charge' from there and so sought to do the best he could to alleviate the damage. He gained promises from the Vandals to spare lives, protect buildings from arson and captives from torture. It may have made some difference but Leo was unable to prevent pillage on the grand scale which went on for two weeks. Treasures and immense wealth were stripped from buildings sacred and profane and then transported to Genseric's vessels. Gibbon comments wryly:

> *The holy instruments of Jewish worship, the gold table and the gold candlestick with seven branches, originally framed according to the particular instruction of God himself, and which was placed in the sanctuary of his temple, had been ostentatiously displayed to the Roman people in the triumph of Titus. They were afterwards deposited in the temple of Peace; and at the end of four hundred years, the spoils of Jerusalem were transferred from Rome to Carthage by a barbarian who derived his origin from the shores of the Baltic. The Christian churches, enriched by the prevailing superstition of the times, afforded plentiful materials for sacrilege; and the pious liberality of Pope Leo melted six silver vases. the gift of Constantine, each of an hundred pound weight, is an evidence of the damage he attempted to repair...it was difficult to escape or satisfy the avarice of a conqueror who possessed leisure to collect and ships to transport, the wealth of the capital.*
> **(*Decline & Fall*, xxxvi)**

Did Leo save Rome? Perhaps the worst excesses of the invader were ameliorated by his diplomacy. Certainly his action showed that the bishop of Rome was beginning to act like a civic ruler. Furthermore, he adopted the title Pontifex Maximus (Supreme Priest) and spoke of the apostles Peter and Paul as being the founding fathers of Christian Rome just as Romulus and Remus had been founders of the pagan Rome. Henceforth he was to speak not just as a priest amongst other priests but as the successor of Peter with all his authority. Leo sought to lead the entire church as the rightful ruler or pope because the authority given to Peter was now his. 'Thou art Peter, and upon this rock I will build my church; and the gates of hell shall not prevail against it.'

As we consider this period of upheaval, it is well to pause and remember that the fall of Rome did not exactly mean the end of an empire. In the East the Byzantine Empire centred in Constantinople avoided the traumas of Rome and a succession of Caesars continued. Unlike the West the eastern church had always been subservient to the state. True there was some independence but it had been granted rather than gained. It is important to remember this when considering later developments in Christianity. The spectacle of an emperor like Theodosius being humiliated by a bishop like Ambrose in Milan could not have happened in the East even though it produced unequivocal preachers like Chrysostom.

In the West, despite the collapse of Rome's political structure, life continued in an orderly if chastened way with the church taking over many of the functions of state. The bishop of Rome played a vital role in maintaining that structure. In later years attempts were made to revive the empire of the West but it was largely the church that provided whatever stability there was for an anarchic age. The church, through the monasteries, made sure that learning survived and the poor and sick were cared for. There were unscrupulous clergy around, attracted by power and wealth, but there was also devotion and inner strength enabling it to ride out upheavals and provide continuity and example throughout dark ages. Indeed, the historian Kenneth Latourette claims that the western experience even enhanced the Christian witness:

> *It is significant that this impulse from Jesus issuing in a vigorous church was most potent in the conditions peculiar to Western Europe. It persisted in the Byzantine Empire but not so markedly, apparently because it was handicapped by a strong even though ostensibly friendly state.*
> **(*The Unquenchable Light*, p 28; Eyre and Spottiswoode, 1945)**

Councils at Ephesus and Chalcedon

Looking back from the vantage point of modern times, it seems incredible to believe that while the fabric of international stability was crumbling to dust ecclesiastical argument continued unabated. The Council of Nicaea had concluded that Jesus and God were of the same substance. Now in 431 the emperor in Constantinople,

Theodosius II, called another Council, this time in Ephesus, to settle a dispute arising from the teaching of a bishop of Constantinople called Nestorius, who had been appointed by the emperor himself. Nestorius was soon unpopular for unprovoked attacks on Jews and heretics and also incurred the hostility of Cyril, the patriarch of Alexandria. Nestorius objected to a title 'Theotokos' given to Mary the mother of Jesus. The title meant Mother of God and Nestorius thought this misleading. He was immediately under attack from Cyril and Pope Celestine I, who not only condemned his theology but deposed him from his bishopric. The Council of Ephesus declared:

If any one does not acknowledge that Emmanuel is in truth God, and that the holy Virgin is, in consequence, 'Theotokos', for she brought forth after the flesh the Word of God who has become flesh—let him be anathema.

Nestorius retired to a monastery where he wrote a book called *Tragedy* justifying his position and ensuring that his teaching lived on in many who followed him.

Interestingly, the emperor had invited Augustine of Hippo to attend the Council of Ephesus, not knowing that he had died the previous year. How the Council might have benefited from the wise leadership of such a man. Instead the disputes rumbled on and another Council was called in 451, this time at Chalcedon (across the Bosphorus from Constantinople). The proceedings were presided over by three legates from Pope Leo who had just circulated the church with a statement of faith usually called *Leo's Tome*. It proved to be a weighty intervention from the see of Rome on doctrine concerning the Person of Christ. A committee of bishops drew up a statement, which included this passage: 'We confess one and the same Christ, Son, Lord, Only-begotten, recognised in two natures, without confusion, without change, without division, without separation—the property of each nature being preserved and combining into one person; not as it were parted or divided into two persons, but one and the self-same Son, Only begotten, God the Word, Lord Jesus Christ'. This was presented to the council along with the Creeds of Nicaea and Constantinople and the council declared that this was the Faith of the Apostles we all follow! There were minor adjustments at two further councils but by and large the main doctrinal questions were settled and the faith of the Catholic Church set forth and safeguarded. No major changes have been made to the substance of Chalcedon since except the addition of the famous *Filoque* in the West stating that the Holy Spirit proceeded from the Son as well as from the Father.

Clovis *(c. 466–511)*

The leaders of the barbarian tribes, which invaded the Roman Empire from the fifth century were heretical Christians, most of them Arians (see Chapter 2). The leader of the Franks however was a pagan, though even he had a Christian wife. Information about Clovis comes almost entirely from the historian Gregory of Tours but it would seem that he was a federate chieftain within the Roman Empire. As the Empire crumbled he asserted himself and when he defeated Syagrius, the last Roman ruler in Gaul, he was in charge of what is now northern France. In a battle on the river Rhine he faced a serious defeat and in his extremity sought help from the God of his wife. His success in battle was attributed to his prayers and like Constantine before him he converted to Christianity. He was baptised by Remigius, the bishop of Rheims, in a dramatic ceremony at Rheims cathedral along with 3,000 of his warriors and the people followed him, 'We will give up worshipping our mortal gods, pious King, and we are prepared to follow the immortal God about whom Remigius preaches'.

Clovis failed to drive the Goths from southern Gaul but established himself at Paris where he built a church dedicated to the apostles and later called Saint-Genevieve. His authority as a Christian was such that he summoned a council at Orleans attended by 32 bishops and was personally involved in the deliberations. Roman power had disappeared in Gaul but a new Constantine had assured the position of Christianity at the heart of the blossoming country of France.

So the ancient world experienced shuddering changes on the political scene and struggled for agreement about what constituted an official explanation for the Christian experience. Meanwhile, the transition from Ancient World to Medieval World was ready to take place and at the helm of the church in Rome was a man for the moment—his name was Gregory.

Gregory I *(540–604)*

Gregory was a Roman, a landowner, a man with good administrative skills and experience in imperial service. About 573 he gave up his public service and wealth to become a monk. Later he was sent to Constantinople as an ambassador. By 590 he was bishop of Rome and facing a desperate future. The Lombards were threatening to destroy the city, citizens were blighted with famine and plague and as Ravenna was uninterested, Gregory assumed total command. He administered city relief, provided a defence, organised generals in the army and negotiated peace with the Lombards. All this without any official authorisation from any imperial source. At a stroke authority was assumed by the bishop and the transition from ancient to medieval world had been bridged.

With this assumption of power Gregory also adopted a stance of universal ruler of Christendom when he put real authority behind the title 'pope'. Gregory was not thinking in purely western terms either and soon let it be known that he disapproved of Patriarch John of Constantinople using the term 'universal bishop' of himself. Officially, Eastern Emperors did have the authority to keep Gregory subservient and all appointments from Rome needed the rubber stamp of Constantinople but in reality Gregory had changed the balance of power. He made no obvious attempt to dominate the Eastern church but was at loggerheads with John of Constantinople and he chose the title 'servant of the servants of God' for himself. He became a ruler, theologian, preacher, liturgical innovator (he even founded a choir school in Rome) and, as his *Book of Pastoral Rule* shows, he was a real shepherd of the flock.

Gregory did more than anybody else to provide the shape of the Roman Catholic Church as we know it today and he is often considered by church historians to be the last of the church fathers after Ambrose, Jerome and Augustine. He is also thought of as the first medieval pope, the one who rejected the Byzantine claim of equality between patriarchs. He was the man who filled the power vacuum left in the decaying Empire and inside the church he provided rules for all Western bishops. He launched great missionary drives against Arian tribes of Europe in an attempt to win them for Catholic Christianity and it was Gregory who, in 597, decided to send a team of monks, led by Augustine, to convert the warlike Anglo-Saxons of Britain. A biographer of Gregory tells how he had been impressed by sturdy, blonde Angle slaves who were being sold in Rome. He called them 'angels' not 'angles' and he bought some to train as monks, later to return to England as missionaries. He also officially recognised the monastic movement of Benedict of Nursia and blessed it as the blueprint for the Western church, ensuring that thereafter Catholic monastic orders were of Benedictine style. He was a prolific writer and some 850 letters of his have survived to this day. These show him to be deeply ascetic, somewhat mystical and always highly political.

Unwittingly, Gregory took decisions which eventually contributed to the divisions with Eastern Orthodoxy and Protestantism, but his legacy to medieval Christendom was considerable. He ruled over much of Italy and, though pope for a mere fourteen years, his indelible stamp of authority still lives with us today.

5 *Christianity in Britain*

Patrick	78
Columba	79
Augustine	80
Aidan	82
Hilda	83

When Augustine arrived in Britain in 597 it was not to a land devoid of Christian influence. How Christianity first reached this misty island must remain a subject for conjecture, perhaps through Roman soldiers, commercial travellers, or even unknown early missionaries. As early as 209 a soldier called Alban had been beheaded for harbouring a Christian priest and bishops from London, York and Lincoln are known to have attended the Council of Arles, called in 314, to sort out the traditor dispute. A missionary had also left British shores by 432, when Patrick crossed the Irish Sea to preach in Ireland.

As the Roman Empire crumbled in the West, legions were withdrawn from Britain leaving the way open to invasion from Scots, Irish, Franks, as well as the Saxons from Germany, amongst whom were the English or Angles. It is these we now call Anglo-Saxons. Conflicts were fierce indeed but though the Saxons have been accused of hating all things Roman, it would be wrong to think the departure of Roman government plunged Britain into a cultural and spiritual black-out. In fact, a distinctive Celtic Christianity flourished with a culture never totally eradicated and these days the subject of much interest. How that culture merged with Latin Christianity we will now consider.

Patrick (389–461)

Patrick was born near Hadrian's Wall in Roman Britain, the son of a deacon and Roman magistrate called Calpurnius. When he was sixteen he and others were kidnapped by marauders from Northern Ireland and sold as slaves. He worked for six years as a shepherd and his conversion dates from this time. He wrote, 'The Lord opened to me the sense of my unbelief that I might remember my sins and that I might return with my whole heart to the Lord my God'. After six years he escaped and returned to the mainland, where he brushed up his education and at some time seems to have travelled to France. Ireland was, however, deep in his heart and a night vision convinced him that he must return.

By 432 he was back in Ireland with a Christian message for a people saturated in magic and occult practices from the Druids. His missionary strategy was to win tribal leaders for Christ so their tribal warfare would come to an end. Tradition says he taught the mysteries of the Trinity with the aid of a shamrock. He was spectacularly successful and many local lords became Christians quickly followed by the

Tradition says he taught the mysteries of the Trinity with the aid of a shamrock.

peasants. Some estimates claim that a hundred thousand converts resulted from his ministry.

Patrick was not a scholar himself but he did encourage learning in others and seems to have been a champion of the monastic life. Monasteries became the centres of organised Christianity and great numbers of monks took their faith into Western Europe during this period. Patrick favoured a private kind of asceticism like that of the Egyptian Antony and it was this Egyptian pattern, typified by extreme rigour and learning, which took root in Ireland. The lack of sizeable towns in Ireland probably gave the monasteries greater influence than usual and soon Celtic monks were familiar figures throughout Europe, indeed many of the continental monasteries were established by them. By the time of his death, the cathedral church of Armagh was a centre of learning and administration and a guarantee that the tenacity and devotion of his ministry would live on.

Columba (521–597)

A man greatly influenced by the Celtic monks of Ireland was an aristocrat from Donegal called Columba. He was a mathematician, poet, musician and scribe with a flavouring of classical studies and theology. He was another who founded several monasteries in Ireland until, in 561, he became embroiled in a conflict and skirmish where several people were killed. Columba was exiled. Along with twelve colleagues he sailed to the small Hebridean island of Iona, off the coast of Mull, and this island became home and base for missions to the northern tribes of Scotland, where he was particularly successful with the Picts. He infiltrated the tribal life of Scotland and larger kingdoms, like Dalriada in the west, adding a Christian component to a culture already producing beautiful crafts in metal, glass, wood, leather and basketry. He formed schools and offered new intellectual possibilities in classical learning, art and writing, sometimes with spectacular results. The *Book of Kells* is probably the finest manuscript produced in Britain during the so-called Dark Ages. It is thought that over three hundred books were produced by Columba, though only one, a Psalter written on vellum, has survived.

Today, Iona is a remote island but in Columba's day it was central to a network of sea lanes linking Ireland and Scotland and perfectly situated to launch missions, oversee schools and monasteries and arbitrate in political events like the royal succession to the kingdom of Dalriada. He was the peace-broker of his day who smoothed out squabbles between Irish and Scot's pretenders. Columba died in 597, the very year Augustine, commissioned by Gregory I, arrived in Britain as a missionary from Rome. In the north of Britain thriving Christian communities already existed and Iona was a place of pilgrimage. This influence did decline with the later marginalisation of the Columban Church and the gravitation towards Canterbury in England and Armargh in Ireland, but the survival of crosses, art and music still bear eloquent testimony to a unique Celtic Christian expression, which received a great impetus from the life of Columba.

Augustine (d. 604?)

Augustine reluctantly embarked on his mission to Britain accompanied by forty monks. They arrived just before Easter in the year 597. Gregory, who was well informed about Britain, had read the situation well for Britain was ripe for evangelism. Ethelbert, the king of Kent, had married a Christian princess of the Franks called Bertha and she had brought a chaplain with her. As Ethelbert's kingdom extended towards the Humber in the north he was an important fish to catch. When the king was confronted by a procession of missionaries chanting in Latin he wasn't meeting something entirely new for Ethelbert was already half converted and his baptism soon followed. Augustine set up his headquarters at a little Roman church at Canterbury and this became the first Episcopal centre in England. Augustine was off to a flying start. Other Anglo-Saxon kingdoms proved more difficult to convert and even when they eventually adopted Christianity some bishops, monks and nuns found the habit of getting drunk difficult to overcome! The historian Bede complained shortly before his death that some villages never saw a priest and peasants were unable to recite the Lord's Prayer.

Celtic Christians, for their part, did not accept Augustine as their Archbishop and they were affronted when he refused to stand in greeting them. They also had differences with him about the date for Easter and Roman traditions about baptism. Augustine's work prevailed however, and by the time he died he left bishops in Canterbury, Rochester and London. Then a missionary from Kent called Paulinus moved north and was well received in Lincolnshire and Yorkshire and converted king Edwin of Northumbria. On Easter Day 627 Edwin was baptised at York on a spot where an imposing stone basilica was ordered to be built. Paulinus then inspired a religious awakening around Wooller where he spent thirty-six days baptising people of the region. Bede, the monk of Jarrow, and the father of English history wrote:

> *From dawn to dusk he did nothing else but proclaim Christ's saving message to the crowds who flocked to hear from all the surrounding villages and countryside; and when he had instructed them he washed them in the cleansing waters of baptism in the River Glen, which was nearby.*
> **(Bede, *Church History of the English People*)**

For a period Christianity held Edwin's realm in thrall and the north of England was so peaceful that it was said a woman with a new-born baby in her arms could walk in safety from sea to sea. Then Edwin was killed in battle and many of the gains made by Paulinus were lost. In an attempt to regain lost ground Oswald, the great king of Northumbria, appealed to the abbot of Iona to send them someone who could put things right and after a false start with an austere monk called Carman, Aidan was chosen and proved to be the man for the hour.

Aidan (d. 651)

King Oswald received Aidan with open arms and offered him any site in his realm as a see. Aidan chose the Isle of Lindisfarne not far from Oswald's capital at Bamburgh, an island partly cut off from the mainland by tides. Perhaps it reminded Aidan of Iona.

Lindisfarne quickly became an inspirational centre for spiritual and educational activity. Bede lavished praise on the work of Aidan, even though his religious sympathies rested with the Roman mission from Canterbury rather than the Celtic centre of Iona.

> *Many Scots arrived daily in Britain and proclaimed the word of God with great devotion in all the provinces under Oswald's rule...Churches were built in several places and the people flocked gladly to hear the word of God, while Oswald gave money and land to establish monasteries and the English both noble and simple, were instructed by their Scots teachers to observe a regular and disciplined life.*
> (op. cit.)

The relationship between Aidan and the king could not have been closer:

> *The king always listened humbly and readily to Aidan's advice...and while the bishop, who was not yet fluent in the English language, preached the gospel, it was most delightful to see the king himself interpreting the Word of God to his thanes and leaders.*
> (op. cit.)

Life at Lindisfarne was simple and frugal. The monks had no property except cattle and all gifts were immediately transferred to the poor. Even when the king dined with them the monks ate sparingly and soon hurried back to their prayers. Aiden's preaching was uncompromising and when it inspired people to offer gifts of money as recompense for their sins, it was used to redeem people falsely sold into slavery. In modern parlance, the monks 'walked their talk' and produced such an attractive and winsome faith that even when Oswald was killed in battle Aiden's work continued to flourish.

When Aiden died he was buried at Lindisfarne. Later, his relics were reputedly moved from there to Iona, Glastonbury and then Durham Cathedral but his spirit remains in his cradle island of Lindisfarne. His life, inspirational to the north, was also invaluable in helping merge Celtic and Roman traditions throughout Britain.

Hilda (614–680)

To further clarify the position between Celtic and Roman Christianity, King Oswin, Oswald's successor, summoned a synod to convene at the royal Northumbrian monastery at Whitby, ruled by the English abbess Hilda. The year was 664.

Hilda was the grandniece of Edwin, the king of Northumbria. She was baptised at thirteen after being converted during the mission of Paulinus and twenty years later she became a nun. Within two years she was abbess of a convent in Hartlepool and she founded Whitby Abbey in 657. It provided accommodation for men and women in adjoining quarters and earned a reputation as one of the foremost religious centres in England, becoming famous for its school of theology and literature. It nurtured five future bishops and also housed a poor farmer called Caedmon who was probably the earliest Anglo-Saxon Christian poet. He wrote poems of such beauty that Hilda persuaded him to join the Abbey as a lay brother.

Whitby in 664 was the place where differences between Celts and Romans were thrashed out. In effect, the outcome was for Celtic influence to decline and for Iona to be eclipsed by Canterbury. Cross fertilisation did continue however, usually harmoniously, and the strengths of both traditions continued in another hero of Lindisfarne called Cuthbert (634–687) who fused practices sweetly until withdrawing to the Farne Islands as a recluse.

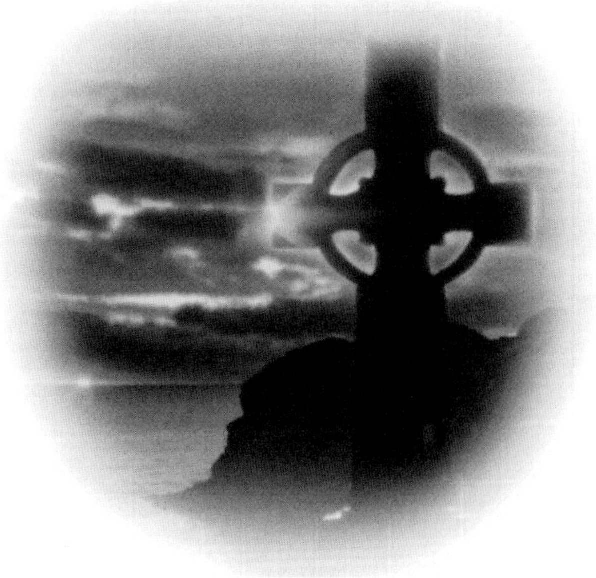

6 The Rise of Islam

Muhammed	86
Abu Bakr	89
Omar	89
Othman	90
The Religion	91
Ali ibn Abi Talib	92
Aisha	92
Fatima	93

Gregory's decision to send Augustine to Britain extended papal influence westward. Meanwhile, he was doing little to forge links with a Byzantine church developing separately and about to face a challenge destined to have great repercussions for the church and the whole world.

In the sixth century Syria and Egypt were part of the Byzantine Empire, while Iraq was part of the Persian Empire. Wars between them kept life on a knife edge and disrupted the trade routes from India and the Persian Gulf. Merchants from Mecca, an important town and religious shrine in the Arabian desert, took advantage of the hostilities and became rich by exploiting the caravan routes. There was a subsequent growth in wealth leading to greed and attempts to monopolise trade. Clan chiefs began neglecting traditional duties of providing for the poor in order to concentrate on commercial activity. So, at about the time Gregory was turning his back on a career in the civil service in order to become a priest, a young Arab was about to challenge Arabian leaders with a new revelation.

Muhammed (570–632)

Muhammed's beginnings were unpromising. His father died before he was born, his mother lived only to see his sixth birthday and the grandfather who adopted him died when he was eight. It fell to an uncle to raise the boy and he took him on trading journeys into Syria. Then a wealthy widow called Khadija commissioned him to look after her goods in the caravans and was so pleased with him that she proposed marriage even though she was forty and twice widowed. Muhammed was just twenty-five. He accepted the proposal and, using her capital well, became a very successful trader. It was a happy marriage blessed with six children, four daughters and two sons, both sons died in childhood.

At the age of forty, this man of the desert was happily married with a family and wealth to provide for them. Then, in a series of strange events, Muhammed, who had each year been in the habit of retreating to meditate in caves on Mount Hira (a Christian custom rather than an Arab one) began to recite messages given to him by mystical voices. He told Khadija about the experiences and she in turn talked to a kinsman called Waraqa who knew the Bible well and could well have been a Christian. Waraqa suggested that Muhammed's experience was similar to that of Moses and persuaded him that the voices were nothing less than a revelation from God. The sense of prophetic destiny broke into his consciousness and was reluctantly, then decisively, obeyed. The similarity to Moses' experience is striking. Moses too found it difficult to speak publicly and later Muslim scholars stressed that Muhammed's messages came from outside himself and one tradition goes so far as to claim that Muhammed was illiterate. Like an Old Testament prophet (he would have been familiar with both Judaism and Christianity) he began to urge the people of Mecca to worship God alone and get rid of their many idols. It was his constant sermon, primed steadily by the recurring messages coming to him. Encouraged by his wife, he grew in confidence even though he knew his sermons were infuriating the rich Arabs who represented the status quo.

Mecca had long been an important religious centre for Arabs as well as the commercial capital, so Muhammed was taking on the establishment on two fronts. The city rulers were the Quraish who dominated the sacred *haram* visited by the pious during monthly pilgrimages. The haram was the area surrounding the Ka'ba which was roughly cubical in shape and had a black stone, possibly a meteorite, built into one corner. When their customs and practices were criticised by Muhammed their reaction was like that of the religious leaders who condemned Jesus for overturning the tables of the money changers in the temple courtyard. He was accused of copying the errors of other religions and there were those who questioned his sanity.

The haram was the area surrounding the Ka'ba which was roughly cubical in shape and had a black stone, possibly a meteorite, built into one corner.

Muhammed, for his part, was demanding obedience to God (*Islam*) and stating that only those who were obedient were righteous (*Muslim*). In rejecting false gods Muhammed was abandoning the whole heathen cultus and instituting in its place a worship of prayer, like the devotions of Christians and Jews. The prayers were individual though Muslims did come together as well. This provoked hostility from the Meccans and forced the Muslims to choose secluded places outside the city for their meetings. Muhammed's conflict with the hierarchy lasted for thirteen years during which time Khadija and his guardian uncle died. His message of one God infuriated the rich Arabs whose faith required many idols and by 622 he and a few of his followers were forced to leave Mecca and move to an oasis two hundred and fifty miles north. This was Medina.

This emigration was the *hijra*, a decisive moment in the development of Islam, in its way as decisive as the Jewish *exodus* from Egypt. Muhammed's message up to this point had been religious and a struggle in defence of freedom of conscience but from the emigration onwards his messages became more political, more concerned with building a power structure and he became an accomplished military leader. It was a move likely to make a confrontation with the Quraish in Mecca inevitable. Skirmishes ensued for the next eight years during which time Muhammed seems to have hoped for an alliance with the many Jews around Medina but they refused to recognise him as a latter-day prophet and relationships soured. Muhammed's five-fold daily prayers changed direction and instead of facing Jerusalem worshippers turned towards Mecca. It was a hugely symbolic moment. In Medina a large house of worship (*mesjed*, mosque) was built where the faithful could perform their private devotions and where they could pray in unison under the direction of Muhammed.

In ensuing battles with the Quraish, Muhammed outmanoeuvred them and eventually gained the right to return to Mecca as a pilgrim. He strengthened his position still further by acquiring Jewish property and annexing neutral tribes. When he made his next move to Mecca he was too powerful to resist and 'manifest victory' was attained and more and more tribes joined his federation. All those subdued by Muhammed became Muslims and were not allowed to attack one another. Therefore the raid (*razzia*), which drove off the camels of unfriendly neighbours and was a normal activity of tribal life, didn't take place and the energies of the tribesmen were directed outwards towards Syria and Iraq. This was the beginning of expansion, a policy vigorously pursued by Muhammed's successors, the caliphs.

In March 632, after a life of struggle and achievement Muhammed made a great pilgrimage (*Hajj*) to Mecca. Three months later he was dead. He had done little to arrange for anybody to succeed him apart from appointing Abu Bakr to lead worship when he was ill, so the struggle to succeed him was fierce, especially as he had married several wives after the death of Khadija. After meetings in Medina leaders chose Abu Bakr to lead the community and he took the title Khalifat Rasul Allah (successor to the messenger of God) from where the title caliph is derived.

Abu Bakr (570–634)

Abu Bakr was Muhammed's father-in-law and closest associate. Sunni Muslims regard him as the first of four 'righteous caliphs'. He had accompanied the prophet on his migration to Medina and sometime later his daughter Aisha became the third and probably the favourite of Muhammed's many wives. Abu Bakr was conspicuous in military campaigns and a greatly respected advisor but his rule lasted just two years. During that time he quashed an attempt by Meccans to break from the federation and reassert their authority and resisted a challenge from a woman called Sajda who claimed to be a prophetess. By 633 Abu Bakr had taken control of central Arabia and paved the way for conquest in Syria, Palestine, Egypt, Iraq and Iran, thus encroaching on the territories of the Byzantine Empire.

Omar (caliph 634–644)

Omar consolidated the gains of Abu and became the real organiser of an empire. He turned the heat on both the Byzantine and Persian Empires and Damascus fell to the Muslims in 635, the following year a decisive battle was fought against the Byzantines beside the river Yarmuk, a tributary of the Jordan, south of the Sea of Galilee. Victory gave access to the Golan Heights and the conquest of Syria. In 637 the ancient lands of Assyria and Babylonia were wrested from the Persians. When Omar was assassinated in 644, the Muslim Empire stretched from Cyrene in the West to India in the East.

Othman *(caliph 644–656)*

Expansion slackened under Othman as the empire reached 'natural' limits. It was a period of consolidation and settlement but it allowed the old aristocracy in Mecca to reclaim lost ground and regain control of armies and the richest provinces. Secularisation set in and the purity of Islam was diluted as a faith empire gave way to an oligarchy. Othman's position grew weaker and when he refused to abdicate he was besieged and killed in his own house.

During Othman's caliphate the process of collecting Muhammed's messages began along with a growing reverence for the 'practices of the prophet'. After all, went the reasoning, if Muhammed was God's prophet then his whole way of life, including arbitrary matters, must also be the result of divine inspiration. Thus the practices of Muhammed (*the Sunna*) became examples of guidance to be placed alongside his words, which became inspirational (*the Qur'an*). The Sunna became particularly important to the branch of Islam followed by the Sunnis. Under Othman the Qur'an obtained status and shape becoming the sacred text of Islam. Historically, Islam begins with Muhammed and the revelations in the Qur'an but religiously the faith goes back to Abraham, Moses and Jesus because these were also prophets who surrendered their wills to God as all good Muslims do.

The messages of Muhammed were in Arabic and tradition says they came via the angel Gabriel. They were committed to memory or written down on palm leaves, animal hides or bits of bone. Then, after the prophet's death, followers put them together in the form we now recognise in the Qur'an. Othman was largely responsible for writing down the text which is divided into 114 chapters (*suras*), each with its own title. These chapters are divided into verses (*ayas*). Altogether the Qur'an is about the length of the New Testament and written in a somewhat complicated mixture of prose and poetry. It is difficult to grasp, hence the need for constant interpretation.

Early messages to Muhammed were assurances that there was one God, merciful and compassionate. He is Allah the creator of all things. Everything declares his glory. Later revelations followed the penetration into Arabia and deal with the organisation of society with laws, procedures and dealing with problems. Familiar names from the Bible appear in the text, like Noah, Abraham, Joseph, Moses, Jesus and Mary and all are honoured but Muhammed himself is revered as the final perfect, prophet of God. Despite the mention of these names, the Qur'an reveals few essentials of the Jewish or Christian religions other than belief in God and a last judgement and it is an interesting conjecture to wonder if Muhammed's knowledge of these faiths was gained from Arab Christians who were poorly instructed. Certainly the misconception that Christians worship three Gods can only result from a vague awareness of Christian belief in the Trinity.

The Religion

The essence of Islam is contained in five beliefs and disciplines:

i) Muslims must confess 'there is no god but Allah and Muhammed is His Prophet'. This does not mean 'only' prophet but it does mean the last of the prophets.
ii) Muslims must observe ritual prayers five times every day, at dawn, noon, afternoon, after sunset and at night, preferably in congregation when the brotherhood of Islam is seen.
iii) Muslims must contribute two and a half per cent of gross wealth to charity. (This is like a Jewish tithe or tenth).
iv) Muslims must fast during daylight hours for one month of Ramadan. The last food and water to be taken before dawn then at dusk the fast is broken.
v) Muslims should wherever possible make a pilgrimage to Mecca and perform the prescribed rituals at a specific time of year (*hajj*) This custom began when Muslims lived near Mecca and is still preserved though pilgrims have to cross continents.

Other practices have become custom even though they are not mentioned in the Qur'an e.g. male circumcision and the wearing of a sari.

Although Islam gradually developed a distinct culture, there is little doubt that originally it shared similar ideas to Jewish and Christian customs and therefore interaction between the faiths was much easier than it is today. Difficulties began when the centre of gravity for Islam moved towards Iraq increasing the oriental influence. As the new religion spread, pagans had to accept Islam or perish but Jews and Christians as 'people of the book' were allowed special status and were happily tolerated as long as they paid normal taxes.

Ali ibn Abi Talib (600–661)

According to Sunni Muslims, Ali is the forth and last of the righteous caliphs. The Shiites regard him as son-in-law of the prophet and the designated and sole legitimate successor and the first of the imams. He is revered as the one with divinely granted knowledge, infallible and a miracle worker. Sufis also regard him as the founder of their mystical movement and trace all spiritual authority back to him. Traditionally, Ali was amongst the first converts to Islam and especially close to the prophet. One of Ali's wives was Muhammed's daughter Fatima. He had sought to be the first caliph but lost to three rivals in turn before achieving his ambition with the assassination of Othman in 656. During Ali's caliphate the first real schism occurred when some objected to the power and influenced gained by 'eleventh hour' Muslims during Othman's time. The resentment smouldered and then burst into flame when twelve thousand people deserted Ali saying he was unworthy of their allegiance. The Kharijites (come outers) believed a caliph should be elected by the voices of all Muslims and not by heredity. The 'come outers' were a puritan group within Islam and like most zealots before them they found it difficult to agree amongst themselves and split up into many factions. It is likely that the Kharijites were behind the murder of Ali in 661.

Aisha (614–678)

Aisha was the third of Muhammed's wives, the most famous and preferred after Khadija. Daughter of the loyal Abu Bakr, she was only eight when given in marriage to the prophet. All Muhammed's wives were esteemed in the community but Aisha is the one usually called 'mother of the believers'. Muhammed spent his last days with her when he was terminally ill.

Aisha remained aloof from politics until Ali's day when she joined an abortive coup. The attempt failed and she was pardoned and allowed to stay in Medina where she lived until her death. Shiites regard her with disfavour and think of her as a spiteful opponent of Ali and his wife Fatima and she is ritually cursed in public. To Sunnis on the other hand she is a paragon of virtue.

Fatima (606–632)

Fatima was a daughter of Muhammed to his first wife Khadija and the wife of Ali ibn Abi Talib. She is the ancestral mother to the imams of Shiite Muslims and to those who claim descent from the prophet. As such she is greatly respected within the Muslim tradition being described as 'infallible' and she is sometimes compared in Shiite literature to the biblical figure of Mary.

The prodigious advance of Islam slowed under Ali but built up another head of steam under the Umayyad dynasty which lasted until 750. The westward advance reached the Atlantic in Morocco and then crossed into Spain and north as far as Poitiers in France before it was decidedly halted. The Moors, as the north African Muslims were called, had a vibrant culture in Spain and a freedom of ideas and religion contrary to much of Christian Europe.

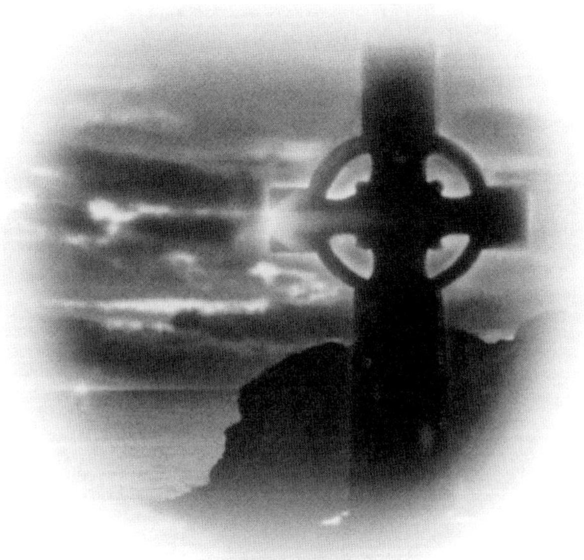

7 Worlds Collide

Boniface	97
Charlemagne	98
Vikings	100
Transubstantiation	102
Confession	103
The Icon Dispute	104
The Great Divorce	105

*T*here were now three distinct 'Religions of the Book' in the territories of the Roman and Byzantine Empires. Sometimes there were fruitful exchanges of ideas amongst them but for Christianity there were enormous problems. The Western Empire had been decimated by Vandals and Africa in particular suffered dreadfully. The churches, which had produced great men like Tertullian, Cyprian and Augustine, disappeared as Muslims surged through North Africa and on into Spain and Southern France. In Spain, Islam won converts but most Christians retained their religion even though they adopted Moorish customs and were known as Mozarabs or 'would be arabs'. Cross fertilisation led to a unique Spanish-Arabic culture with positive results, which Baron Carra de Vaux had to acknowledge even though he was not an admirer of the Arabs:

> ...they became the founders of the arithmetic of everyday life; they made algebra an exact science and developed the foundations of analytical geometry; they were indisputably the founders of plane and spherical trigonometry which properly speaking, did not exist amongst the Greeks.
> **(*The Legacy of Islam*; Clarendon, Oxford, 1931)**

They made great strides in astronomy as well for the practical reason that they needed to know the direction of distant Mecca for their prayers. They developed their own medical schools and made careful lists of plants useful in pharmacology.

Jews were an important part of life in the Muslim world of Spain. The majority of Jews in the world today are descendants of either the Ashkenazim Jews of central Europe, who developed medieval German as their language (Yiddish), or the Sephardic Jews of Spain, who developed a language mixture of Spanish and Hebrew. Their proximity to Muslims enabled them to form their own intellectual culture and in cities like Cordoba, Grenada, Toledo and Seville wealthy Jewish communities were established where craftsmen, traders and doctors flourished and built up a rapport with liberal caliphs. Even in Israel today Ashkanazi and Sephardic Jews have their own rabbis.

Christians did join in the cross fertilisation but this was not a characteristic of normal relationships where religious differences led to hostility. Some European Catholics actually equated Muhammed with the beast of *Revelation*. Muslims, for their part, would countenance allegiance to no other than Muhammed. The evolution of Christianity had reached a crucial stage. It was under pressure in the West and had also to come to terms with the widening gap between Rome and

Constantinople. A token show of authority from Constantinople still existed in an imperial presence at Ravenna but, since the days of Gregory, popes increasingly dominated Italy. The great problem was that Byzantine politics were being dominated by a struggle with Islam and there was little enthusiasm to get involved in the difficulties of the western areas of the empire. The struggle with the Lombards had kept popes faithful to the Byzantine emperor but when their token presence in Ravenna disappeared in 751, the papacy turned for help to France and the Frankish king Pepin III. Papal claims to power were backed up by one of the great forgeries of the Middle Ages in the form of a document, which came to be known as the *Donation of Constantine*. This stated that when the emperor had moved from Rome to his new capital city of Constantinople, he had bequeathed the western part of his Empire to the bishop of Rome. This document was spurious but it indicates clearly the efforts being made in the West to regain lost ground. In this they were successful despite the forgery. Kenneth Latourette writes:

> *The church in the west remained the most stable institution in an age of disorder when civil authorities came and went and violence was rampant...It was chiefly through the church and its monasteries that education and learning survived and was handed down to later generations, that the poor were succoured, that the marriage tie was given sanctity, that the sick were cared for, that travellers were sheltered and that morality was inculcated.*
> **(*The Unquenchable Light*; Eyre & Spottiswoode, 1945)**

The time had come for the Anglo-Saxons, who had benefited from Augustine's mission to Britain and from Celtic missionary endeavour, to repay something of their debt and carry the gospel back to Europe. Heading the new spearhead was Wynfrith of Crediton, better known as Boniface.

Boniface (680–754)

A claim could be made that Boniface was the most successful Christian missionary since the Apostle Paul. Born in Devon, he became a monk in Exeter then moved to Southampton. He was ordained at the age of 30 and in 716 heard of missionary work going on in the border regions of Germany and the Netherlands. He obtained permission from his abbot to go and arrived just as the land had been laid waste by a pagan prince. He moved on to Rome where he received the pope's blessing to undertake missionary work in Germany. He based his early activities in the Low Countries where a Northumbrian monk called Willibrord had preceded him. He then moved south to the German state of Hesse and was so successful that he was recalled to Rome to receive the bishopric of the whole of Germany East of the Rhine. It was here he took on the pagan gods by sawing down the great oak tree, the legendary abode of Thor, the god of Thunder. He used the timber to build a chapel, an enterprise so audaciously stunning to the local populace that many were converted to Christianity. Others arrived from England to join in his work and bishoprics were established in several places, including Bavaria where he became Archbishop. He also revived the church of the Franks and was supported in this work by the powerful Carolingian family who were beginning to dominate the politics of France and Bavaria. This support was appreciated and encouraged by the papacy because it provided effective resistance to the aggressive Muslims who were crossing the Pyranees and invading southern France. There were tensions between church and state but Boniface was a skilled diplomat and kept friendships sweet. Several rulers had been raised in the monastery of St Denise near Paris where Boniface had great influence and this proved invaluable in cementing relationships. Acting as papal legate, Boniface anointed Pepin as a Carolingian ruler and he was the father of Charles the Great, better known to us as Charlemagne.

Even though Boniface was Archbishop of Mainz and had authority over the whole of Germany he resigned his position and at the age of 70 went back to the north and continued his missionary activity. It was while in the north, on June 7th, 754, he and 52 companions were butchered by a band of ruffians whose motive seems to have been robbery rather than religious dispute. Thus, almost by accident, Boniface was added to the list of Christian martyrs.

Charlemagne (765–810)

The Carolingian kingdom opened up a new era in the West, providing a confidence which pushed the papacy into a final effort to wrench itself free from Constantinople. Charlemagne's Empire included the regions of modern Germany and France, with Aix-la-Chapelle (Aachen) as his capital. On Christmas Day in the year 800, the pope invited Charlemagne into St Peter's Church in Rome and there publicly crowned him as Roman Emperor, the first emperor in the West since 476. Having placed the crown on his head the pope then knelt before him and did him homage. The people acclaimed him *imperator et augustus*. That was in the West, in the East his authority was not recognised. Nevertheless, it was a moment to savour, the man of destiny had breathed new life into the ancient Roman Empire after an interval of three hundred years and the Holy Roman Empire was born. How the concept of a Holy Roman Empire was construed varied between political and theological ideas but Charlemagne was acclaimed as nothing less than God's deputy here on earth:

> *Always remember my king, you are the deputy of God your king. You are set to rule all his members and you must render an account for them on the day of judgement...Our Lord Jesus Christ has set you up as the ruler of the Christian people, in power more excellent than the pope or the Emperor of Constantinople...On you alone depends the whole safety of the churches of Christ.*
> **(Karolini Epistolae, AEVI ii 503)**

The title seems 'over the top' to modern ears but it was given in the euphoria of victory over the Lombards and the control of those parts of Italy held by Eastern Emperors of Byzantia. Charlemagne accepted the title, at first humbly enough, but he soon grew into the position and deferred less and less to papal benevolence. He set to work with a will and began a series of far reaching and impressive educational reforms. For this enterprise he was greatly indebted to an Anglo-Saxon scholar from York called Alcuin. He headed the court at Aix-la-Chapelle and inspired generations of students who spread their learning in schools and monasteries throughout the empire. It was impressive work and revived interest in biblical scholarship, theology and church order. Studies also included the classics of Greece and Rome and classes were open to ordinary people as well as the nobility. Having joined the court Alcuin dedicated himself to learning of all kinds, he was so busy and in such demand that he only returned to York for two brief visits during the rest of his life.

Charlemagne's earliest biographer, Einhard, described how the emperor delighted in learning, read avidly and was especially fond of Augustine's *City of God*. He honoured scholarship and was interested in the arts and mathematics. Much of his fortune was spent on churches, especially in Rome, though he only went there four times during his life. He was greatly interested in church life and clergy were sometimes brought to book over issues like celibacy, drunkenness and inappropriate relationships with women. Charlemagne also introduced permanent professional judges and royal envoys, thus extending his authority in the realm. He was clearly in charge of both church and state, exercising a paternalism irksome to some but which certainly established a common culture for the Western world.

The new empire scarcely outlasted Charlemagne and was soon torn asunder by political strife and political chaos. The weakness invited renewed attacks from Muslims in the South and from Magyars (Hungarians) from central Asia. It also provided opportunities for a fearsome new invader from the sea, Norsemen from Scandinavia—the dreaded Vikings. A united empire would have been able to resist but minor kinglets were no match for this new ruthless and determined invader.

Vikings

> *Men will quake with terror*
> *Ere the seventy sea-oars*
> *Gain their well earned respite*
> *From the labours of the ocean*
> *Norwegian arms are driving*
> *The iron studded dragon*
> *Down the storm-tossed river*
> *Like an eagle with wings beating.*
> **(*King Harald's Saga* by Snorri Sturrluson)**

Viking invaders had an eye for easy prey and when they came across unguarded and vulnerable monasteries they must have thought they had won the middle-age lottery. Lindisfarne, isolated on the east coast, quickly succumbed to Viking attacks and the sacking of such a sacred spot sent shock waves across Europe. Alcuin wrote from Aix-la-Chapelle:

> *Lo, it is nearly 350 years that we and our fathers have inhabited this most lovely land, never before has such terror appeared in Britain as we have suffered from a pagan race, nor was it thought possible that such an inroad from the sea could be made. Behold the Church of St Cuthbert spattered with the blood of the priests of God, despoiled of all its ornaments.*

Viking invaders had an eye for easy prey.

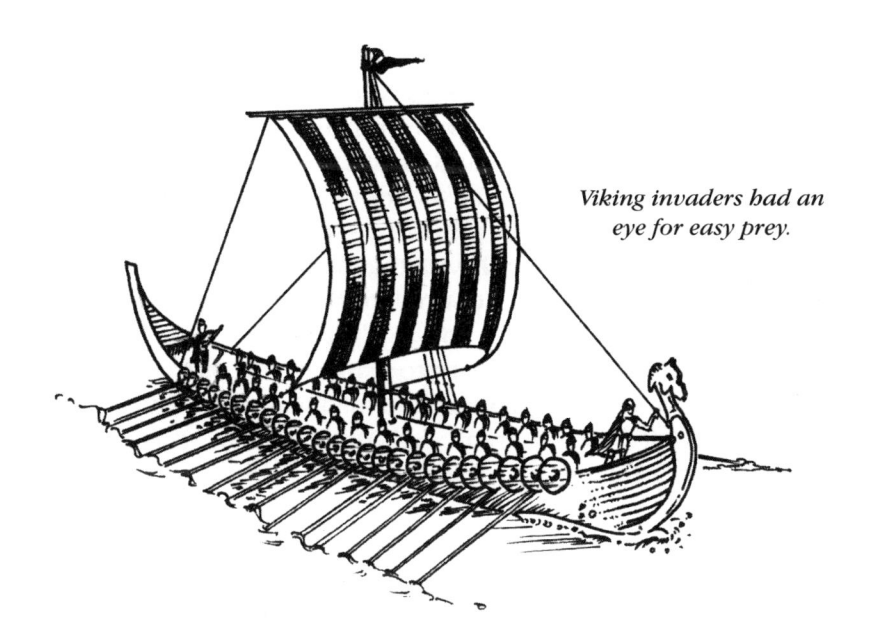

The Saxon king Edmund was martyred by the invaders and his remains taken to Suffolk, where the market town of Bury St Edmunds grew up around the abbey built at his shrine. Simion of Durham was later to write of the Vikings:

> ...*stinging hornets, spreading on all sides like dreadful wolves, they robbed, they tore and slaughtered not only beasts of burden and sheep and oxen, but also even the priests and deacons and companies of monks and nuns.*

Some of the people vanquished by the Vikings were transported north as slaves taking their faith with them. They are not recorded in any chronicles but astonishingly, from artefacts, inscriptions and trickles of information, it can be detected that these people became ambassadors to the very people who had ravaged them. Slowly but surely, the religion of Thor and Odin was transformed from hammer to cross as the blood red religion of the Vikings was overcome by the 'Pale Galilean'. The Viking princedom of Kiev (the land of Rus) became Christian when King Vladimir was bowled over by the splendour of Orthodox worship in the Cathedral of St Sophia, which he described as 'heaven come down to earth'. By 988, Orthodox Christianity was the official faith of the land of Russia and has been so ever since, despite the Communist Revolution of the twentieth century.

In Britain, Alfred, king of the Saxon kingdom of Wessex, suffered set backs at the hands of the Vikings but, just when it seemed that Christianity might be driven underground, he succeeded in defeating them at the Battle of Edington in 878 and demanded that their king be baptised. Alfred himself acted as godfather to the Viking. Alfred believed the Vikings had been sent by God as a punishment for neglecting to study the Bible. It was this belief which motivated his efforts to educate the people not only for their own sake but for the stability of God's kingdom in the country. The king's own contribution to the betterment of the state was to translate the first fifty Psalms into English, no small achievement for a man who received no formal education as a child. He also translated Pope Gregory's *Pastoral Care* and helped spread the influence of Catholic Christianity.

Transubstantiation

We have already indicated that under the Carolingians there was a revival of learning and a new interest in theology. One theological speculation concerned the Lord's Supper. Obviously this sacrament had been a corner stone of Christian worship from the very beginning but few had ever given much thought to the *nature* of the bread and wine when consumed. John of Damascus, perhaps the most important eastern theologian of the eighth-century, had formulated a transubstantiation doctrine of the Lord's Supper and this began to gain credence in the West. Sacrament means 'sacred symbol' and as such it was easily understood. Now believers were told that as the bread and wine were being consecrated in worship they were effectively changed into the body and blood of Christ, though to the sight and taste they appeared unchanged. Carolingian theologians disagreed and taught that Christ was in the Lord's Supper but only in a spiritual sense and not physical. It was a dispute not likely to go away and it has been with us ever since. In 1079, Pope Gregory II made Berengar of Tours declare contrary to his own teaching:

> *I believe in my heart and confess with my mouth that the bread and wine which are placed on the altar are, by the mystery of holy prayer and the words of our Redeemer, substantially converted into the true and proper life-giving flesh and blood of Jesus Christ our Lord.*

Transubstantiation was with us. The simplicity of a farewell last meal in the upper-room had become a mystery tour impossible to comprehend and guaranteed to lead to future discord amongst believers.

Confession

Another development of this period was that of penitential discipline. The origins of personal, public confession are found in the monasteries where infractions against rules of the order were confessed before assembled brothers. Fasting and prayer were offered as remedies to make good shortcomings. This discipline then extended to lay folk and required private confession to a priest with accompanying penances. In the Celtic Irish Church manuals were drawn up with a penance designed for each different sin. It started slowly but gained momentum during Charlemagne's rule when he ordered all priests to hear confession of parishioners, though this did not become law until 1215 at the Fourth Lateran Council:

> *Every Christian of either sex who has come to years of discretion must privately confess all his sins truthfully to his own priest at least once a year, and endeavour to the best of his ability to fulfil the penance imposed upon him.*

After penance came absolution, a guarantee that sins were forgiven and the penitent relieved of eternal punishment. Later followed the idea of indulgences, which meant that people who did generous acts, such as dedicating a church or contributing to a cause, were free of penance because of their devotion or generosity. Thus, by 1095 Urban II could reward crusaders by discarding penance:

> *Whoever out of pure devotion and not for the purpose of gaining honour or wealth, shall go to Jerusalem to liberate the church of God, may reckon that journey in lieu of all penance.*

Such ecclesiastical jurisprudence was certain to result in corruption and misuse and to urgent appeals for reform. Meanwhile, the Christian odyssey was becalmed in the kind of legal specialisation Jesus had given his life to overcome.

The Icon Dispute

The worship of images had always been anathema to Jews. When Roman generals sought to bring their insignia into the precincts of the Temple of Jerusalem it was enough to spark off a riot. The Greek word for an image was *eikon* and in the East images of Christ played an important part in Byzantine and later Orthodox devotion. The pious believed them to be a direct point of contact between worshipper and the image depicted. John of Damascus (c. 657–749) said that Christ was not venerated *in* the image but *with* the image. Others claimed they were merely a throwback to paganism and therefore something to be avoided like the plague. It was a somewhat blurred distinction and it provoked a heated religious controversy. In 717, the Eastern Emperor, Leo III, began to repress the use of images and passed an order that the huge statue of Christ standing before the Imperial Palace and facing Hagia Sophia in Constantinople, should be pulled down. There was a riot and the hapless official appointed to implement the emperor's wish was murdered by outraged housewives. Undeterred, Leo decreed that all imagery, apart from the cross, should be smashed and all liturgical vestments burned. Pope Gregory II decided to get involved and suggested in a letter to the emperor that he should leave religious affairs to religious experts. The emperor sent ships to arrest him but they sank en route to Rome and this mollified the situation. However, Leo's son, Constantine V, was even more of an iconoclast than his father and he, quoting from the second commandment, 'Thou shalt not make unto thyself any graven image', provoked such an argument that some monks even had their beards set on fire! To and fro went the dispute, until the affair was finally resolved in favour of the icon when Empress Theodora called a Council of Constantinople, which restored images as aids to worship.

Thereafter, Eastern Christianity developed the icon as an artistic form that probably reached its zenith in the 14th century when a man called Sergius moved to a monastic community twenty-five miles north of Moscow to a place called Zagorsk, now the headquarters of the Russian Orthodox Church. He remained a monk all his life but his artistic expression had a profound effect on the piety of Russian peasants. Most icons are painted anonymously and only a few names like Andrei Rubiev, Theophanes the Greek and Daniel Chorney live on.

The Great Divorce

The controversy over icons spilled over to the West and increased the strain on relationships between the Roman and Byzantine worlds. Leo III had tried to gag Pope Gregory II during the icon dispute and went so far as to remove his ecclesiastical power in Italy. To the popes in the West however, this was mere bluster because the nominal imperial presence in Ravenna was weak and soon succumbed to the barbarian Lombards. The coronation of Charlemagne as emperor in the West was eloquent testimony that the Latin Church was prepared to take its destiny into its own hands.

The confrontation leading to a final rift between East and West blew up in the Balkans, frequently the powder keg igniting great historical events. Rome and Constantinople had long vied for influence there and the Byzantines were furious when papal envoys in Bulgaria insisted that the *Filoque* teaching about the Holy Spirit proceeding from the Father and the Son should be added to the Nicene Creed. This proved to be the focus of dispute between the churches, though cultural differences were probably more important than the theological argument. The argument rumbled on for years, until 1054 when acrimonious correspondence between Pope Leo IX and Patriarch Michael Cerularius was followed up with a legation from Rome led by a man called Cardinal Humbert. He was a man not blessed with patience and when the diplomatic going got tough he marched up to the high altar during an act of worship in the Hagia Sophia and slapped down a Bull of Excommunication against Cerularius. Cerularius, far from being intimidated, responded in kind. The rift was ratified, the divorce was complete and the universal Church has been split by the schism down to the present day.

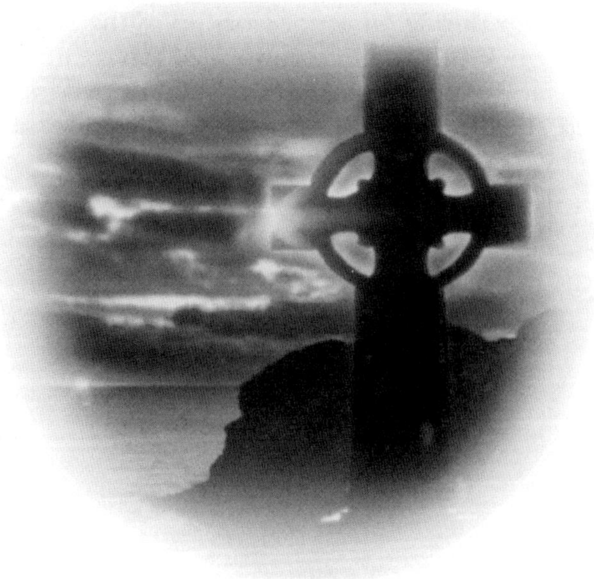

8 Teachers, Preachers and Builders

Anselm	109
Abelard and Heloise	110
Bernard of Clairvaux	113
Churches and Cathedrals	114

It was at this time the first universities grew out of the cathedral schools and monastic libraries, gradually gaining in prestige and replacing the schools. Soon major cities boasted universities, first Paris, then Oxford, Bologna, Padua and Cambridge. During the Middle Ages eighty universities were founded and many of them have had a distinguished history from that day to this. Students attached themselves to universities and paid fees to professors who read the text of handwritten books and expounded on them. Books were rare, valuable items and much had to be committed to memory. The universities were quite small at first with perhaps 2,000 students who read grammar, logic, rhetoric, arithmetic, astronomy, law, medicine and, 'the queen of the sciences'—theology. University interest in theology followed from the fact that many of them had developed from monastic schools. Paris University, for instance, grew out of the cathedral school of Notre Dame, so theology was a natural continuation of interest. Organisation was loose, any lecturer with a licence to teach could set out his stall and if he was good or controversial his classes grew. It was a system encouraging independent thought and was a womb for new ideas. Universities were given birth by religious institutions so they copied cathedral and monastic patterns.

The great scholars of the time were monks and clerics who had inherited the classical thought of Greece, the Bible and the early Christian Fathers but, as the independence of universities increased, new scholarship sought to resolve mysteries by logic rather than tradition and authority. Scholars or 'schoolmen' were a departure from all that had gone before and they developed a certain style to their thinking. Reason was the discipline they used to uncover truth. Problems posed by theology and philosophy about the ultimate nature of reality sparked off a spirit of inquiry the western world had not known since the great age of Greece. Applying a logical systematic method to a better understanding of Christianity is called Scholasticism. Strictly interpreted this means 'that taught in schools' but really it is the method of argument setting out an affirmation of truth then tested by a critical doubt. This leads to a debate bringing about a rational conclusion or synthesis. There was great confidence in this method of coming to truth so it was used to ask the ultimate question—can the existence of God be proven? Anselm, usually regarded as the founder of Scholasticism, set himself to answer that question.

Anselm (1033–1109)

Anselm was an Archbishop of Canterbury, who came to England when the Norman influence on the country was growing rapidly after the invasion of William the Conqueror. Before that he was a monk in the Benedictine abbey of Bec in Normandy. Bec had a great tradition of philosophy and Anselm became an eager student. His biographer speaks of him 'wearying his body with late nights, with cold and hunger'. He became familiar with Aristotle and textbooks of logic and soon was writing books eagerly read all over Europe.

The country suffered much during the invasions but there were blessings too. Viking attacks had undermined squabbling petty kingdoms, which had warred for generations, but under the Normans, Wessex, Mercia and Northumbria disappeared leaving England more united than it had ever been before. The pope had supported William's invasion so not surprisingly the king's ecclesiastical policy was to bring England firmly under the religious authority of the pope. When sees became vacant the tendency was to fill them with foreigners. William II (Rufus) was more tyrannical than his father and one of the ways he filled the royal coffers was to refrain from replacing deceased bishops and abbots and pocket the revenues from church land. Canterbury was vacant for four years and this led to a breakdown in church government. In 1092, a great petition begged the king to appoint Anselm to Canterbury but it was only when a serious illness threatened the king's life that he eventually submitted. Anselm was called to the king's bedside to be appointed archbishop. It was the beginning of a protracted struggle between church and state, a battle the gentle and scholarly Anselm took no delight in. 'You have yoked a savage bull to a weak old sheep', he joked. Constantly at odds with the king, he was frequently exiled and in 1097 decided to live in Rome until the king's death.

Anselm is today largely remembered for his scholarship even though he was something of a reformer who encouraged regular church synods, enforced celibacy on his clerics and tried to suppress slavery. As a scholar he highlighted the value of reason but did recognise that faith directed his mind and said 'I believe in order that I may understand'. To Anselm is accredited the first of the philosophical proofs for the existence of God, usually called the 'ontological argument'. It is an argument illustrating well the scholastic method. It runs thus:

God is a Being greater than anything else that can be conceived; but an idea which existed only in the mind would not be so great as one which existed in reality as well as the mind; therefore God must be thought as necessarily existing.

It is unlikely that such 'proofs' have ever played much part in producing religious conviction and, though useful as a philosophical exercise, their value has diminished even more in modern times. Anselm's book, *Why God Became Man*, argues than sin builds up such a debt with God that is impossible for men to repay it. Hence, the necessity of finding one who can free us from the debt by repaying it in full. Only the merit of Christ's death gives us that salvation and wipes the slate clean. This is Anselm using the thought patterns of his day to work out the New Testament belief that 'Christ died for our sins'.

Anselm's struggle with royalty continued with William II's successor Henry I. A fundamental dispute blew up between them about the appointment of bishops. In England, as on the Continent, bishops had lands like barons. The king appointed them and invested them with a ring and a crosier, therefore a bishop paid homage to the king and had his office confirmed by the pope. When the pope claimed the right to appoint bishops, Anselm upheld the pope's position and Henry saw in the prospect of an independent church a threat to his authority. Just before his death Anselm was instrumental in hammering out a compromise, which allowed cathedral canons to elect their bishops under the control of the king. The church thereby obtained rights of investiture and the king retained the homage. It was an uneasy compromise Thomas Becket was to trip over in future years. Anselm also had problems with Canterbury's monks who wanted him to establish the primacy of Canterbury over York. He did not listen to the monks but it was at Canterbury that Anselm was happiest 'Just as an owl is glad when she is in her hole with her chicks'.

Abelard and Heloise (1079–1140)

With Peter Abelard the scholastic method took an interesting turn. Christianity had now passed its first millennium and Abelard concluded that there was no consensus of tradition that could be traced back to the New Testament with infallible authority for belief. He revealed conflicting teaching between various church fathers and claimed that such contradictions could only be resolved by critical, systematic theological thought. Helen Waddell, in her beautiful novel *Peter Abelard*, has the scholar reading through the writings of the Church Fathers for help with a problem about whether it is lawful for a man to marry a woman with whom he has committed fornication:

> *Well, what had they to say about it? He settled down to read sardonically. St Ambrose: for any Christian to enter upon marriage with her whom he hath stained with unlawful defilement, was even as the sin of incest. Augustine, on the other hand, that legitimate marriage with good intent may well follow an illicit union, and that true marriage may follow even adultery...Gregory the Great, as grim as Ambrose. Council of Chalons, against. Council of Aix-la-Chappelle, against...Abelard thrust the manuscript from him and was on his feet snarling...Anything was more tolerable than this insufferable patronage of the saints... 'NEITHER DO I CONDEMN THEE; GO AND SIN NO MORE.' He stopped his trampling up and down the room. He did not know where the words had come from.*

His emotional life was also to throw light on the idea of romantic love, which was something of a rebellion against the prevalent view of marriage where landowners arranged marriages to consolidate property and monarchs to enlarge kingdoms.

The loose organisation of universities suited Abelard well for he was a dynamic and charismatic teacher who attracted thousands of students dazzled by his Paris lectures. His turbulent career reflected the times through which he lived for he was no plaster saint or isolated hermit. Born in Brittany, he studied in Paris, before falling out with his masters and moving to nearby Melun. In 1108 he returned to Paris and rapidly acquired a reputation as an outstanding teacher and original thinker. His barbed debating style soon brought him enemies but that could not prevent him becoming the university's brightest star.

In 1117, at the age of thirty-six, he began to tutor Heloise the teenager niece of Fulbert, a canon at the cathedral of Notre Dame. They fell in love and soon Heloise was pregnant and gave birth to a son they named Astrolabe. They married secretly and at first Fulbert, who was the girl's guardian, seemed satisfied with the arrangement but later Heloise was persuaded to take holy vows at the Benedictine Abbey of Saint-Argenteuil and Fulbert decided to exact terrible revenge. Using the services of hired thugs Fulbert had Abelard cruelly castrated. The lovers were forced to separate, Heloise joined an order of nuns and Abelard retired to the Abbey of St Denise in Paris. Later still, he was forced to leave there and he founded a chapel and oratory called the Paraclete before being elected abbot of a monastery at Saint-Gildas-des-Rhuis, where he wrote the autobiographical *History of Misfortunes*. Abelard and Heloise began to exchange the love letters that have become classical letters of romance into which were often woven deep theological ideas:

> *Dearest sister, are you not moved to compunction by the sight of the only begotten of God who, although he was innocent, yet for you and for all men was taken by the impious, was scourged, mocked, spat upon, crowned with thorns, and executed between thieves by so frightful and shameful a death? Look upon him, your bridegroom and the bridegroom of the Church... With his own blood he bought you and redeemed you. What I ask, did he, who lacked nothing, see in you that he should do battle for you in the agonies of a death so ignominious? What did he seek in you except yourself? He is the true lover who seeks not yours but you.*

Perhaps it was Abelard's own suffering that inspired his theory of Christ's atoning death. Christ's suffering at Calvary was only a snapshot of the heartache endured by God all the time. Rings go down the whole length of a tree but when you cut across it you see only a sample of something there throughout. Calvary was one example of something eternal.

Abelard's love affair with Heloise damaged his reputation.

The love affair damaged Abelard's reputation and for much of his life authorities harassed him. Bernard of Clairvaux accused him of polluting the minds of the young and of heresy. None of this dimmed his popularity with students however, and attendance at his lectures increased still further. They recognised him as one of the major Christian thinkers of his day. His book, *Yes and No*, explained the association of faith and reason and claimed that Christianity was intellectually sound and consistent with philosophical thought. This didn't prevent a council of Soissons condemning him unheard and burning a book of his on the Trinity.

In 1140 Abelard set off for Rome hoping to appeal against a papal condemnation of his teaching but he died on the way there and it was many years before his worth as a scholar and teacher was fully recognised. His body was taken to the Paraclete and when Heloise died, twenty-four years later, she was buried alongside him, concluding one of the great love stories of all time. He is still best remembered for his affair with Heloise but even without that his place as an outstanding theologian of the Middle Ages was assured.

Bernard of Clairvaux (1090–1153)

Abelard's work was criticised by Bernard, the abbot of Clairvaux and probably the most influential Christian leader of his day. His piety was renowned, as was his fearless condemnation of fools and knaves. His was a voice people listened to, especially in disputes about papal succession. His own rectitude, personal devotion and mysticism guaranteed his authority and he was constantly dragged into political issues when his own desire was for prayer, devotion and chivalry. Bernard secured recognition for the order of Knights Templar for whom he wrote a rulebook. His overriding loyalty was to the Cistercians, a Benedictine order, which emphasised poverty, simplicity and solitude. He had joined the order at twenty-two when he moved into the monastery of Citeau. It was struggling for survival in those days but by the time of Bernard's death, aged sixty-three, it had 339 houses and the community he founded at Clairvaux had 68 daughter houses—all recognised as superb examples of the way monasteries should be run. The Cistercians returned to a literal observance of the rule of Benedict, with its emphasis on simplicity and industry and as a result they became extremely successful and often wealthy. They cultivated wasteland, reduced forests to fields and turned swamps into meadows. They introduced intensive farming, milling, weaving and experimented with greenhouses. They pastured sheep on their meadows and produced so much wool they moved into marketing and the wool became famous. The endeavour and skill of the monks influenced the economic advance of northern Europe to a remarkable degree and paradoxically they became embroiled in the very world they sought to escape. They were the chief religious influence in the West and received many favours from Pope Innocent II after Bernard had taken his side in a papal election controversy.

Summarising Bernard's life is not easy, for he met with popes and scholars yet remained poor and devout himself. He could be aggressively self-righteous, as he was with Abelard and Heloise, yet he believed and practised a conviction that sexual love could be transformed by love for God. He was a contemplative mystic yet acutely aware of what was going on in the world. His own personal devotion to the Mother of God gave great impetus to the cult of the Virgin in the West and his order of Knights Templar helped introduce the concept of chivalry into Christian warfare. He was a marvellous preacher and a person of such moral strength that he was often called away to adjudicate disputes in the Church and beyond. Today, Bernard's piety is recalled in hymns attributed to him like 'O sacred head now wounded', 'Jesus, thou joy of loving hearts' and 'Jesus, the very thought of thee'.

Churches and Cathedrals

Our faith odyssey has so far dealt with people who testified and died for their beliefs and with the people who worked out those beliefs in classroom and creed. We pause for a moment now to think about the largely anonymous people who expressed their faith in building and design. In these matters, Western Europe trailed behind the East, where new technology and skill amazed the world with buildings like the Hagia Sophia (church of the Holy Wisdom) in Constantinople. A church had stood on the site from the year 532, but it was the building of Justinian, which became a showpiece of the empire and a tribute to the skill of architects Anthemius of Tralles and Isadore of Miletus. Hagia Sophia is a square, capped by a dome of enormous proportions, dwarfing anything ever attempted before. The enterprise was completed in just six years, with thousands of men involved in the grand scheme. It was ornately decorated with ivory, silver, glass and mosaics and when the candlelight flickered on the materials it gave the impression of gentle movement. When Justinian entered the completed building he is reputed to have said, 'Solomon, I have outdone thee'. In later years Crusaders were to stand transfixed by the wonder of such a church. It still stands to be marvelled at today, albeit with added Muslim features over what is now a museum. Another remarkable building of the East is the Dome of the Rock, dominating Jerusalem from Mount Moriah as once Solomon's Temple had done. Built by Abd el Malik between 685 and 705, its construction is Byzantine but the décor is Oriental. When the crusaders entered Jerusalem in 1099, they commandeered the building and topped it with a cross that remained in place for eighty-eight years.

While these impressive buildings were being erected in the East, very simple structures appeared in the West. In Britain, wayside crosses indicated where travelling monks were likely to preach their faith. Rough wooden shelters from the elements then appeared, later replaced by stone. They were simple buildings with a small chancel for the altar at the East End and a nave for the people with a floor covering of straw or rushes. The stone was often taken from Roman ruins as at Escomb in Durham, where the handbook describes the building as 'a simple, tiny, dog-kennel of a church wherein lies its strength and unique beauty'.

Escomb, 'a simple, tiny, dog-kennel of a church'.

The Saxon crosses in the churchyards were more elaborate than the churches themselves and many are still to be seen in the north of England. The plague village of Eyam in Derbyshire has a particularly good one dating back to the eighth century. Rudyard Kipling has captured the Saxon simplicity in a poem about Eddi, the priest of St Wilfred:

> *Eddi, priest of St Wilfred,*
> *In the chapel of Manhood End,*
> *Ordered a midnight service*
> *For such as cared to attend.*
>
> *But the Saxons were keeping Christmas*
> *And the night was stormy as well,*
> *Nobody came to the service*
> *Though Eddi rang the bell.*
>
> *'Wicked weather for walking',*
> *Said Eddi of Manhood End,*
> *'But I must go on with the service*
> *For such as care to attend'.*
>
> *As the altar candles were lighted*
> *An old marsh donkey came*
> *Bold as a guest invited*
> *And stared at the guttering flame.*
>
> *The storm beat on at the windows*
> *The water splashed on the floor*
> *And a wet yoke-weary bullock*
> *Pushed in through the open door.*
>
> *'How do I know what is greatest,*
> *How do I know what is best?*
> *That is my Father's business',*
> *Said Eddi, Wilfred's priest.*
>
> *'But three are gathered together,*
> *Listen to me and attend,*
> *I bring good news, my bretheren',*
> *Said Eddi, of Manhood End.*
>
> *And he told the ox of a manger*
> *And a stall in Bethlehem,*
> *And he spoke to the ass of a rider*
> *Who rode to Jerusalem.*

They steamed and dripped in the chancel,
They listened and never stirred,
While, just as though they were bishops,
Eddi preached them the word.

Till the gale blew off on the marshes
And the windows showed the day
And the ox and the ass together
Wheeled and clattered away.

And when the Saxons mocked him,
Said Eddi of Manhood End,
'I dare not shut this chapel
On such as care to attend'.

The simplicity of Anglo-Saxon churches shows clearly a lack of building skills. Doors and windows were small and narrow, so as not to weaken the structure and the inside was dark and gloomy. All that was to change after the Norman invasion of 1066. The intense ardour of religious feeling, which pervaded the Middle Ages, is still to be seen in the stones and mortar of hundreds of churches and cathedrals which were built between the eleventh and fourteenth centuries. Millions of tons of stone were quarried and transported to build great edifices to tower over towns and cities all over Europe. Cathedrals, the seat of bishops (cathedras), were the most spectacular buildings and soon they were rivalling the glories of the East. In Paris, Notre Dame soared to 114 feet, Chartres to 123 feet, Amiens to 138 feet, while Cologne cathedral boasted a tower of 512 feet. In Britain, remarkable building skills were displayed in York where churches were continuously built on the same site until the thirteenth century. The present York Minster was built with a central tower rising to 234 feet and had hundreds of stained-glass windows, some of which dated back to the tenth century. (York interestingly, like nearby Beverley, retains its Anglo-Saxon word 'minster' as the name for its large church.) Cathedrals were more than places of worship; they were also community houses where business was conducted in the naves and where only the chancel was sacred. It was a feature of the Middle Ages to separate the chancel from the nave with a wooden or stone screen, often elaborately carved and surmounted by a large crucifix called the rood. In Amiens the Cathedral, when first built, could hold ten thousand people and was large enough to house the total population of the town. Cathedrals belonged to the whole populous because the people built them. The wealthy provided the funds, the artisans their skills, the artists their art, even the children harnessed themselves to carts to drag building materials to the site. Because religion dominated the lives of people it was thought right and proper that human activity in all its forms should be performed there. Out of the services of worship grew the plays, from the saint's days came the feasts and dances, and from the fund raising came the markets in the churchyard with stalls even set up in the church porch.

Norman churches rarely remained unaltered. As people grew richer so their churches were altered and enlarged. Windows were replaced by larger windows and filled with magnificent stained glass. Aisles were added, chapels were added, roofs were raised, and columns were capped with capitals, sometimes intricately carved and often displaying grotesque figures. Behind screens were rows of seats beneath which, were ledges or misericords where monks could rest themselves during long sessions of worship. These were often covered with carvings of biblical and local scenes depicting caricatures of priests or others. Nobody seemed to mind a joke. Builders experimented with arches and vaults and competed with neighbouring towns to own the most spectacular houses of God. In short, church building was built for life, for sound, for fun, for beauty and for practicality. The sacred merged with the secular and God ruled all the affairs of man. Perhaps it is a concept to be rediscovered in the next millennium.

Cathedrals were more than places of worship.

9 Crusades

Urban II	121
Jewish Massacre	122
Peter the Hermit	123
Western Princes	124
Knights Templar and Knights of St John of Jerusalem	126
Godfrey of Boillon	127
Second Crusade	128
Saladin	128
Richard the Lionheart	130
Further Crusades	132
Children's Crusades	133
Crusades in Russia	133

*A*t the close of the first millennium an uneasy truce existed amongst the three monotheistic religions, Judaism, Christianity and Islam. There was co-existence amongst them, sometimes amiable as in Spain and North Africa but other times hostile as in John Chrysostom's eight *Sermons Against the Jews*, which became a pattern for anti-Jewish tirades. Islam became a proselytising faith yet in the tenth and part of the eleventh centuries Christians and Jews remained the majority of the population even in areas where Muslims ruled. But Islam was in transition and as Turks, originally from central Asia, migrated south westward, conquering Persia, invading Armenia and Iraq, where they captured Baghdad, so the nature of Islam changed and the relationships with Christians and Jews became more acrimonious. Turkish movements began to threaten the Byzantine Empire. The Byzantines regarded themselves as the heirs of the old Roman Empire with Constantine's city of Constantinople, the new Rome. The Byzantine Emperor was seen as the successor to Roman rulers dating back to Augustus, a claim ridiculed by Christians in the West who were getting confident enough to reassert themselves against Muslims, regaining the city of Toledo in 1085 and achieving a notable victory at Valencia under the generalship of El Cid.

A watershed for relationships between the religions occurred in 1009 when the caliph of Egypt, al-Hakim, started to persecute all Muslims who refused to acknowledge the exclusive claims of Ali to the caliphate. Then he persecuted Jews and Christians for good measure. He seems to have been totally insane but that didn't prevent claims being made on his behalf that he was a god. He openly broke with Islam, the cult eventually becoming the Druze faith, which rejects many traditional Islamic teachings and claims its own sacred books. Hakim ordered all Christians and Jews to wear sashes round their waists along with distinguishing badges, women were forced to cover their faces and were not allowed to walk the streets or use the public baths. He cursed early Muslims in writings on mosque doors. This clampdown coincided with a dreadful time of famine when the Nile failed to flood, food became scarce and sickness struck several towns. Hakim's response was to order the destruction of the church of the Holy Sepulchre in Jerusalem. His measures became more and more bizarre until he was finally assassinated in his thirty-sixth year. His followers claimed that one-day he would return, a belief which gave hope to Druze followers. More significantly, news of the destruction of the Holy Sepulchre reached the West and produced the first spark of crusading zeal. It was to be some years before the spark produced a flame but the smouldering had begun. Muslim pressure on the Byzantine Empire had been steady and had led to a series of wars against Muslims and Armenians. The empire held its own until a new foe appeared in the form of the Seljuk Turks. They were a fierce adversary and a Battle of Manzikert in 1071 ended in defeat for the Byzantines and the loss of half their realm. Emperor Alexius Comnenus appealed to Pope Urban II for help. It was a momentous decision.

Urban II (1035–1099)

On 27th November 1095, the pope responded to Alexius' appeal by preaching a sermon to a council gathered at Clermont in Southern France. The sermon evoked such a response that we still live with the reverberations to this very day. Appealing to the feelings of veneration for the Holy Land, with its biblical associations, strengthened by generations of pilgrimage and piety, Urban told a dreadful tale of a barbaric race slaughtering Christians and depriving them of their lands. It was a tale of plunder, rape, desecration, torture and fire. Recalling the greatness of Charlemagne he appealed to knights.

> *O most valiant soldiers, descendants of invincible ancestors…Start upon the road to the Holy Sepulchre, to tear that land from the wicked race and subject it to yourself.*

The response was immediate and the crowd shouted, 'Deus Vult! Deus Vult!' (God wills it). So the cause was established and the battle cry resounded around Europe, 'God wills it!'. The age-old call to gallantry and sacrifice went forth and ladies said good-bye to their husbands, not wanting to lose them but sure they ought to go. The cream of Europe's aristocracy signed up; Robert of Normandy, Raymond of Toulouse, Robert of Flanders, Godfrey of Bouillon, Baldwin of Boulogne, Stephen of Blois. Alongside these leaders stood men of lesser rank, monks, women and children, all committed to ridding the holy places of the wicked race.

Yet despite the response, crusaders knew it was a risky enterprise. Crusader poetry reveals the extent of their sadness as they abandoned loved ones:

> *Good Lord God, If I for you*
> *Leave the country where she is that I love so,*
> *Grant us in heaven everlasting joy,*

My love and me, through your mercy,
And grant her the strength to love me,
So that she will not forget me in my long absence,
For I love her more than anything in the world
And feel so sad about her that my heart is breaking!
(Arnold, *Documents of Medieval History*; 1981)

They feared the journey, worried about supplies being available and felt vulnerable to illness and disease knowing that a scratch could lead to lingering death. The prospects were grim, the enemy was unknown, the allies strange and unreliable. Moreover, knights bankrupted themselves to raise funds for the journey and left wives and relatives struggling to manage estates and homes. What led them to do it?

The answer lies in the outlook of the age, which was both religious and militaristic. Violence was a way of life but it was closely allied to honour, chivalry and vendetta. Urban's message was interpreted in terms equating love for God with the killings of infidels who were known to have dishonoured the Saviour. More difficult to understand is the appeal crusades had for thousands of peasants who responded to the pope's appeal even though it was not directed at them. Perhaps Jerusalem was important to them and the assurance that whatever sins they had committed in this life would be forgiven in this great act of penance. Whatever the cocktail of motives the result was between 100 thousand and 140 thousand people taking crusader's vows. The majority came from France, Italy and Germany and the aim was to reach Constantinople where they would muster and recharge themselves before moving on to the ultimate goal—Jerusalem.

Jewish Massacre

This great moralistic adventure got off to the worst of starts in May 1096. A battalion of crusaders commandeered by Count Emich of Leiningen decided to start their journey by massacring Jews. Many were dragged from the homes of Christian friends who sort to protect them. 'Convert or die', was the ultimatum and most chose death, many of them committed suicide. Some took refuge with the Bishop of Ruothard, the most important priest in Mainz, and were hidden inside his home but Emich attacked the bishop's palace and dragged Jews into the courtyard where they enveloped themselves in their prayer shawls. They were slain without mercy. The old Jewish cemetery in Worms bears witness to the eight hundred Jews who died at the hand of Emich and his crusaders in just three days.

Peter the Hermit

The pope had tried to limit the number of crusaders but the response was so great it could not be controlled. One popular preacher called Peter the Hermit, who had suffered at the hands of the Turks in a previous pilgrimage to Jerusalem, went through France whipping up support with great success. People regarded him with something like adoration and thousands joined him for a 'Peasants' Crusade'. There were petty nobles on horseback but most were prepared to walk the 2000 miles to Jerusalem.

> *Peter was generous in the way he made very liberal gifts to the poor out of things given to him: he bestowed prostitutes as wives and provided their dowries; he settled disputes and restored peace on all sides with wonderful authority. Indeed, whatever he did or said seemed godlike, to such a degree that hairs were pulled from his mule as relics'.*
> **(Guibert of Nujent, *Historia Hierosolymitana*)**

His route to Constantinople was via Hungary and remarkably they made such good time they were at the gates of the Byzantine capital by August 1096. Anna Comnena, daughter of the Emperor Alexius described them:

> *There was such eagerness and enthusiasm that every highway had some of them; along with soldiers went an unarmed crowd, more numerous than the suns or stars, carrying palms and crosses on their shoulders, including even women and children who had left their own countries.*
> **(op. cit.)**

The emperor did not welcome Peter's army with open arms, especially as they had been involved in skirmishes with his own army. Peter had not found it easy to control undisciplined elements in the ranks who had been unable to resist sacking Belgrade and setting fire to mills. Nevertheless, Peter was granted an audience with the emperor who gave him gifts and advised him to camp outside the city walls and await the second wave of crusaders on their way from Western

Europe. Sightseeing tours were organised for small groups who were astonished at the opulence and splendour of Constantinople. Like modern tourists they were aghast at the Basilica of St Sophia with its marble floor and columns holding the enormous dome, 107 feet in diameter.

Indiscipline could not be stamped out however, and soon Peter's army was shipped across to Asia Minor away from the capital. The army was by now about 25,000 strong, many of them non-combatants but all with stomachs to be fed. Soon they were foraging for food and even sacking houses and churches of Greek speaking Christians. One day when Peter was back in Constantinople obtaining supplies, his army, divided into factions, was led into a Turkish ambush and slaughtered. Their base camp was then surprised and some were killed in their beds. Byzantine forces rescued a few and Peter survived but the army was virtually wiped out.

Western Princes

A second and more organised wave of crusaders followed on the heels of Peter the Hermit. Princes of Europe, including the son of Henry I of France, William the Conqueror's son and son-in-law and other dukes and nobles, headed for Constantinople with knights and soldiers in their command. Some wives travelled with their husbands and whole families with neighbours and friends swelled the numbers. They journeyed through Italy and others through Hungary and Slavia before reaching Greece, the Byzantine territories and Constantinople. It was tough going, provisions were scarce but they reached the capital within five months, anxious to receive permission from Alexius to cross the Bosphorus into Asia and head for the Holy Land. The emperor was alarmed at the numbers involved and demanded assurances from the princes that due homage would be paid to him along with promises that any conquered lands would be restored to his empire. By May 1097 all the armies were in Asia.

Several major cities had to be stormed and secured along the route, Nicaea, Dorylaeum, Heraclea, Caesarea, before climbing the Taurus mountains to the great city of Antioch. The Turkish Empire was in disarray and unprepared for such an invasion. There were pockets of stiff resistance and some bloody battles but nothing to prevent the princes pressing on. They lacked unity but buoyed up with booty of gold, silver, horses and livestock they were not demoralised even when food became scarce.

In one dreadful period in the Taurus Mountains a chronicler records how horses and mules lost their footing in the winter mud and plummeted to their deaths. Knights were left to carry their own provisions and armour and many perished. Against the odds and despite internal squabbles Antioch was taken and the population, made up almost entirely of Christians, rejoiced at their liberation. For over a year the armies billeted in Antioch, regaining their strength, fighting off a serious epidemic and overcoming a breakdown in law and order. Then, it was onward to Jerusalem.

By June 7th 1099 they were in sight of their goal. From the Mount of Olives, Jerusalem would not have looked so different from the view today. The troops would have marvelled at the Dome of the Rock built between 685–705 and covering the spot where Abraham prepared to sacrifice his son. Sharing the same plateau, where Herod's Temple had once stood, was the El Aqsa Mosque, which the crusaders thought of as the Temple of Solomon.

After six days attacks started and were beaten off. A penitential walk followed. 15,000 men and women circled the city bare-footed while the Turks rained abuse on them from the walls. Then, with help from Genoese and English ships in the port of Jaffa, huge timber siege towers were built to attack the walls. By the 15th July crusaders were inside the walls and cutting their way past Muslim resistance. The battle was won and devout penitents prostrated themselves before the ruins of the Holy Sepulchre. The crusaders, steeped in blood, knelt before the spot where they believed the Prince of Peace had been laid after his crucifixion.

Victory had been achieved. The holy places were back in the hands of Christians and soldiers began to think of home and the journey back to Europe. A small army remained, strengthened by later crusaders but numbers were always a problem. Meanwhile, news of victory sped home accompanied by thanksgiving and emotion, all too late for Pope Urban II who died days before the news could reach him. At face value the pope's call for a crusade to free the holy places of Jerusalem had been a glorious success. Closer examination however, revealed that the toehold gained by the crusaders was extremely tenuous and had been achieved at the expense of alienating Christians in the East. Crusaders now controlled Jerusalem and Antioch but left Emperor Alexius furious that he had been overlooked in the settlement. The crusaders, for their part, felt betrayed because they said he had been carving out treaties with the Turks while they had been locked in mortal combat. The lack of trust did not augur well for the future. Renewed streams of pilgrims gave an illusion of strength as ships from Venice and Genoa regularly arrived in the Holy Land, but it was impossible to keep a strong and stable army established and supplied without full support from Constantinople.

Knights Templar and Knights of St John of Jerusalem

So instead of a strong permanently based military force backed up to the hilt by the Emperor of Constantinople, the notion of chivalrous Knights was transferred from the West to Jerusalem. The original purpose of Knights Templar was to offer aid and protection to pilgrims on their way to the Holy Land. They acted in conjunction with Knights of St John or Hospitallers who tended sick pilgrims in Jerusalem itself. Templars were warrior Knights who took vows of poverty, chastity and obedience just like monks. They were cavalry forces, originating in Burgundy and Germany, who opposed invaders like Muslims and Vikings. The church expected them to be virtuous and put their swords to the service of the poor and needy. Boys as young as seven were sent to live with knights so they could acquire the necessary skills and qualities. Then when their skill with weapons was acknowledged, they were slapped with the flat of the sword and called 'Sir Knight'.

Knights Templar or Knights of the Temple of Jerusalem, were so called because their first quarters adjoined the building called Solomon's Temple in Jerusalem. The pope sanctioned their order and, as we have already seen, Bernard of Clairvaux drew up a monastic set of rules for them. They were allowed to wear a distinctive dress of white mantle with a red Latin cross. Their vows of poverty did not prevent them from handling money sent from Europe to finance the work and this led to a banking system, which was both efficient and lucrative. They grew immensely wealthy and their banking operations spread to Europe, where they evoked the hostility of royal houses.

When Jerusalem fell in 1187 and Christians were expelled from the Holy Land after the fall of Acre in 1291, the Templars became more military in outlook. Later headquarters in Rhodes and Malta meant that the order continued to exist and even today they do maintain hospitals and medical centres for war casualties and refugees. The eight point Maltese cross is the symbol of the St John's Ambulance Service in Britain.

Godfrey of Boillon (1060–1100)

The problems of maintaining a military presence in the Holy Land are well illustrated by the life of Godfrey, who was a native of Ardennes near Brussels. He led a crusade of French and German-speaking Lorrains and financed them by mortgaging ancestral lands and taking protection money from Jewish communities along the Rhine. Many in his army were his own kinsmen and others he financed from his own resources. He was popular, a good general and when others preferred to head back to Europe, he stayed on to lead a crusader army in Jerusalem. He was known as 'Prince' rather than 'King' to satisfy those who felt that 'King' should only apply to Christ himself. As crusaders returned home Godfrey was left with just three hundred knights and some two thousand-foot soldiers. It was never going to be enough. Courageous, astute and zealous he undoubtedly was but his rule lasted one year. An illness killed him, though an Armenian chronicler called Matthew claimed a Muslim amir in Caesarea had poisoned him.

It was the same chronicler who claimed that Emperor Alexius betrayed the crusaders by sending them into the Anatolian wilderness in high summer, where Turks ambushed them. William, duke of Aquitaine lost his entire army.

> *What a sight! The air was full of the harsh sound of arrows thudding from bows, horses reared up in terror and the mountains reverberated with the din of battle. The Frankish duke wept bitterly to see his soldiers massacred.*
>
> **(Matthew of Edessa, Chronicle in the *Recuil des Historiens des Croisades*; Paris, 1841–1906)**

Yet, despite such setbacks, a Latin presence in the East was established. The County of Edessa was formed in Turkey, the Principality of Antioch included the Taurus Mountains, the County of Tripoli was a narrow strip of land between Mount Lebanon and the coast, and the Kingdom of Jerusalem began north of Beirut in the Golan Heights and stretched to Gaza on the coast and the Dead Sea. By and large these crusader states governed themselves and had oversight of a mixture of races and religions. The superimposed society, funded from the West, sometimes worked with great success. A Muslim wrote:

> *We passed through a series of villages and cultivated lands all inhabited by Muslims, who live in great well-being under the Franks…One of the chief tragedies of the Muslims is that they have*

> *to complain of the injustices of their own ruler, whereas they cannot but praise the behaviour of the Franks, their natural enemies.*
> **(Wright, W. (ed.), *The Travels of Ibn Jubair*; London, 1852).**

This toleration also extended to the Temple Mount in Jerusalem where the Templars provided space for Muslim prayer at the al-Aqsa Mosque.

Second Crusade (1140)

Such sweet reasonableness was not about to last. Imad-ad-Din motivated by the idea of *Jihad* or Holy War attacked and took Edessa. It was a great shock to the West and largely provoked the Second Crusade. Bernard of Clairvaux used all his eloquence to advocate it and the response was immediate with special enthusiasm being shown in England. Several routes again led armies towards the Holy Land where as many as 50,000 troops congregated outside the walls of Damascus, but it was an army undermined by petty squabbles and lacking a unity of purpose and soon the enthusiasm for battle ebbed away. Again, Europe was badly shaken and more papal calls for more crusaders fell on deaf ears. The crusaders were facing hard times especially when a new Muslim champion entered the stage, his name—Saladin.

Saladin (1138-1193)

Born at Takrit in modern Iraq, he was raised in a Khurdish military family. At the age of fourteen he was serving in the army of the Syrian Nur-ad-Din and accompanying his uncle Shirkuh on expeditions to Egypt where the crusaders were attacking the vulnerable caliph Fatmid. By 1171 Saladin had seized power in Cairo and brought Egypt under the control of the powerful Sultan Nur-ad-Din. Egypt became Saladin's power base and he revived the economy and successfully repelled the crusaders. When Nur-ad-Din died Saladin was quick to marry his widow and quickly assume the role of successor by seizing his territories. He was remarkably successful and by 1181 was undisputed leader of a unified Muslim army capable of taking on the crusaders. The driving force of Saladin was his devotion to *Jihad*, the Muslim

Saladin's religious idealism motivated his life.

response to the Christian *crusade*. His religious idealism motivated his own life and he sought to recreate the zeal of the first generation Muslims. His idealism also did much to make him a civilised and courteous man respected by friends and foes alike.

Reynold of Chatillon, a prince of Antioch who had survived sixteen years in Nur-ad-Din's jail had become a pain in Saladin's side because of his constant raids on rich Muslim caravans and pirate raids in Red Sea shipping lanes. The clashes escalated into a major confrontation. A crusader army of some 20,000 was amassed, which included 1500 knights. They assembled in Galilee where a piece of the true cross was transported from Jerusalem so that the bishop of Acre could carry it into battle. Saladin's forces, substantially greater in number, were divided into two, one group bivouacked in Southern Galilee and the other attacked Tiberius. The crusaders marched on Tiberius. In full chain mail and under blistering sun their slow progress was hindered further by lightning Muslim sorties. Still some way from Tiberius they rested for the night near the twin peaks of the Horns of Hattin overlooking the Sea of Galilee. On the 4th July 1187 a decisive battle was fought:

> *The opposing forces were lined up at a place called Hattin in the hill behind Tiberius...so many were slain, so many wounded and so many thrown into chains that our own people were a pitiable sight even to the enemy. Worse still, the Cross of our Salvation, that life giving wood was taken into the hands of the Muslims and along*

> with it fell its bearers, the bishop of Acre and the preceptor of the Holy Sepulchre...Guy of Lusignon, King of Jerusalem, saw the cross fall and rushed forward and flung his arms round the cross, hoping to snatch it back, or die beside it...Reynold of Chatillon was brought before Sultan Saladin and the tyrant struck off that proud and venerable head with his own hand. All the Templars he ordered to be beheaded determined to wipe them out, for he knew their reputation in battle.
>
> **(Stubbs, W. (ed.), *Itinerarium*; London, 1864)**

After Hattin the price of a Christian slave in Damascus fell to that of a single shoe. Denuded of soldiers Tiberius fell to Saladin, then Acre and Ascalon. By August only Tyre, Gaza and Jerusalem remained in crusader hands. Jerusalem, full of refugees, many of them women and children was no match for the besieging forces as 'arrows fell like raindrops'. Wounded filled up the hospitals and within two weeks surrender terms were negotiated. After eighty-eight years under crusader control Saladin received the city and not a building was looted nor a person injured. Syrian Christians were allowed to keep their churches and Jews were encouraged to return. Christian holy places were returned to the Orthodox Church of the Byzantine Empire. The magnanimity of Saladin even liberated thousands of captives and allowed them passage to Tyre.

Richard the Lionheart (1157–1199)

The defeat at Hattin was a bitter pill to swallow in the West. Pope Gregory VIII sent out an appeal for a new crusade and called on people to fast each Friday as atonement for the sins, which had made such a disaster possible. A tax to fund the crusade (Saladin's Tithe) was imposed and the cross was taken up by the King of England, Richard I. He put everything he had up for sale—castles, titles, possessions, even whole towns. The biggest and best ships were acquired from the Cinque Ports, Normandy, Brittany and Aquitaine. King Philip of France teamed up with Richard, which on paper looked a formidable alliance but in reality the distrust both kings felt for the other made the coalition paper-thin. Relationships were not improved when Richard refused to marry Philip's sister Alice to whom he had been betrothed for twenty years.

When the crusade venture began, several ships were lost in gales and unruly elements made the army difficult to control before a successful campaign against a Cypriot friend of Saladin's boosted morale. A siege to recapture Acre had been in operation for two years and the new crusaders joined it. Fortunes ebbed and flowed until a final squeeze made the defenders sue for peace. Richard held three thousand hostages, claimed 200,000 gold pieces as the price of victory, acquired numerous weapons and also demanded back the relic of the true cross. By this time Philip was ill and tired of crusading so he returned home leaving his army under the control of the Duke of Burgundy. Richard believed Saladin to be slow in returning the relic of the cross and sought to speed him up by massacring two thousand of his hostages. He then marched towards Jerusalem. He fought off raids along the way and in so doing did much to dispel the myth of Saladin's invincibility. At one point Richard's forces captured a fortress a mere thirty miles from Jerusalem but as the great prize beckoned he again had to contend with division in the alliance. He was also receiving information of a plot by his brother John to take over his English realm and of plans by Philip to attack Normandy. Richard's crusading impetus was running down. Saladin was also feeling the

Richard fought off raids along the way.

pressure of a life of constant warfare and so these adversaries, who had grown to respect each other greatly, worked out a truce. Richard was granted all the coastal cities as far south as Jaffa and pilgrims were assured safe passage to the holy places. The Lionheart sailed homeward, taking a last look at Acre on October 9th, 1192. A few months later Saladin himself was dead aged just 54. When relatives scrambled for pieces of his Empire they discovered Islam's most generous ruler of all had not left enough money to pay for his own funeral. Baha-ad Din-Shaddad wrote:

> *Since Islam and the Muslims lost their four caliphs, never had our faith suffered such a loss. The whole world was filled with a grief so profound that only God could realise its true depth...On that day, if I and others had been asked 'Who will lay down his life in exchange for the sultan's?'. I am convinced that each of us would willingly have done so.*
> **(Sultanly Anecdotes, *Recueil des Historians des Croisades*; 1872–1906)**

Further Crusades

Expeditions to the East continued but with less single-mindedness than before. Instead of concentrating on regaining the Holy Land, the great city of Constantinople became the prize. Soon its legendary walls were under siege. Venetian ships used their long spars to enable soldiers to leap onto the battlements and by-pass the defences. In 1204 the city fell and western crusaders sacked the city and placed their own emperor on the throne. The Patriarch's throne was desecrated when a whore climbed the throne and sang an alehouse song. The long-standing rivalry between Rome and Constantinople had reached its nadir.

Crusades continued to be called by popes like Innocent III but with decreasing returns until the city of Acre, the last crusader link to the Holy Land fell in 1291.

> *That day was appalling, for nobles and citizens, women and children were frantic with terror; they went running through the streets their children in their arms weeping and desperate; they fled to the seashore to escape death and when the Saracens caught them one would take the mother and the other the child, they would drag them from place to place and pull them apart.*
> **(*Chronicle of the Templar of Tyre*)**

At Acre 60,000 Christians were slain or captured. The great surge of religious enthusiasm which had ignited Europe had burnt itself out, never to be rekindled.

Children's Crusade

One grotesque crusade that illustrates the emotional frenzy of the time was the Children's Crusade of 1212. It lacked official sanction and was deplored by the church but it still went ahead. Its origins were in Cloyes, near Vendome, in France and in Cologne. In Cloyes, a young shepherd boy called Stephen convinced many that a vision of Jesus had commanded him to raise an army. In Cologne, a young preacher called Nicholas raised followers in the Rhineland and Lorraine. He was even more successful than Stephen.

> *The whole of Germany was affected by the movement as well as parts of France and Burgundy. Their parents and friends were unable to restrain them from taking part in the march, so great was their determination. Things reached such a pitch that everywhere in towns and in the countryside people dropped their tools and gear and joined those who were passing by.*
> **(Annals of Marbach, *Monuments of Germaniae Historica*; Hanover, 1826)**

Some children arrived in Genoa, others in Marseilles. A handful reached Rome and some may have found passage to the Holy Land. The youngsters took over clergy roles and administered sacraments but eventually the movement fizzled out and the great majority disappeared without trace, probably to Arab slave markets.

The Children's Crusade was a pathetic reminder of the grip the Holy Land had over Europeans for many years. The legend of the Pied Piper of Hamlin probably originated with this strange footnote to crusading history.

Crusades in Russia (1242)

One other crusading incident remains to be mentioned because of the long term effects on relationships between Catholic and Orthodox Christianity and the brush with Genghis Khan (Very Great King).

Christianity had spread amongst Slavs largely because of the missionary activity of two brothers, Cyril and Methodius, who had used a devised alphabet of the unwritten language as a tool of evangelism. This became so successful it provided the basis for writing now used in southeast Europe and Russia. Indeed, the name 'Cyrillic' ensures Cyril's name lives on. The books of Cyril and Methodius reached Kiev and so Russians gained an advantage denied to Britain and other European countries of the time, namely, scriptures in their own native tongue. Despite this independence of language they remained staunchly in tune with the Orthodox Christianity of Constantinople. Latin Christians, the Catholics, were regarded as heretics. Their distrust of Catholics was increased when they found themselves invaded by German crusaders who sought to take advantage of chaos caused by Mongol raids on Russia. The vast Mongol Empire, which extended from China to the Caucasus and from the frozen north to the Himalayas, had been infiltrated by Franciscan friars who had even gained access to the court of Genghis Khan. A string of Christian missions extended from Constantinople to Peking and there was a time when Mongol rulers seemed ready to adopt Christianity as their 'official' religion. Islam won the day however, and Christian missionaries began to find it difficult to travel through their territories.

Genghis Khan himself was dead but his sons, with seemingly unlimited supplies of mounted warriors, covered the steppes of central Asia like locusts. Soon they had overrun Central Russia, the Ukraine, Poland, Hungary, Iran and Asia Minor and the highly mobile army seemed capable of creating a world empire. Seeking advantage from these raids German crusaders launched an attack on Northern Russia but were repulsed by a leader called Alexander Nevsky, who was later honoured as a saint for his achievement. Nevsky preferred to submit voluntarily to the rule of Mongols and Russia did so for over two hundred years, until they gradually reasserted themselves and gained liberation. The Mongols never interfered with Russia's Orthodoxy and when liberation was achieved Moscow emerged as the leading Orthodox City of the world. A monk called Philotheus wrote:

> *The Church of Moscow, the new 'third Rome' shines throughout the entire world more brightly than the sun.*

10 Dramas in Europe

Thomas Becket	136
Francis of Assisi	138
Dominic	141
Thomas Aquinas	142
Dante Alighieri	143

Thomas Becket (1118–1170)

While crusaders were battling in the Holy Land Europe was acting out its own dramas. In England, the struggle between church and state was reaching melting point when King Henry II had a personal feud with his friend Thomas Becket.

Becket was a Norman, the son of a London merchant of some standing. His father groomed him for a life in the church, he was educated at Merton Priory in Surrey and later in Paris. Plans went awry when Becket's father fell on hard times, making it necessary for him to earn his own living. He worked as a clerk and auditor, then when he was 25, he found a job with the Archbishop of Canterbury and saw at first hand the world of politics, power and influence. He grew close to the king who shared a love of hunting, hawking and shooting. He had many promiscuous companions and while there is evidence that he himself remained chaste, frugal and pious he certainly was acquainted with life in the fast lane. He took orders as a deacon and was appointed Archdeacon of Canterbury until the king surprisingly made him his Chancellor. He held this job for eight years and was unstinting in his service to the king, at the same time becoming extremely wealthy and a big land owner. He lived in some style maintaining a group of knights, keeping open-house and even acting as governor of the Tower. He was criticised by churchmen but kept the affection of the king.

When the Archbishop of Canterbury died Becket was surprisingly appointed in his stead. Perhaps the king believed that his friendship with Thomas would ensure he kept the church in his pocket. If that was the case he misjudged his man. Becket warned the king that the appointment would spoil their friendship but Henry would not be dissuaded. Becket's life-style changed immediately, he adopted a more rigorous discipline and took his ecclesiastical duties very seriously. He was no longer a follower of hounds but a shepherd of souls. Conflict was inevitable and not long in coming. Henry wanted to reduce the power of the church courts, which insisted on trying all churchmen for their alleged crimes. The king felt, with justification, that the term 'churchmen' was being interpreted too widely, allowing clerks and lawyers to appear before church courts that could only pass sentences of excommunication and discipline, avoiding the harsher sentences of the civil courts. Henry's case was that the laws and customs of the realm should apply to everybody. Becket agreed but added the proviso '*except where they interfered with the rights of the church'*. Henry wanted criminals tried before ordinary courts *after* trial by church courts but Becket said no man should be tried twice for the same offence. Henry wanted to ban appeals to Rome without royal consent but Becket said this was state interference in church matters and he wanted an English Church which was free to keep an untrammelled relationship with Rome. Agreement was not about to be reached so Henry decided to take action and deprived Becket of his possessions, accusing him of treason before a council at Northampton. Becket appeared in full ecclesiastical regalia and refused to recognise the authority of the tribunal. He left the court amid great enthusiasm from the crowd and then secretly sailed to France the following day. The king immediately seized his property and banished all four hundred of his dependants.

For six years Becket lived in exile while the Western world took sides in the dispute. Meetings were arranged between them and Becket did promise submission to the king but always with the reservation, *'saving the honour of God'*. In 1170 the king had his son crowned as 'under king' at Westminster and in Becket's absence the ceremony was conducted by the Archbishop of York. Shortly afterwards a reconciliation was worked out between king and cleric and Thomas returned to England to a rapturous welcome from the people. Without delay he excommunicated the Archbishop of York and then, in a Christmas Day service, excommunicated other clergy and barons of the king. Henry was in France at the time and in a fury cried out in anger, 'Are there none of the servants who eat my bread, who will not avenge me against this upstart priest who insults me?'

As he prayed the knights rushed in and murdered him beside the altar.

Four knights heard the king and interpreted the outburst as a call for Becket's murder and set off for England. They arrived in Canterbury on the 29th December and ordered the archbishop to remove the excommunications forthwith. He refused. The knights then went away to arm themselves, giving Thomas the chance to escape but it was time for Vespers and as he prayed the knights rushed in and murdered him beside the altar. Terrified monks buried him in the crypt. Henry, on hearing news of his old friend's murder, locked himself away for three days in deep mourning but the murderers were never brought to justice and when the pope sent out legates to receive the king's penance, Henry had gone to Ireland.

A Becket cult followed, in 1173 the martyr was canonised by Pope Alexander III and Canterbury became one of the most popular of western shrines. Becket's commitment to a belief in liberty for the church, even before a bullying king, has never been forgotten and remains an example of Christian conscience upheld to the limit. Later, the *Magna Carta* of 1215, did enshrine in law the church's right to be free along with the assurance that no freeman should be imprisoned, fined, exiled or put to death without a trial before his equals or by the law of the land. Pilgrimages to Canterbury, which started from the Tabard Inn in Southwark, were the occasions which gave rise to Chaucer's *Canterbury Tales*—stories of romance, chivalry and the everyday doings of country folk, told to wile away the hours of the journey. In modern times, T.S. Elliot's *Murder in the Cathedral*, Fry's *Curtmantle*, and the film *Becket*, have all rekindled interest in the most famous of all Canterbury's archbishops.

Francis of Assisi (1182–1226)

By the end of the twelfth century the medieval world was in the throes of enormous social, cultural and religious change. Ideals of courage and chivalry remained but this had been seasoned by the culture of Islam and increasing demands for individual's rights. Previous certainties were in the melting pot, the structures of society were changing and spiritual hunger could not be satisfied by authority alone.

Into such a world came a man whose faith vividly brought back to life all the idealism and beauty of Jesus in the first century. He was Francis Bernadone from the Umbrian city of Assisi. His Christianity was so passionate it was capable of embracing men and women whatever their condition or however poor. It even spilled out beyond human beings, embracing the creation he saw radiant with the sunshine of divine glory. Yet it was a life begun with little promise.

He was a carefree young man who promised to be a personable knight well endowed with wealth from his father's cloth business. Then he became involved in a local war and was kept as a prisoner for twelve months. In prison he befriended a man ostracised by everybody else and he started to show a real independence of spirit. After his release he fell ill and made a pilgrimage to Rome and it was there he began to take the religion of Jesus seriously.

> *The Kingdom of Heaven is upon you. Heal the sick, raise the dead, cleanse lepers, cast out devils. You received without cost; give without charge. Provide no gold, silver or copper to fill your purse no pack for the road, no second coat, no shoes, no stick: the worker earns his keep.*
> **(Matt. 10:7–10)**

He started to act out the words of Jesus literally and on one occasion dismounted from his horse to embrace a leper and give him money before riding on. He received a vision to rebuild the derelict old shrine of St Damian in Assisi and immediately sold his horse and several bales of his father's cloth to raise the money. His father was not amused and had his son locked up. The dispute dragged on until it culminated in Francis declaring dramatically:

> *Up to this time I have called Pietro Bernadone father, but now I am a servant of God. Not only the money but everything that can be called his I will restore to my father, even the very clothes he has given me.*

He piled his garments into a heap, tossed money on top and, having received a blessing from the bishop, he walked out half naked and began to rebuild the church with his bare hands. His life changed completely. From carefree youth with aspirations of knightly glory, he became a beggar with nothing to call his own. Yet from this zero position he could say, 'Blessed is he who expecteth nothing, for he shall enjoy everything'. With a handful of friends (friars) he walked the countryside begging from the rich and giving to the poor. He preached sermons, full of kindness and charm winning more followers. Then, in 1210, Francis gained approval from Pope Innocent III for his 'lesser brothers' to be recognised as an order and from then on they met yearly at Portiuncula near Assisi. Two years later a society for women was formed when an heiress of Assisi was converted and commissioned. Within a century there were more than 25,000 Franciscan friars preaching from over a thousand friaries throughout Western Europe

Was Francis an impractical idealist out of touch with the real world? People certainly thought so when he decided to go on a mission to the Saracens of Syria. His idea to bring the crusades to an end by conversion rather than conquest was a simple idea but, as G.K. Chesterton said of his scheme, 'It was in one way a simple idea, as most of his ideas were simple ideas. But it was not a silly idea'. After all it is better to create Christians than to destroy Muslims. Remarkably Francis did reach the crusader front-line at the besieged city of Damietta, found the headquarters of the Saracens and secured an interview with the sultan. He did not succeed in converting the sultan, indeed they probably thought him mad, but it was typical of him that having had an idea he plunged in with energy in an attempt to bring the idea to fruition.

Returning from his personal crusade Francis found his own order changed in character so he withdrew his leadership and retired to a hermitage on Mount Alverno, where he experienced the stigmata (Christ's wounds on his own body). He wrote quite a lot in his retreat and his *Admonitions* tell us much about the way he thought life should be lived:

> *Blessed that friar who loves his brother as much when he is sick and can be of no use to him as when he is well and can be of use to him. Blessed that friar who loves and respects his brother as much when he is absent as when he is present and who would not say anything behind his back that he could not say charitably to his face.*
> **(Admonitions XXV)**

The Franciscan Order has changed but there can be no doubt how great has been the influence of Francis over the years. Five Franciscans have become popes, many have benefited from scholarships from the order and the missionary and social work done by them has been outstanding. His idealism is still a vibrant force in Christianity.

> *Lord make me a channel of thy peace*
> *Where there is hatred, let me show love,*
> *Where there is injury ,pardon*
> *Where there is doubt, faith;*
> *Where there is despair, hope;*
> *Where there is darkness, light;*
> *Were there is sadness, joy;*

O Divine Master, grant that I may not so much seek
To be consoled, as to console;
Not so much to be understood as
To understand;
Not so much to be loved
As to love;
For it is in giving that we receive;
It is in pardoning that we are pardoned;
It is in dying that we awaken to eternal life.

Dominic (1170–1221)

A contemporary of Francis who founded another order of preaching friars was Dominic. The Dominicans took similar vows of poverty but put more emphasis on the intellect and were particularly concerned with combating heresy. They became the intellectual driving force of the medieval Church.

Born into a pious family in Castile, Dominic was educated by an uncle before moving to Palencia University where he proved to be an exemplary student. Afterwards he became a canon at Osma Cathedral near Castile and accompanied Diego, his Bishop, on a diplomatic mission to Denmark. It was here he came across Albergensians, a heretical group who believed that all flesh was intrinsically evil. Dominic was impressed by their life-style but not by their beliefs so he decided that the only way to persuade the heretics was by a continuous mission by preachers who, in a similar way to the Franciscans, travelled on foot and relied on local generosity for their well-being. They had some success with their preaching, particularly with women converts and they opened the first Dominican convent at Prouille.

When Diego died Dominic took over the leadership of the preaching group and when a gathering of bishops was convened by Pope Innocent III (the Fourth Lateran Council) to find out the state of Church pastors, Dominic hoped his group of poor friars would be allowed to found a new order. Permission was not granted and so the sixteen or so members decided to adopt an Augustinian discipline, which gave them flexibility of operation. In effect preaching and study were given priority over prayers and chanting. They became very popular and eventually were granted permission to continue their order with special responsibilities for combating heresy. They wore a black mantle and became known as The Black Friars, soon to be seen lecturing in the many universities opening up all over Europe.

Thomas Aquinas (1225–1274)

Thomas Aquinas was destined to be the most famous Dominican friar of them all. He was born to a wealthy family at Aquino near Naples. At five years of age he was placed in the monastery of Monte Cassino and stayed there for nine years until the emperor expelled all the monks because they were too obedient to the pope. He then went to the University of Naples where he decided to join the Dominican friars. His mother was so furious that she kidnapped him and confined him to the family castle for more than a year. When eventually he was released he went to Paris to continue his education. It was in Paris he was nicknamed Dumb Ox, probably because of his size and thoroughness but his tutor Albertus Magnus predicted that one day, 'this ox will fill the world with his bellowing'.

He was right. By 1256 he was a doctor in theology and a Professor of Philosophy in Paris. Three years later he was called to Rome by Pope Alexander IV and asked to act as adviser and lecturer in the papal court. He returned to Paris later to become embroiled in the real argument of the age, which concerned Christians, Jews and Muslims alike. The subject of the debate was Aristotle, who had been translated into Latin along with accompanying commentaries by the Islamic scholar Averroes. Until the thirteenth century Augustine had dominated Western philosophy but the 'rediscovery' of Aristotle with all its vigour and clarity did much to restore confidence in knowledge gained from the senses as opposed to knowledge coming through special revelation. Aristotle, as interpreted through the Averroists, could not be ignored because it stated bluntly that religious knowledge and rational knowledge were sometimes in disagreement and could also be contradictory. Aquinas responded with a cogently argued case that truth through faith and truth from experience, as presented by Aristotle, are complimentary rather than contradictory. His writing was prolific, filling eighteen huge volumes and including commentaries on the Bible, discussions about Aristotle and sundry arguments and sermons. His ideas show the confidence and the achievements of the Middle Ages. In *Summa Theologica* he asks how can we know God then argued his case:

> *Our natural knowledge begins from the senses. Therefore our natural knowledge can only extend as far as it can be led by the object of the senses. On the basis of sensory objects our intellect can not go so far as to see the essence of God, because sensory creatures are effects of God which are not equal in power to their cause. Hence we cannot know the full power of God on the basis of the objects of the senses and consequently we cannot see his essence. However, because they are effects that are dependent on a cause, we can be led from them to know that God exists, and to know the characteristics that he must possess as the first cause of all things that transcends everything caused by him. Hence we know about his relationship to his creatures that he is the cause of all, and that creatures differ from him in that he is not a part of the things that he has caused, and that they are separate from him not because of any deficiency on his part but because of his transcendence...*

Even in his own day not everybody was won over by the arguments of Aquinas but his interpretations of Aristotle, Augustine, Averroes, and other Muslims and Jewish thinkers, like Maimonides, opened up discussions in a completely new way and led to a synthesis of rational and religious truth. Initially Rome shied away from his conclusions but his work gained prominence and he was canonised in 1323 and officially named Doctor of the Church. His first biographer, William of Tocco said of him:

> *Brother Thomas raised new problems in his teaching, invented a new method, used new systems of proof. To hear him teach a new doctrine, with new arguments, one could not doubt that God gave him power to teach, by the spoken and written word, new opinions and new knowledge.*

Aquinas taught at all the great Dominican houses in Rome, Orvieto, Viterbo and Perugia until he had a trance like experience in 1273 after which he wrote little, saying that his work was mere chaff. A year later, at the age of 49, he died. But the influence of Aquinas and the Dominicans was enormous and did much to shape the character of the new universities, where all the ingredients of developing civilisations were being mixed together in a spiritual milieu now being provided by Christianity, Judaism and Islam.

Dante Alighieri (1265–1321)

European art forms began to develop in their own style through the thirteenth century and when Dante was born the city of Florence was poised to launch a great era of culture and art quite breathtaking in its achievement. The painter Cimabue had started a breakaway from Byzantine art forms by giving figures three dimensional appearance and he was followed by Giotto with his clever use of perspective. The dawn of the Renaissance was bringing with it new life.

Dante, writer of poetry and prose and speech-maker thrown in, is undoubtedly Italy's greatest writer ranking alongside Shakespeare and Goethe as a giant of European literature. His output was prodigious and writing in Italian rather than Latin, he moved European literature decisively away from Latin. His early work reveals a love-sick youth mooning over Beatrice, a young girl who does not respond with enthusiasm to his affection. Undeterred, he continued his adoration and was devastated when she died in 1290. Even when he turned to his writing for consolation she continued in his mind and repeatedly appears in his poems. His masterpiece, *The Divine Comedy* consists of three sections—Hell, Purgatory and Heaven and in each there are visions of the supernatural realm. In the first it is Good Friday in the year 1300 and he is lost in a dark wood. After a tormented night, he heads for the sunshine only to be blocked by a leopard (lust), a lion (pride) and a wolf (avarice). The Roman poet Virgil guides him through the wood and the infernal realm and through the second journey up to the mountain of Purgatory. Virgil is then replaced by Beatrice who leads him to Heaven by the loving power of her glance and here Dante enjoys a brief, sublime vision of God. The work is more than a journey from Hell to Heaven but starting with a concept from Aquinas that created things exist through the being of God, he builds his poem around it. He actually meets Aquinas in the third part of the *Divine Comedy*, where the great teacher is in the company of past saints, which include Francis and Dominic. He was tied to the cosmology of the time but for all that the work is packed with concrete images and moral passion. His message is clear, happiness in this life is achieved by moral and intellectual virtues and celestial happiness by the virtues of faith, hope and love. The poem is an allegory of Dante's own pilgrimage of faith and a map to be followed by all those who seek meaning for this life and the next.

Dante's work has influenced succeeding writers through the ages, including Milton, Bunyan, Byron and T.S. Elliot and his images were readily taken up by the great painters of the Renaissance who were picking up their brushes as Dante lay down his pen.

11 Renaissance and Reformation

John Wyclif	146
Catherine of Siena	148
Jan Huss	149
Joan of Arc	150
Johann Gutenberg	151
William Caxton	152
Savonarola	153
Leonardo da Vinci	154
Copernicus	155
The Borgias	156
Michelangelo	157
Erasmus	158
Indulgences	160
Martin Luther	161
Thomas More	166
Henry VIII	168
Thomas Cranmer	170
William Tyndale	171
Philip Melanchthon	172
Zwingli and Bucer	173
John Calvin	174
John Knox	176

Towards the end of the thirteenth century the unheard of happened. Pope Celestine V abdicated. He was replaced by Boniface VIII (1294–1303) who immediately started to reform the papacy and reassert power over the powerful monarchies, especially France. Boniface claimed the right of full temporal and spiritual power, a claim totally rejected in France. A feud ensued, which ended with Boniface excommunicating the French king Philip IV. The king in turn used forgery, defamation, intrigue and all else before resorting to violence and attacking the pope at Anogni. Citizens helped the desperate Holy Father to escape but he died in the Vatican a few weeks later. Clearly national monarchies were not prepared to relinquish power of any sort to the pope and Boniface had misread the signs of the times. French pressure led to the election of Clement V (1305–1314) as pope and, as he was Archbishop of Bordeaux in southern France, he chose Avignon as his official residence. For most of the fourteenth century no pope lived in Rome, a situation regretted by many staunch Christians. Meanwhile, the running costs involved in the vast bureaucratic machine of papacy increased dramatically, which did little to increase its popularity. Pope Gregory XI's regime needed half a million gold florins to finance it and not a few people began to ask where the spiritual leadership was coming from in the rush for riches. One loud questioning voice in England belonged to a man called John Wyclif, perhaps the greatest of the English reformers.

John Wyclif (1329–1384)

Wyclif was a Yorkshireman born in Richmond, who rose from humble beginnings to become the master of Balliol, Oxford, and the greatest scholar of his day. He lived in hard days. During his early life the Black Death visited England and within eighteen months had killed nearly half the population. It was bubonic plague, so called because of the swelling, or buboes, seen in armpits and groins, which was spread by fleas on rats. It surged through Europe killing some 25 million people This agony coincided with a thoughtless declaration from Pope Gregory that a Jubilee Pilgrimage should be made to Rome. It was an idea to swell papal coffers but it cost a million lives. The Franciscans alone lost 30,000 men during the pilgrimage.

The plague caused a scarcity of labour, landlords and even the clergy quit their posts and crowded into London. Serfs roamed the country-side looking for work and many became outlaws, stealing for food. Richard II chose this moment to introduce a poll-tax of 4d for every person, no matter what age, it was so unpopular that the fires of peasant revolt led to the slaughter of tax-collectors, the destruction of buildings, the burning of court roles and the beheading of the Archbishop of Canterbury.

In this social cauldron Wyclif taught at Oxford and preached in his church at Lutterworth in Leicestershire. He launched scathing attacks on monks, friars, and clergy castigating them for their greed and wantonness. He denied that preachers needed to be licensed by Rome before they could preach and saw no reason why clergy should not be allowed to marry. Wyclif believed that a farmworker's prayers were just as valid as a priest's and declared that the real yardstick of faith could only be the Bible. But he was not merely a denouncer. He made the first translation of the Bible into English at a time when worship was conducted in Latin and legal matters took place in French. The pages were painstakingly and beautifully written out by hand and then spread amongst people who, for the very first time, could read the Bible in English. He sent out 'poor priests' whose preaching was based on the handwritten pages and not on traditions and superstitions, their success was so great that the following century was saturated with biblical knowledge. The preachers dressed in distinctive woollen robes as brown and rough as a russet apple and they relied for hospitality on the goodwill of their hearers, who gave readily in response to a reading or a Wyclif sermon. Respectable clergy derided them for their appearance and called them Lollards, which meant 'babblers' or 'hymn-singers'. They had to face persecution from heresy hunting bishops and, though they quickly went underground, many died.

Wyclif was pronounced a heretic. The pope issued five bulls against him but he was unyielding:

> *There is one thing stronger than the strongest authority that was ever set up and that is the spirit of revolt against wrong based on an overwhelming conviction of the truth.*

The Chancellor of Oxford forbade him to teach and he was compelled to leave the university, his brilliant career over. Oxford could ill afford to lose him. Books written by Wyclif or his followers were burnt and destroyed in a thoroughly Hitlerish way and nearly all those beautifully prepared pages were lost to the flames. The blame for the Peasants' Revolt was placed firmly at Wyclif's door and a process of vilification stepped up in an attempt to discredit his work. It was a process so successful that even today the full stature of Wyclif has not been fully recognised.

However, ideas cannot be burned like books, and the spirit of religious and political independence seeped into the thinking of all classes. It was said, 'Lollardy was the keystone of the arch upon which the liberties of Englishmen were supported'. Wyclif spent the last two years of his life at Lutterworth gathering his writings together and he remained industrious to the end despite two heart attacks. Persecution followed him beyond death when the Council of Constance ordered Wyclif's bones to be exhumed, burned and scattered into the river Swift. But his place in English history is assured, for Wyclif was not a mere hors d'oeuvre to the Reformation but the Reformation's dawning or Morning Star.

Catherine of Siena (1347–1380)

Few women are recorded in this odyssey of faith because their lives were lived in the shadow of their husbands. They might well be the wind beneath many imperious wings but this was scarcely recorded in official records. Occasionally however, even official documentation had to acknowledge that religious institutions could not possibly have survived without the support and endeavour of women. It was ever so.

Catherine Benincasa was born to a humble family in Siena where her father was a wool dyer. She was one of twenty-five children, thirteen of whom survived to adulthood. Death was a frequent companion, especially in 1348 when the Black Death in Siena decimated many families. Perhaps the tragedies of her childhood were responsible for her shunning the idea of marriage and children for herself. Her energies were poured into a life of devotion and fasting which were so extreme she might well have been considered anorexic today. She pursued a life of deliberate deprivation in an effort to get nearer to God. In childhood she claimed to see visions and had an air of spiritual intensity about her, unusual in one so young. She mastered reading early but was unable to write until she was quite mature. At sixteen she joined the Dominicans, her devotions and work with the poor gained her a reputation and won scores of admirers who hung on her words. It was with some moral authority therefore, that in 1376 she journeyed to Avignon to meet Pope Gregory XI and tried to persuade him to return to Rome and close his exile in Avignon. The Great Schism of 1378, which saw three claims to the papal throne, depressed her deeply and she trekked all the way to Rome to support the claim of Urban VI, though she always stressed the need for unity. She was an ardent worker for peace in an Italy divided by petty kingdoms and vendettas, though that did not prevent her from advocating a further crusade to win back the Holy Land. She died, still a young woman of thirty-three, and did not live to see how her pleading and vision would be ignored in the years about to follow.

Jan Huss (1372–1415)

Catherine's disquiet and that of others like John Wyclif spread far and wide as power in the church was flagrantly abused. In Bohemia (now Czechoslovakia) Jan Huss, a priest who spent much of his life teaching in Prague University, used the vernacular of Czech instead of Latin in an attempt to get the gospel across to the ordinary people. He preached in Czech and, like Wyclif, went back to the Bible for his authority, emphasising that Christ alone was the Head of the Church and not ecclesiastical officialdom, which by nature was sinful and prone to corruption. His preaching, powerful and persuasive, urged people to accept their own responsibility in the search for truth, pointing them away from doctrines having no sanction in Scripture. He berated his congregations for their idol worship, their gullibility in being led towards superstitious pilgrimages and the purchasing of indulgences that were supposed to relieve dead relatives of years in the torment of Purgatory. Even the Communion Service came in for criticism because ordinary people were being denied the cup of wine lest the blood of Christ be spilt, a logical extension of the doctrine of transubstantiation now widespread.

In 1408, complaints about the preaching of Huss began to arrive on the desk of his Archbishop and a ban was slapped on his ministry. The following year Alexander V, one of the contending popes of the time, issued a bull (papal edict) condemning the work of Wyclif and ordering that all his books be burned. Huss had a problem with that because he used Wyclif's books and agreed with his teaching. In 1410, Huss was inevitably excommunicated. But how do you stop a man preaching when the convictions he holds are burning a hole in his heart? He continued to preach and became a hero, gaining vast popular support, which culminated in riots throughout Prague. His position was weakened gradually by the removal from office of Huss supporters and he was hustled out of the city by friends who feared for his life. During his forced exile he wrote his main work *The Church*, setting out systematically the views he had expounded in his sermons.

The next official move was to summon him to appear before a Council of Constance, called to suppress heresy once and for all. Huss naively travelled to the Council under the emperor's, so-called, safe conduct, thinking he would be allowed to express his views. He was wrong. As soon as he showed his face in the Council he was arrested and the hearing became a trial. The trial was a travesty. His views were misrepresented and Huss found himself being called upon to recant. He refused categorically, was condemned by the Council and burned to death at the stake. The martyrdom of Jan Huss infuriated the people of Prague, who refused to accept the verdict of Constance. Resistance to authority increased and became organised, others began to take up Huss's mantle preaching contentious and passionate sermons from his pulpit. Led by Jakoibek of Stribo, demands were made that priests be allowed to preach directly from Scripture and the chalice and host should be returned to the people during communion. Further demands stated that clergy should take vows of poverty and return land to owners and that vestments and Latin liturgy should be abolished. Meeting resistance, a Hussite church was formed and became strong enough to force Pope Martin V to declare a crusade against them, a tactic which failed so miserably that Hussites achieved virtual autonomy within the Catholic church. Just as Wyclif's voice could not be silenced, so the burning of Jan Huss could not be forgotten and the blue touch paper of reformation continued to burn.

Joan of Arc (1412–1431)

Another life to come to an end in the flames at this time was that of the Maid of Orleans, the patron saint of France. Theology was not the prime reason for her death but there were definitely religious overtones to her life and end. Like Catherine of Siena, she was born to a peasant family and as a thirteen year-old convinced influential people that she saw visions and heard celestial voices. These 'voices' were telling her to help the Dauphin (later Charles VII of France) fight off the English at Orleans. A board of ecclesiastics rubber stamped her claims and amazingly she was given troops to help her fulfil her mission to save France. Dressed in full armour and carrying the fleur-de-lys, she accomplished a great victory and was rewarded by a position of honour at the king's coronation in the cathedral of Rheims.

She led later military operations against the English in efforts to swing the Hundred Year's war in France's favour but she was captured by Burgundian soldiers in a battle at Compiegne and sold to the English. She was interrogated by an ecclesiastical court for fourteen months, accused of wearing men's clothes and claiming direct access to God rather than through the Church. She was sentenced to death but then she repented. Finally, she went before a secular court and was tried again as a relapsed heretic. She was burned to death at Rouen on May 30th 1431, aged just nineteen.

Johann Gutenberg (1400–1468)

When books were painstakingly written out by hand it was possible to conceive of plans to totally rid the world of ideas from radical thinkers like Wyclif and Huss. No doubt some work was totally destroyed and lost to the world forever. Any such future possibilities were about to end. The spread of ideas through the written word were about to receive a boost with the invention of the printed word and one of the first books to be printed was the Bible. Printing was an invention that transformed the Middle Ages as dramatically as television changed life in the twentieth century.

Printing was an invention that transformed the Middle Ages.

There had been attempts to use moveable type in China, perhaps as early as the ninth century, but the German Gutenberg was the first person in Europe to print with moveable type using a method only replaced in recent times. Strangely, his name does not appear on any of the works confidently assigned to him and records of his life are few and far between. He was born in Mainz, trained as a goldsmith and moved to Strasbourg where he got involved in disputes with other guilds in Mainz. His official work involved cutting gems and producing mirrors but secretly he worked away at his printing invention. He moved back to Mainz and records show that he borrowed 800 guilders from a wealthy man called Fust and two years later another 800 guilders bought Fust a partnership with Gutenberg. Fust seems to have been after a quick financial return on his money, whereas Gutenberg was searching for a perfect machine and was not working fast enough for his partner. The outcome was a court dispute and Gutenberg was ordered to pay Fust 2,026 guilders for the two loans plus compound interest. Gutenberg was ruined and he must have been heartbroken to see his work printed after the trial, work which included a forty-two-line Bible, which was really his masterpiece. Another fascinating work attributed to him is a warning against Turkish invasion, a distinct possibility in 1453 when the Turks had successfully defeated the Byzantines and brought to an end that great empire. For a long time efforts had been made to bridge the gap between the church in East and West dating back to the Emperor Constantine, now with the stronghold of Orthodox Christianity captured by Muslim Turks the ancient conflict was partly resolved.

Towards the end of Gutenberg's life his eyesight deteriorated badly and a sympathetic friend took him in and provided a living for the destitute inventor. His work lived on and thousands were able to read the Bible for themselves as a result of his labours.

William Caxton (1422–1491)

As with Gutenberg, little is known of Caxton's early life but he was born in Kent to parents who had fallen on lean times. He was apprenticed to a man called Robert Large. By 1446 he had served his articles and begun his own business in Bruges, where he printed *The Recuyell of the Historyes of Troy*, his first book in English. Later, he set up a press in Westminster where he published about one hundred books, including *Canterbury Tales*, which ran to over seven hundred pages. Caxton's printing did much to fix the literary dialect of the English, though even in Caxton's day most people could not read and even nobles read little or nothing. His work, therefore, was directed to churches, monasteries and schools. It was work not considered technically brilliant but he was a pioneer and printing like his did much to speed the Renaissance and ease the transition from the Middle Ages to the modern world. Printing was also the means by which reformers like Luther and Melanchthon reached a wide public with their ideas.

Savonarola (1452–1498)

In 1452 two people were born, who in their lives, illustrate the upheaval shaking the Western world of the fifteenth century. They were Savonarola and Leonardo da Vinci.

Savonarola was a Dominican who began to stir public life in Florence by his preaching. With papal approval he was appointed Vicar-General of the Dominicans in Tuscany, with a brief to reform the order. His preaching was uncompromising and included strong warnings about the sinfulness of contemporary life, with special reference to the Medici family who ruled Florence. When Florence was attacked by the French the Medici fled for their lives and it appeared as though they had received their just desserts. The French soon left and a Republic was set up under the guiding hand of Savonarola and without Medici interference. He had an ambition to transform Florence from a corrupt, pleasure loving city, into a Christian commonwealth, a blue-print for a new Italian golden age. Tax reforms were introduced helping the poor. The legal system was reformed and then, in one great carnival night, crowds made a bonfire of their cosmetics, false hair pieces, pornography and gambling paraphernalia. Savonarola then turned his eyes on Rome, where the infamous Borgias were bringing the papacy into total disrepute. He denounced Alexander VI and the whole papal court. Rome responded by demanding he answer a charge of heresy and when he refused to show up, he was forbidden to preach and his authority as Vicar-General was revoked. Savonarola disregarded the order.

The struggle with Rome distracted him and possibly dissipated his energy and cracks began to appear in the administration in Florence giving the Medici family opportunity to recover lost ground. At this delicate juncture Rome excommunicated him and began to threaten Florence. Savonarola said the excommunication was invalid and refused to be gagged. Plague was the next visitor to Florence and Savonarola threw himself into work with sick monks but there were continuous efforts to discredit him and in 1498 he was officially pronounced a heretic, guilty of seditious teaching. He was sentenced to death. Along with two members of his order he was hanged. But before the execution he administered the sacrament to his colleagues and himself. An official announcement declared that Savonarola was 'excommunicated from the church on earth *and in Heaven*'. 'That is beyond your power!', he retorted. Savonarola never departed from his Catholic theology but he became a hero of the early Protestants who applauded his courageous opposition to the papacy.

The disputes with reformers showed the papacy quick to use excommunication as a weapon of ecclesiastical discipline and it is interesting to read a decree from the Council of Trent sixty-five years after the murder of Savonarola:

> *Although the sword of excommunication is the chief weapon of ecclesiastical discipline, and very useful for keeping the people to their duties, it is to be used only with sobriety and circumspection, for experience teaches that if it be used rashly and for small reason it will be more despised than feared, and will work more evil than good.*
> **(Decrees of the Council of Trent XXV, Dec 4th 1563)**

Leonardo da Vinci (1452–1519)

We turn now to one of the great figures of the Renaissance, whose life epitomises the profound leaps in knowledge, which made this period in history so special. Leonardo was artist, architect, engineer and scientist all rolled into one. Born in Vinci, a small town near Florence, he was the son of a wealthy secretary and a peasant mother. He received the best education on offer and with his easy wit and sharp intellect soon rose through Florentine society. At fourteen he was apprenticed to a painter and sculptor called Andrea del Verrocchio and during a lengthy training contributed much to that painter's work. It was not until he was twenty-six that he was considered to be a master in his own right.

In 1482 he wrote a letter to the Duke of Milan claiming that he could build portable bridges, catapults, ships, armoured vehicles, canons and sculpt in marble, bronze and clay. Such a CV impressed the Duke, Leonardo was set on and became principal engineer and architect. He also found time to paint, often labouring over work he seemed reluctant to finish. A masterpiece, *The Last Supper* (only recently restored) took him over two years to paint and because it was a mural painted in oil on plaster it did not wear well and had started to deteriorate as early as 1500. In 1502 Leonardo started working for Cesare Borgia, the son of Pope Alexander VI. He was chief architect and engineer working on fortresses for the pope. He painted numerous portraits during this period all of which are lost, with the notable exception of the *Mona Lisa*. This picture must have meant much to him because it accompanied him on his travels for the rest of his life.

In later life Leonardo worked in Milan, Florence, Rome and France but sadly much of his work is lost and his brilliant draughtsmanship can only be seen in his many drawings. As a scientist his work was inspirational and his notebooks testify to his acute observation and precise scientific method and reveal extraordinary knowledge about subjects as diverse as blood circulation, the effects of the moon on tides, fossils, flying machines and hydraulics. He was a one-off, a man before his time, but even he was only part of the explosion of knowledge taking place in the fifteenth and sixteenth centuries. Another man turning the world on its head was the astronomer Copernicus.

Copernicus (1473–1543)

Nicolas Copernicus was a Pole who developed the idea that the earth was in constant motion around a static sun and therefore could not be the centre of the cosmos but only one planet amongst others. He was invited to Rome in 1533 to lecture on his theories before Pope Clement VII, who approved of Copernicus and his method. Despite this papal favour it was many years before his research was published and it is said that a copy of his research, *De Revolutionibus*, was given to the astronomer on the last day of his life. Copernicus was better known to his contemporaries as a compassionate physician but it was his astronomical theory which caused such a profound shock to his generation. His work affected every branch of learning, not least in philosophy and theology. His theory was explained simply:

In the middle of all sits the sun on his throne, as upon a royal dais ruling his children the planets which circle around him.

Galileo and Kepler would be left to develop his theories in later years when the doctor's work would be seen as a truly 'Copernican revolution'.

The Borgias (1455–1507)

Unfortunately for the Western Church the new knowledge igniting Europe occurred when, for much of the time, the papacy was occupied by the Borgia family from Spain. Their name became a byword for infamy and vice.

There were two Borgia Popes, Callistus III (1455–1458) and his nephew Alexander VI (1492–1503). Alexander (Rodrigo Borgia) attained his election by bribery and he plundered much of the wealth of the Church. His second son Cesare Borgia, the child of his favourite mistress, was general of the Church armies and once the slur of illegitimacy had been removed by papal decree, he was also allowed to hold ecclesiastical office. Father and son were totally immoral and Machiavelli described Cesare as a 'ruthless new prince'. Church duties interested him only slightly and he became famous for his hunting parties, mistresses and opulent life-style.

In an attempt to consolidate the family's power, Cesare was married to Charlotte, the sister of the king of Navarre and he received the title Duke of Valentinois from Louis XII, king of France, provoking the nickname Valentino. He embarked on a plan to secure a Borgia state in Italy but he made enemies and this started off a ruthless campaign to kill off all opposition. Backed up with seemingly endless papal funds, he might have achieved all his ambitions but his father died in 1503 and his successor Julius II was not well disposed to the Borgias. Cesare spent his last years escaping from people who wished him dead. He met his death in a skirmish with rebels in France.

Much of our knowledge of Cesare Borgia we owe to Machiavelli (1469–1527) whose principal work, *The Prince*, was based on the life of Cesare. Machiavelli worked out a political theory from observing the prince at work and concluded that to win and maintain power sometimes means overlooking Christian morality, in the belief that a noble end can justify any tyranny that proceeds it. (A modern parallel might be to suggest that the slaughter of millions of Russian peasants in the twentieth-century could be justified if the eventual result was to usher in a communist state.) Machiavelli has been praised as a practical realist and damned as a dangerous cynic. Perhaps he was neither of these for his writings reveal a complex, passionate man who could be extremely generous, was ardent about his religion and longed for virtue to be established in his beloved Italy. He wrote of himself:

> *I laugh, and my laughter is not within me;*
> *I burn and the burning is not seen outside.*

Michelangelo (1475–1564)

Another giant of the Renaissance who was employed by the Borgias was Michelangelo. Although not born in Florence he had a fond attachment to the city. Most of his adult life was spent in Rome but when he died he left instructions that he should be buried in Florence. The Medici family patronised his work as painter, sculptor and architect but he was also an outstanding poet. When the Medici family were expelled from Florence during Savonarola's Republican years, Michelangelo moved to Bologna and then to Rome where archaeology had uncovered some classical statues, the inspiration for his larger than life marble sculpture, *Bacchus*. This is one of the few works of his not having a Christian subject. The stunning *Pieta*, now in St Peter's, followed and his successful career was assured. At the age of twenty-five he was the outstanding sculptor of his day, when he returned to Florence his work increased in intensity and the colossal 14 feet marble of *David* was sculpted and placed outside the Florentine town-hall.

Pope Julius II called him back to Rome to work on the new basilica of St Peters with a remit to paint frescos on the ceiling of the Sistine Chapel, a project which occupied him for four years. For good measure, St Peter's itself, designed by Donato Bramonte, was passed over to Michelangelo to complete. Then a vast sepulchre, with forty life-size figures, was ordered by the pope, and this became a project which harassed him for years with quarrying problems, poor assistants, papal pressure and inconsistent finance. It was a task never concluded and he was threatened with lawsuits by the pope's family, who wanted to bind him to completing the work, long after the pope's death. Not surprisingly perhaps, the great artist complained of every illness imaginable from time to time and spoke of his 'imminent death' forty-eight years before it occurred! When he did die, aged eighty-eight, he said at his last confession:

> *I regret that I have not done enough for the salvation of my soul and that I shall die just as I am beginning to learn the alphabet of my profession.*

It is a mistake to think of Michelangelo as a tortured genius who laboured away in isolation on his many projects. New records, found in archives in Florence, show that he rarely worked alone. Thirteen people helped him with the Sistine ceiling, twenty carved the tombs of the Medici Chapel in Florence and during the 18 years working on the Laurentian Library in Florence, he supervised a team of at least 200. He listed the names and the wages of each of these employees, sometimes writing down their nicknames. Michelangelo's innermost thoughts are contained in poetry written without thought of publication. They are intimate glimpses into the life of a man who brushed shoulders with the powerful men of his day on almost equal terms and he reveals himself as a lonely man desperate for love. He describes his art as a 'false idol' which had robbed him of years he could have spent searching for God. It is personal poetry, laughed off as mere novelty, but it was greatly valued by those who knew him best. These friends published them after his death.

Erasmus (1466–1536)

A need for church reform had become a necessity and there were people asking pertinent questions about how that reform should come about. The Dutchman Desiderius Erasmus wanted to see an end to worldly popes and unlearned monks and pointed to more biblical knowledge and a study of the early Church Fathers as a way forward. He was an illegitimate child who, by great effort, overcame his bad start in life to become the most respected scholar of his age. His guardians persuaded him to enter an Augustinian monastery but he hated the life and escaped the cloister by becoming secretary to the bishop of Cambai.

He was a restless traveller, working as tutor and lecturer and disputing with the learned and wise. He often travelled to England and he formed close friendships with John Colet of St Paul's School, London and with Thomas More, the Lord Chancellor of England. He taught Greek at Cambridge University and did much to establish humanism in the country. He linked Greek studies to Christianity and was fascinated by old manuscripts which he translated meticulously. 'Back to the originals', was a motto of his because he thought it necessary for accurate translations to be passed on for ordinary people to read for themselves:

> *The mysteries of kings it may be safer to conceal but Christ wished his mysteries to be published as openly as possible. I wish that even the weakest woman should read the gospels and epistles of Paul...I long that the husbandman should sing portions of them to himself as he follows the plough, that the weaver should hum them to the tune of his shuttle and that the traveler should beguile with their stories the tedium of his journey.*

Erasmus was a witty writer whose reputation was made with a collection of Greek and Latin proverbs called *Adages* but he applied himself to many projects, which revealed his concerns about life inside the church and his desire for biblical knowledge. A book, *The Praise of Folly*, written in a few days whilst staying with More in London, was a bitter satire on a Church more concerned with external devotions and ceremony than with inner experience. 'Oh, the folly of those who revere a bone of the apostle Paul encased in glass and feel not the glow of his spirit enshrined in the epistles!' He mocked those who claimed miracles had been wrought by one of Thomas Becket's slippers which, he said ironically, could do more when he was dead that his whole body could do when he was alive! On matters of doctrine he was concerned with things essential to salvation and pointed out that God would be unlikely to damn people for not believing in something they found incomprehensible. But ridicule was not the whole of Erasmus for he was eager to get people to know the Bible. His Greek New Testament, published in 1516 and dedicated to Pope Leo X, attracted many admirers and he saw Scripture as the bedrock of education. He wanted people to read and to think and advocated that elementary Latin and basic Christianity should be taught at home before official education began at seven. His educational technique, which started with language as conversation before the restraints of grammar, sounds very up-to-date to modern ears, as does his belief in physical education and the need to make learning fun.

Church reformers took inspiration from Erasmus and some even think of him as the Father of the Reformation. He certainly associated and disputed with reformers but he himself remained a Catholic, even though he was aware of all the church's follies. Was Erasmus a reformer at heart but afraid to declare himself? Was he the forerunner of Luther, the man who produced the egg that Luther hatched? Or was he his own man, an independent thinker who refused to join any camp? Neither Catholics or Reformers seemed comfortable with him. Clearly his motivation was to dispel ignorance and shun superstition, which led to his work being listed in an index of forbidden books by the Council of Trent in 1563. His own toleration did much to make the Netherlands into the environment offering refuge for religious thinkers and prisoners of conscience who were being harassed in their own lands. Towards the end of his life there was talk of a Cardinal's hat for Erasmus but by then he was not looking for any kind of preferment and was happy to work on a paraphrase of the Psalms for an old friend. He died in Basle where the friend wrote of him:

> *As was his life, so was the death of this most upright of men. Most holy was his living, most holy his dying*

Indulgences

The building of St Peter's Church in Rome was a monumental undertaking, demanding all the resources and skills of the finest builders and artists of the Middle Ages. Linked with the martyrdom of the Apostle Peter, who was thought to have been crucified at the foot of Vatican Hill, the new basilica replaced one built in 324. Twenty popes and ten architects, including the aged Michelangelo, worked on the project with Michelangelo's dome rising to 452 feet. It was very expensive. For those who contributed funds Pope Julius II offered benefits in this life and beyond and his successor Leo X continued to offer these benefits. But questions were being asked. Why should people in Britain or Germany be expected to finance the building of a church in Rome when their own parish church needed its roof patching up? Why should the faithful in England finance the siege of Bologna by Pope Julius II? To ensure that funds did not dry up the pope appointed the Archbishop of Mainz as his chief collector of funds. He, in turn, employed a Dominican friar called Tetzel to preach indulgences, granting remission of all sins committed in this life and cancelled pains in purgatory too. Souls already in purgatory benefited from contributions as well because indulgences could be obtained on their behalf. Tetzel became preacher and money raiser and organised the plan for the contrite to visit seven churches, recite five paters and aves and *most importantly* make a contribution rated according to status, occupation and income. This could vary from one to twenty-five gold florins.

The preaching of indulgences was a new doctrine too far and the one which led to protests of such vehemence that it swelled into a protesting church. Martin Luther was to say, 'Why does not the pope, who is richer than Croesus, build the single church of St Peter out of his own money, instead of out of the poor believers?' Luther was about to become the voice of a reformation.

Martin Luther (1483–1546)

Wyclif might have been the Morning Star of the Reformation and Erasmus the Father of the Reformation but there can be no doubt that the Reformation itself began on October 31st 1517, when Martin Luther, an unknown professor of Biblical Studies at a new University in Wittenberg, Germany, nailed ninety-five theses onto the door of the Castle Church in Wittenberg. It was a familiar action for church doors were often used as notice-boards but the contents of this notice filled Europe with excitement. Suddenly, the Christian faith was defined anew and the foundation of the new teaching went back to the New Testament. Luther had no intention of waging war upon the Catholic Church but he did want to open up a debate. He must have been terrified by the explosion which followed.

Luther was the son of a miner, born in the Saxon town of Eisleben. Unlike Erasmus he travelled little even though his father through enterprise and graft, became quite well-off. What prosperity did do was provide a sound education for his son. Initially it was to be an education in law with a professional career beckoning beyond that, but fate decreed otherwise. One day in 1505 he was caught in a violent thunderstorm, an experience which shook him rigid and provoked a religious strain of thinking not suppressed until he had entered the Augustinian monastery at Erfurt. It was a monastery well known for its ascetic life-style and he entered it with enthusiasm, striving earnestly with his prayers and meditations to find peace with God. Peace eluded him. Then in 1510 he was sent to Rome and having walked over the Alps into Italy he was shocked to find the centre of Christianity so devoid of depth and spirituality. It was an experience he was never to forget.

He gained his doctorate in 1512 and was appointed Professor of Biblical Studies at the University of Wittenberg, a position he held for the rest of his life. The professorship compelled Luther to concentrate on biblical texts and this began to show in his sermons and teaching. It was a short step from reading the texts to comparing them with life in the churches, where the practice of indulgences was having dreadful effects on the lives of ordinary Christians. The Medieval World had a dread of purgatory because of teaching which claimed that nobody could reach heaven unless they had been cleansed of all sin. Penance took away that sin and indulgences shortened the painful cleansing process in purgatory. It was a belief summed up in ribaldry:

As soon as the coin in the coffer rings,
The soul from purgatory springs.

Luther was shocked to find the centre of Christianity so devoid of depth and spirituality.

There were further claims that the Church knew the penance appropriate for every sin and had the power to forgive those sins and restore people to a relationship with God ensuring a safe seat in heaven. The Church was the holder of the keys of heaven, confirmed by Christ in a sentence to Peter, 'I will give you the keys to the kingdom of heaven, what you forbid on earth shall be forbidden in heaven and what you allow on earth shall be allowed in heaven'. (Matt. 16:19.) People wanted heaven and paid up for indulgences with their contributions. It was a racket worthy of Al Capone and milked to the full by Pope Leo X who allowed bishop Albert of Brandenburg to sell indulgences to pay off creditors, so long as half the proceeds were diverted to expenses for the building costs of St Peter's.

The heart of Luther's message in the ninety-five theses was an understanding of penance gleaned from his study of the New Testament:

> *When our Lord and Master Jesus Christ said, 'Repent'* **(Matt. 4:17)** *he willed the entire life of believers to be one of repentance* **(thesis 1)**

This meant that each Christian was responsible for his own sin and his own penance and any intermediary, like a priest, was totally unnecessary because it clouded what the gospel was all about. What that meant was clear:

> *Any truly repentant Christian has the right to full remission of penalty and guilt without the need for letters of indulgence.*
> **(thesis 36)**

Luther wrote a diplomatic letter to Leo X explaining, without rancour, his beliefs. The letter, *Freedom of a Christian*, sets out things he had rediscovered in his Bible study. He pleaded that grace and forgiveness were not things the Church could administer condescendingly. God alone provides the grace to transform even the most odious of people into saints. The last are indeed capable of becoming first. Sadly, the Church's response was, not to set up a theological debate as Luther wanted, but to charge him with heresy. The heavy guns were out again. His opponents compared him to the Czech Jan Huss and in 1520 Pope Leo X officially declared Luther a heretic. Kindling for the fires began to be gathered and Luther now saw a need to limit the power of the pope and worked out conclusions to his study of the apostle Paul's letters:

> *We are justified by faith and by faith also we receive peace, not by works, penance or confessions.*
> **(*Luther's Works* 31,99 Concordia Publishing House)**

Luther had grasped what Paul had meant when he quoted the prophet Habakkuk, 'The just shall live by faith'. It was an insight opening the gates of paradise for him. Criticism of the pope continued and in an essay *On the Papacy in Rome* he concluded that the papacy was not founded by Christ at all. The keys of heaven had not been given to Peter alone but to the Christian community. This conclusion was eventually worked out as the Priesthood of all Believers. Luther reduced the number of sacraments from seven to two, baptism and communion, because these were instituted by Christ himself. The Mass was not a repetition of the sacrifice of Christ, for that had taken place on Calvary once and for all. It was in fact a fellowship meal for all the faithful and therefore the cup was to be shared by laity as well as priests, just as Jan Huss had said.

Books by Luther were thrown on bonfires in some German cities but he himself was protected by Frederick, the prince of Saxony. His excommunication however, opened up a division in the Church to add to that between East and West, a division that led to the beginnings of the Protestant Church. In 1521 Luther was called to give an account of his beliefs before Emperor Charles V and a German Parliament (Diet) at Worms. Luther refused the offer to recant with the words:

> *Unless I am convinced by the testimony of the Scriptures or by clear reason (for I do not trust either the pope or in councils alone, since it is well known that they have often erred and contradicted themselves), I am bound by the Scriptures I have quoted and my conscience is captive to the Word of God. I cannot and will not retract anything, since it is neither safe nor right to go against conscience. HERE I STAND, I CAN DO NO OTHER. MAY GOD HELP ME.*

Luther was declared an outlaw and people were forbidden to give him protection. But Frederick did protect him and secretly Luther was smuggled back to a castle in Eisenach, where he remained unrecognized for several months. It was unclear whether he was alive or dead. In fact he was working furiously to translate the New Testament from Greek into German. It was a significant work because printing presses now made his books available to mass audiences. His ideas were set free in the world and papal decrees were incapable of arresting them. The die had been cast and the Church would never be the same again.

Still heretic and outlaw, Luther returned to Wittenberg and sought to oversee the process of reform and rein in the people who were wanting more radical changes that Luther's teachings warranted. Christians were free but not free for anything:

> *A Christian is a perfectly free lord of all, subject to none, but he is a perfectly dutiful servant of all, subject to all.*
> **(Luther's Works, Concordia Publishing 31;344)**

Frederick's refusal to obey the edict of Worms or the emperor, divided German princes and set others against the pope. Luther gave up his monastic vows and at the age of forty-two, married Katherine a former nun who bore him six children, two of whom died in childhood. Until his marriage Luther had never received a personal salary and he refused to take the royalties from his books. His last years were spent in theological dispute, including famous arguments with Erasmus and Zwingli. He also became embroiled in a struggle for freedom, which became known as the Peasants' War. This was not in origins a religious war but an attempt by peasants to break the chains of feudalism, which deprived them of access to woods, rivers and meadows. Luther was not unsympathetic to their claims but was appalled when they began to run amok, pillaging, plundering and guzzling the wine of the monasteries. Luther urged the authorities to take control and he was unfairly accused later of inciting the repressive measures, which led to the deaths of one hundred thousand peasants. It has been claimed that Luther's position in the Peasants' War led to the working classes leaving Luther's churches but in Wittenberg that is definitely untrue, the congregations had manure on their boots throughout Luther's life.

The Peasants' War was a sad episode in the life of a man who, although robust in debate, was without arrogance and never claimed to be the custodian of all truth. In essence, he was a man convinced by truth he had gleaned from the Bible. He never aspired to be a reformer so much as someone who sought to hold up the Scripture in such a way that it might reform the Church. Nevertheless, it remains true that of all the people who played parts in the Reformation it was Martin Luther who led the orchestra.

Thomas More (1478–1535)

While Luther was orchestrating the Reformation in Germany another dramatic battle of conscience was being contested in England. It centred on a friend of Erasmus—Thomas More.

More was born in London to a family we might describe these days as 'upwardly mobile'. His father was a judge, a profession he was keen his son should follow. Thomas worked in the household of the Archbishop of Canterbury and was soon familiar with the life and ways of the ruling classes. He qualified for the bar when he was twenty-three but lived in a monastery until his marriage to Jane Colt. They had four children. His friendship with Erasmus was already established, a friendship he valued a great deal and which lasted until the end of his life. Four great influences in his life were now in place; a love of the law, a deep spirituality, the stability of home and family and a Christian humanism espoused by people like Erasmus. His wife Jane died after six years of marriage but he remarried quickly to Alice Middleton, a widow with one daughter, who shared More's interest in education and ideas including working with the underprivileged. His daughter Margaret worked with prisoners in Newgate prison. The domestic bliss More enjoyed was such that Erasmus likened it to Plato's *Academy* in Christian form.

> *But I do the house an injury in likening it to Plato's Academy. I should rather call it a school or university of Christian religion. For there is none therein who does not study the branches of a liberal education. Their special care is piety and virtue.*
> **(Erasmus, letter to John Fisher)**

A letter of More's to a tutor William Gonell, tells them to:

> *...put virtue in the first place, learning in the second, and in their studies to esteem most whatever may teach them piety towards God, charity to all and Christian humility in themselves.*

The educational themes More advocated were unusual for his age as was his concern for the education of women. His daughter Margaret could hold her own with anybody, including More himself, and she was a respected member of the Erasmus circle.

Two books point clearly the way More's thinking was taking him. One, *The History of King Richard III*, reveals how good government can be destroyed when power crazed autocrats are met with weak compliance. It is a startlingly modern book with a message underlined time and time again in modern history, namely, all it takes for evil men to prosper is for good men to do nothing. The second book is *Utopia*, an imaginary society devoid of all the mistakes and injustices of European states. The new world of America had been discovered by this time so perhaps possibilities of new beginnings were in his mind. The book highlights injustices in England, the rich grinding the faces of the poor into the dirt, people hung for minor offences, self-interest overriding justice. In the New World private property would not exist and wealth would be evenly distributed. In *Utopia* people had worked out an advanced civilization where religion and intelligence merged to work out man's destiny, which was to live as mirrors of their creator. As in a Jewish kibbutz, all citizens shared manual labour but had access to artistic and intellectual pursuits. The vision is of a commonwealth infused with spiritual depth and compassion. Equality was not something to put off until the grave but was possible in Utopia. He writes:

> *...even if one religion is really true and the rest false, the true one will sooner or later prevail by its own natural strength...each person is allowed to choose what he would believe.*
> **(Utopia 98)**

As More was writing *Utopia*, Machiavelli was writing *The Prince*, and he observed that 'how we live is so far removed from how we ought to live, that if a good man made a profession of goodness he must come to grief amongst so many not so good'. True wisdom then, for Machiavelli, might lie in recognizing and manipulating human self-interest, as it did with Cesare Borgia. These were theories about to be tested in the rest of Thomas More's life.

Immediately after writing *Utopia* More became a member of King Henry VIII's Council. Four years later he was elected Speaker of the House of Commons. Six years later he succeeded Wolsey as Lord Chancellor of England. During this period of advancement he was licensed to confute Protestant writings and saw the beginning of proceedings to annul Henry's marriage to Katherine of Aragon. They were events that brought out paradoxes in the character of Thomas More.

Law applied with mercy and compassion is a keynote of his writing but this mercy did not stretch to people like Martin Luther or William Tyndale. During Wolsey's chancellorship nobody was killed for their religious beliefs, whereas in More's term of office six men were burned at the stake. He wrote to Erasmus:

> *I find that breed of men loathsome... My increasing experience with these men frightens me with the thought of what the world will suffer at their hands.*

Heresy trials highlighted legal differences arising out of the development of law in England, especially differences between Canon Law (of the church) and Common Law (civil law). Thomas More might have been expected to lean towards Common Law but in fact heresy cases pushed him towards Canon Law and this led to his problems with the king. Marriage seemed to be clearly within the jurisdiction of Canon Law and when Henry, a king without a male heir, wanted his marriage annulled to leave him free to marry Anne Boleyn, it is not surprising that an ecclesiastical court decided against this and referred the matter to Rome. More, a layman skilled in Common Law, might have been expected to find in Henry's favour but instead he came down on the side of Canon Law. When Thomas Cranmer, the Archbishop of Canterbury, did grant an annulment leaving the king free to marry Anne Boleyn, More refused to attend the wedding. He was accused of treason. Electing to defend himself, he argued that the universal law of the Church had priority over that of a single kingdom like England. He was a faithful subject of the king *but* he was God's subject first. Ironically, here was More claiming for himself the freedom of conscience he denied Luther and Tyndale but for a different reason. His priority seems to have been to preserve the unity of the Church in face of pressure from kingdoms of Europe pulling hard for independence. In the end, this man for all seasons, professed:

> *I do nobody harm, I say none harm, I think none harm... but I wish everybody good. And if this be not enough to keep a man alive, in good faith I long not to live.*

At the last More could not accept the illegitimacy of Mary, the daughter of Katherine of Aragon, and refused to accept the Act of Supremacy making Henry head of the Church in England. So he was not allowed to live. On the 6th July, 1535, Thomas More was beheaded in the Tower of London.

Henry VIII (1491–1547)

It had become dangerous to get too close to the king. Wolsey was dead. More was executed. Then, an Act was passed which made it a treasonable offence to even speak against the sovereign. When a woman known as the Nun of Kent prophesied the death of Henry because of his divorce from Katherine, she was executed immediately. Thomas Cromwell, a former clerk of Wolsey's, was appointed new Chancellor in place of Thomas More and given the title Vicar General. He ordered a visitation of all monasteries with a view to dissolution, thus declaring war on the last stronghold of papal power in England. Soon a report was drawn up called the Black Book, which condemned smaller monasteries for their luxury and profligacy. The report was not published but on the strength of it monasteries were closed and all money transferred to Henry himself. The suppression of the monasteries was the green light for dreadful vandalism and wanton desecration. To many, even those who embraced reforming ideals, the sacrilege seemed like an attack on religion itself and built up great resentment against Cromwell. More than six hundred monasteries were destroyed and an income of £150,000 was dissolved.

Meanwhile, the king was going from wife to wife. No sooner had Katherine died, leaving Anne Boleyn to cry, 'Now I am indeed queen', than Henry fell for Jane Seymour, one of Anne's ladies. Anne was beheaded and Henry married Jane the next day. She only lived a year so Cromwell arranged a wedding with Anne of Cleves, a Protestant princess from Germany. Henry was not pleased with his new wife and Cromwell was arrested and executed. The marriage was annulled and the king moved on to Catherine Howard who, within a year, was found guilty of profligacy and beheaded. His final marriage was to Catherine Parr, a beautiful woman who tended Henry during his final years of failing health.

The Reformation had been extremely useful for Henry's purposes and it allowed him to overthrow the pope's authority in England but he did not please the reformers either. He passed an Act, called by Protestants, 'the whip with six strings' because it stressed six articles they found impossible to swallow. Among them were transubstantiation, confession and celibacy for the clergy. Hugh Latimer, the bishop of Worcester, resigned and Archbishop Cranmer shipped his wife off to Germany. The Act did nothing to stop Reformation ideas spreading through England and catching fire in Scotland, where rampant people welcomed them with warmth. The Bible was now available in English, the Great Bible of Coverdale was introduced into worship and Latin began to disappear.

The promise of Henry's early years disappeared as soon as he ditched Katherine for Anne Boleyn and his reign declined into turbulence and intrigue as he became increasingly headstrong and tyrannical. But the Reformation he had unwittingly set in motion in England spread like a prairie fire and could not be denied, even though Queen Mary (1553–1558) tried hard to restore Catholicism during her subsequent reign.

Thomas Cranmer (1489–1556)

Walking a very precarious tightrope through the reigns of Henry, Edward VI and Mary was Thomas Cranmer, the man mainly responsible for giving shape to the Church of England. He was a Nottinghamshire man, son of a village squire, who gained a doctorate at Cambridge University and taught at Jesus College before he was ordained. He offered help to Henry in his attempts to end his first marriage and became the king's ambassador to Charles V. He remained abroad for some years and married the niece of a reformer, a marriage which became something of an embarrassment when he was nominated Archbishop of Canterbury in 1532. His inclination was to stay abroad but papal bulls confirmed his nomination and Cranmer could do little but accept. He was consecrated as Archbishop on March 30th 1533 and within two months declared Henry's marriage to Katherine invalid. Five days later he announced the king's marriage to Anne Boleyn as a fate accompli. Amazingly, Cranmer kept his office while people to right and left died in a welter of executions. His duties grew until he was in effect an English pope. Allegiance to Rome was withdrawn, references to the pope were removed from prayer books and Henry was pronounced head of the Church in England.

Was Cranmer a time server? Did he simply tune his instrument to the king's music or was he a wise reformer who did what he could in dreadful times? His achievements were notable. He was responsible for introducing Coverdale's English translation of the Bible into churches and he was the driving force behind the revision of Creed and Litany in the church. In 1536 he introduced, through the Convocation in Canterbury, Ten Articles of Faith, the first doctrinal offerings from England during the Reformation. Another Six Articles followed in 1539 at the instigation of the king and, as these included celibacy for the clergy, Cranmer was obliged to send his wife and daughter back to Germany. After Henry he secured permission for clergy to marry and so was free to welcome back his wife with great rejoicing. He maintained a Catholic aura about much of the Church in England though he revised the worship, which led to the Book of Common Prayer. At the same time he kept doors open to European reformers. Personally, he was a sensitive man given to persuasion rather than confrontation, perhaps a perfect foil for a bullish king.

When Henry died the tightrope Cranmer had been walking began to swing against him. All seemed well under Edward VI, where hard hitting preachers like Hugh Latimer, the bishop of Worcester, became popular. His preaching style with dramatic use of alliteration was hugely popular. He spoke of gallant gentlemen 'pampering their paunches', 'munching in their mangers' and 'moiling in their gay manors and mansions'. In a sermon before Edward VI he said:

> *The drop of rain, maketh a hole in the stone, not by violence but by oft falling.*

Things changed under Mary Tudor however, and Cranmer was arrested and confined to the Tower. The queen sought to reintroduce Catholicism and Cranmer was charged with treason and tried for heresy before a Church court. He was subjected to solitary confinement in Oxford and constantly interrogated until he signed seven separate recantations of his teachings. He saw his friends Latimer and Nicholas Ridley burning before his eyes and perhaps heard Latimer cry:

> *Be of good comfort Master Ridley and play the man. We shall this day light such a candle in England that by God's grace shall never be put out.*

Inevitably, the day came when fires were lit for Cranmer and he repudiated all the recantations he had made. He thrust the hand he had used to sign the recantations first into the fire. But his work did not die with him, for as Latimer had said, 'Whenever you see persecution there is more than a probability that truth is with those being persecuted'. Today, if Cranmer could see the Church of England he would surely recognize it as the Church he did so much to bring into being.

William Tyndale (1492–1536)

Bible translating was a risky job in the Middle Ages. Wyclif had found this out in the fourteenth century and it was even more dangerous in the sixteenth. Tyndale, like Wyclif, was educated at Oxford then after ordination he went to Cambridge. There he began translations of the Bible from Greek to English. He was disgusted by the biblical ignorance of some clergy and said to one:

> *If God spares my life, ere many years pass, I will cause a boy that driveth the plough to know more of the Scriptures than thou dost.*

That aim became his life's work. With little encouragement at home he went to Germany where he met Martin Luther and became an ardent reformer. He began printing his English version of the New Testament in Cologne but he was nearly arrested, so he moved to Worms and finished the work there. It was a punchy translation, not to the liking of leading clergy in England maybe but it was quality work, so good it passed almost completely into the King James Version of 1611. Phrases like, 'Let there be light', 'We live and move and have our being', 'fight the good fight', and 'salt of the earth', have become common parlance and we owe them to Tyndale. People like Thomas More, who bitterly criticized Tyndale, probably thought his translation tilted too much towards reformism but the common people read it gladly.

William Tyndale was eventually taken into custody in Antwerp where he suffered sixteen months imprisonment. He was strangled then burnt. His last words were:

> *Lord, open Thou the king of England's eyes.*

Philip Melanchthon (1497–1560)

The tidal-wave of Reformation swept on in Europe even after the death of Martin Luther. Melanchthon had been noticed by Luther when he gave an address at the University of Wittenberg following his appointment as a Greek lecturer. When, after his trial, Luther was confined to Wartburg Castle, Melanchthon was his obvious replacement at the University, his work did much to clarify the ideas of the reformers and he also worked hard on Luther's German translation of the Bible. In 1526 he was one of twenty-seven commissioners who put down in constitutional form the reformers' beliefs. Shortly afterwards he was a representative at the Augsburg Confession, which presented twenty-one articles of faith. They were so conciliatory in tone that it is difficult to think of Melanchthon as any other than a reconciler or peacemaker but, conciliatory or not, it was still rejected by a Catholic delegation.

Luther had never wanted his beliefs in 'justification by faith', 'biblical authority' and 'the priesthood of all believers' to become *new* teaching because he saw the reformers as renovators of faith rather than innovators. However, after Luther's death his teaching became Lutheranism and Melanchthon found himself opposed by Roman Catholics and Lutherans, who believed that he had conceded too much for the sake of peace. In Germany, the tyranny of priests was over and the freedom to read the Bible led to great theological insight and debate. It also led to wrangling amongst the reformers themselves, just as Luther had anticipated. Melanchthon was standing in the centre ground but quite unable to resolve disagreements between them. As in England, acceptable European religion fluctuated with the reigning monarch and heads rolled both ways.

Zwingli (1484–1531) and Bucer (1491–1551)

Another man to make a telling contribution to the Reformation was the Swiss reformer Zwingli. Born within two months of Luther he was educated in Basle, Berne and Vienna and was a friend of Erasmus. He became a parish priest and was a scholarly and popular preacher. He was very much a man of the people and was elected as people's priest of the Minster Church in Zurich in 1519. He made himself familiar with Luther's work and shared some of his ideas and disputed with him warmly about others. Switzerland was already independent in its civic authority, subject to no prince or bishop. When Zwingli began to reform church life in Zurich therefore, he met with no great opposition as he tried to rid the Church of abuses. Scripture was his authority and taking this as his bench-mark he was highly successful in public disputes with conservative opponents on issues like fasting, clerical celibacy, the Mass, monasteries and icons in churches. These things lacked biblical authority, said Zwingli, so they were discontinued. He himself married and fathered four children.

Zwingli became popular throughout Switzerland and his followers reached into southern Germany as far as Strasbourg, where reformers leaned towards the Swiss movements rather than the German. Martin Bucer, a Dominican friar who left the order to marry a former nun, tried to mediate between Zwingli and Luther but without great success. He later moved to England where he helped Cranmer with *The Book of Common Prayer.* The Catholic/Protestant struggle was now firmly entrenched and Zwingli died in a battle with Catholics at Kappel, while Bucer's body was exhumed and burned during the Catholic years of Queen Mary in England.

John Calvin (1509–1564)

It was a French, second generation reformer, who most clearly worked out a theology of the Reformation and that man was John Calvin. A student at Orleans, Bourges and Paris, he was a somewhat introspective scholar who revealed himself only slowly. He became familiar with Luther's teaching in Paris and about the same time experienced a conversion which he described in the words, 'God subdued and brought my heart to docility'. It led him to break with Roman Catholicism and prompted a move to Basle where he started to work out his theology. It was published in 1536 and became known as *The Institutes*, a clear defence of Reformation belief. He did not begin with justification by faith but with the inscrutable decrees revealed to us by God himself. God was omnipotent and knew already who was to be saved and who damned. It was a harsh faith and yet Calvin seemed sure that if they believed the true faith, lived good lives and received grace at the Lord's Supper, they could find assurance that they were amongst the elect. Calvinist certainties made them fearless in their preaching and industrious in their labours for life was short.

Calvin was invited to oversee the Reformation in Geneva where he called on all the townspeople to swear loyalty to Protestantism. Disputes ensued and Calvin and his friend Guillaume Farel were expelled. He moved to Strasbourg where he met Bucer who encouraged him a great deal and helped his work with exiled Frenchmen. He married a widow called Idelette de Bure and they had a child who died in infancy. He produced a string of biblical commentaries and enlarged *The Institutes*. Then, after four years, he was invited back to Geneva where the citizens welcomed him with more enthusiasm and accepted his mandate to change the city's laws and bring the whole populace under the moral discipline of the church. Some task! He became pastor of the Cathedral of St Peter with a house, salary and 250 gallons of wine per year.

Luther had shown little interest in the organisation of the church and left such things to civil rulers but Calvin believed he saw within the New Testament a pattern for the Church with a ministry of pastors, teachers and elders whose job was to maintain order, morals and discipline. Deacons were to be the charitable arms of the Church which relieved the oppressed. Not surprisingly some people objected to this foreign upstart who was determined to preach to them every day but he remained in the city for the rest of his life, even after the death of his wife. Despite the salary from the state he never officially held office there and did not become a formal citizen of Geneva until 1559. Geneva was constantly threatened by Catholic armies and became a walled fortress as well as a moral enclave. Dissenters were expelled and one man, Michael Servetus, was put to death for heresy.

Calvin drew up ordinances for the government, the basis of a constitution covering secular and religious affairs. He also threw his support behind good hospitals, earthy things like better sewerage, care for the poor, development of industries and even the erection of protective rails on balconies to prevent children falling off. He was behind a comprehensive school system for all children with an Academy for the brightest. This became Geneva University with Theodore Beza as the first rector, a mecca for European theological students. Calvin was aiming for a visible 'City of God' on earth. All these things were stimulating experiments but it was his writing that proved to be his lasting contribution to the Church. He was a systematic theologian who wrote commentaries on most biblical books, an influential catechism and hundreds of sermons, letters and hymns. The Bible was his foundation but he did know the writings of the Church Fathers and quoted from many of them. He also believed that his doctrinal statements were in accord with the creeds of Nicaea and Chalcedon.

As already indicated, stress was always upon the total sovereignty of God and those elected or preordained for salvation. It was a theology of the gathered church, very persuasive for nonconformity during the seventeenth century. It is this doctrine most often seized upon as the central doctrine of *Calvinism*. The social implications of Calvin's teaching like thrift, industry and hard work entered the fabric of the Reformation and provided the 'Protestant ethic' eventually leading to business success being a yardstick of God's approval. It also weakened feudalism and gave a kick-start to capitalism. Liturgically, Calvin held that only baptism and communion were to be considered sacraments—baptism was the way people entered the church and in Communion Christ was *spiritually present*. He therefore rejected transubstantiation where priests 'made God' but he also disagreed with Zwingli, who thought communion to be merely a symbol.

By the seventeenth century, Calvinism was adopted in Holland, was the accepted theology of the Huguenots in France, behind the Puritanism of Cromwell in England and the Presbyterianism of Scotland. It was also a force which fired the Pilgrim Fathers and shaped the religious character of North America.

John Knox (1514–1572)

The Geneva experiment made a profound impression on a Scotsman called John Knox who described Calvin's Geneva as:

> *The maist perfyt schoole of Chryst that ever was on the erth since the dayis of the Apostillis.*

Scotland was slow to take up the Reformation but was sparked into action when Patrick Hamilton was burned at the stake for Lutheranism in 1528. Knox had been ordained by the bishop of Dunblane but converted to the reformer's cause in 1543 and was supporting them at St. Andrew's Castle when the castle was captured. Knox was taken to France and made a galley slave. When released he went to England as preacher in Berwick where his sermons attacked the Mass as idolatrous. He was a marked man and felt it expedient to leave for the continent after Mary's accession to the throne. Calvin urged Knox to become the pastor of an English congregation in Frankfurt for a time but he was soon back in Scotland openly preaching the Protestant cause. He was called to answer a charge of heresy but was let off. Then he went to Geneva to become pastor of another English congregation and it was while there he wrote, *The First Blast of the Trumpet against the Monstrous Regiment of Women*, where he argued that female sovereigns contravened natural and divine law. It was a blast aimed at Mary Tudor but shortly afterwards Elizabeth came to the throne and was not amused. Calvin was not pleased either, so when Protestant lords sought his presence in the heather, he returned to Scotland. The return coincided with that of Mary Stuart who worshipped openly as a Catholic. Inevitably sparks began to fly and Knox denounced her masses and court life at Holyrood House. He had at least three face-to-face encounters with Mary and even demanded her execution. She married a Catholic called Darnley and embarked on a series of affairs worthy of Mills and Boon. Ironically, after the execution of Mary it was a son to Darnley who became James VI of

Scotland and later, James I of England. He succeeded in uniting England and Scotland, a dream Knox had hoped for most of his life.

Knox was a man of conviction and courage whose passionate denouncements of idolatry hid a much warmer side to his nature. But it was Knox who established the Reformation in Scotland and dressed it in the Presbyterianism it still wears today.

The Reformation had separated a large part of Europe from the Catholic church. Starting as a protest against abuses of ecclesiastical power it had gained momentum and become political. Ordinary people welcomed the relief it gave from Church taxes but human nature was reluctant to change and attempts to usher in a godly society proved as illusive as ever. Protestant searchers for the spiritual life did not retreat to monasteries but sought to work out their salvation within the world and this search for inner purity took many names. In Britain the searchers were 'Puritans', in Holland they were called 'Precisians' and in Germany 'Pietists'. The authority of the Church had been replaced for many by the authority of Scripture but this led to different emphasis being placed on different parts of the Bible. This, in turn, led to further divisions which we will consider later. Before that however, the Roman Catholic church was poised to try and recover lost ground.

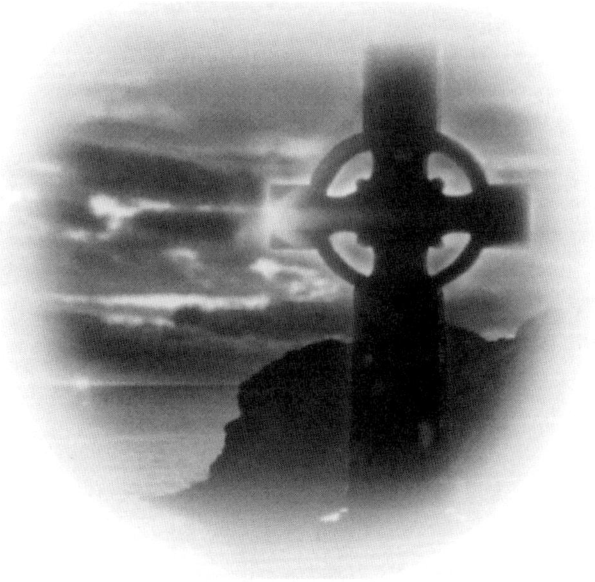

12 Counter Reformation

The Council of Trent	180
Inquisition	181
The Jesuits—Storm Troopers of the Pope	183
Francis Xavier	185

*P*rotestants breaking with the papacy had sought to free the gospel from the shackles of ecclesiology and now it was 'dangerously free' through much of Europe. The Church had always lived with heretics, who had come and gone over the years, but in the twelfth and thirteenth centuries there had been an increasing tendency to preach an alternative Christianity to that of Rome. Bernard of Clairvaux had shown his alarm when he spoke of:

> *Churches without people, people without priests, priests without respect, Christians without Christ, the holiness of holy places denied, the sacraments no longer sacred and holy days without their ceremonies*

The trickle of alternative ideas, which had alarmed Bernard, had become a flood during the Reformation. Something had to be done.

The Council of Trent

Popes had long resisted calls to convene a council that would address abuses within the Church because they feared challenges to papal authority but, confronted with Lutheranism, they eventually yielded. Alessandro Farnese was elected Pope Paul III in 1534 and he sought a universal council, which would include reformers. He was an unlikely man to start a reform inside the Church, having kept a mistress and had four children to her, but he did, and called the council to be held at Trent, a city on the Italian side of the Alps. Alas, the pope insisted on presiding at the council and Lutherans were not prepared to accept that. A reform commission had produced a report on abuses within the Church and, far from being a whitewash, it accepted blame for corrupt practices like the papal sale of privilege, devious dealings of higher clergy and the poor education of parish priests. The Council of Trent was finally opened in 1545. Four cardinals were in attendance, four archbishops and 21 bishops. The council lasted for eighteen years during which time hundreds of other bishops attended and a few reformers made nominal appearances though they were not allowed to vote.

The council did not get rid of tensions between Protestants and Catholics, indeed it seemed to prove the belief of Erasmus that the breach was irreparable. Nevertheless, there were gains. Not least was the sense of repentance dominating the opening proceedings of the council when Cardinal Pole declared, 'It is our ambition, our avarice and our cupidity which have wrought all these evils on the people of God'. It was a promising start but Luther's insistence on Scripture as the sole authority for the teachings of the Church was not accepted and tradition was given equal standing. The Vulgate translation of Scripture was declared the only authentic version to be used in all disputations. Clerical celibacy was enforced. Seven sacraments were insisted on. The sacrificial nature of the Mass and transubstantiation were affirmed and defined. The existence of purgatory was reiterated, as was the preaching of indulgences, though the active selling of them was abolished. The council also issued an index of books, called the Tridentine Index, which censored nearly seventy-five per cent of all books printed in Europe. This index was continually updated until 1966 when it was abolished.

The council was not successful in reconciling Protestants but it did give to Roman Catholics a new sense of their identity and afterwards there was a much greater emphasis placed upon the education of the clergy and greater clarity about what constituted Catholic faith. There was also an acknowledgement that the laity had a place in church life just as valid as that of priests. Although heretics were not acceptable, at least there was a recognition of their existence and an understanding that any dreams of one empire and one religion were at an end. An aftermath of the council was for Catholics and Protestants to purge their own moderates and a zealous Catholic orthodoxy, particularly in Spain, brought out all the machinery of inquisition against Lutherans, Erasmian liberals and even Jews.

Inquisition

Catholic reaction to the council was both negative and positive. Negatively, authority began to crack the whip and put down people and movements out of step with orthodoxy. Investigations into belief had begun as early as 1231 in Gregory IX's papacy, when a formidable instrument of inquisition had been instituted and entrusted to Dominicans to enforce. In Spain, procedures were introduced not unlike those of the Gestapo or KGB. Accusers and witnesses were kept secret from those accused and hearings were behind closed doors. There was a presumption of guilt and torture was a legitimate method used to extract a confession. It was the justice of the day and sentence, when it came, was with the authority of church and state. Heresy therefore became the same thing as treason.

Investigations began with a general inquisition. This meant a visit to a town from a preacher who asked people to report anybody suspected of holding heretical beliefs. After a period of grace to allow for confession and reports the 'special inquisition' began. This dealt with suspects who were detained and put on trial. It was heavy stuff. Aquinas had declared heresy to be a crime worthy of death because corruption of faith was graver than counterfeiting the coinage, a capital crime everywhere. Inquisition was attempting to put a halt to contagion. It was a spectacular misrepresentation of Christianity and instead of bringing peace, hope and harmony to communities it brought instead fear, despair, and suspicion. Trials could go on for years, suspects could be locked away for years and inquisitors were judge, prosecution and jury all rolled into one. Defence lawyers avoided inquisitions like the plague lest they found themselves guilty by association and therefore condemned. Reasonable people were caught up in the search for heretics. Arthur Miller expresses the contagion well in his play *The Crucible*:

> *You must understand sir, that a person is either with this court or he must be counted against it, there can be no road between. This is a sharp time, now, a precise time—we live no longer in the dusty afternoon when evil mixed itself with good and befuddled the world. Now, by God's grace, the shining sun is up, and them that fear not light will surely praise it.*
>
> (Act 3)

In Scandinavia, Holland, Germany, Bohemia, Britain and, to some extent France, where Huguenots were the reformers, the Inquisition changed nothing but in Italy and Spain the Reformation was halted. The Spanish Inquisition came under secular control and the Spanish monarchs, Ferdinand and Isabella, made it a royal instrument of oppression. It was used against reformers but also against Jews and suspect Jews leading to 32,000 deaths at the stake. Objections from Rome claimed that such persecutions offended natural justice but nevertheless, they continued. Persecution of Jews lasted for twelve years and when the old Moorish kingdom of Grenada fell to the Spanish state even more Jewish communities were brought under the Inquisition. Some Jews converted to Christianity, some fled to Africa and Portugal and by 1492 the full expulsion of Jews had been achieved. Paul Johnson in his *History of the Jews* describes the destruction of Spanish Jewry as the 'most momentous event in Jewish history since the mid-second century'. The dispersal sent them throughout the Mediterranean and Muslim world, though Poland became the most popular haven.

The Jesuits—Storm Troopers of the Pope.

At this time, six men, following the leadership of a Spanish Basque called Ignatius Loyola, climbed the hill of Montmartre in Paris and bound themselves to God and each other by vows of poverty and chastity. They hoped to make a pilgrimage to the holy places of Jerusalem but in the turbulent world of Turks, Moors and Protestants this proved impossible so, instead, they dedicated themselves to the pope, prepared to tackle any task, suffer any hardship and travel anywhere in the world at a moment's notice.

So the Jesuits, the Society of Jesus, was born. Destined to be the largest of Catholic orders, they were esteemed by some and hated by others. Himmler organised the infamous SS on the Jesuit principles of adaptability and allegiance to one leader; Napoleon feared their military style discipline; Bismark was perturbed by their lack of national loyalty; Robespierre guillotined them; and even John Adams, the President of the United States declared:

> *If ever there was a body of men who merit eternal damnation on earth and in hell it is the Society of Loyola.*

Ignatius was a Spanish soldier nurtured in the Medieval ideas of chivalry and when a cannonball shattered his right knee a painful convalescence deprived him of female companions and opportunities to show his gallantry. Bored, he searched for something to read and the only things available were a few lives of the saints. He read them and, as he read, the challenge of following Christ took root in his mind and his former passion for chivalry began to fade. He began a search for virtue with single minded devotion. In a typically dramatic way he ceremoniously hung up his sword at a shrine in Montserrat and put on a robe of sackcloth. His pilgrimage begun, he intended to stay at Manresa for a few days but plague in Barcelona detained him for a year and here his devotion became obsessive. Spending seven hours a day on his knees he slipped towards a nervous breakdown and contemplated suicide. Then, gradually the preoccupation with himself subsided and Ignatius began working out a series of spiritual exercises. Written in poor Spanish and no larger than an average pocket-diary, these exercises have proved to be the bonding stone of Jesuit devotion ever since.

Having passed through personal crisis, Ignatius began to educate himself and it was while studying in Paris that he met the companions who later made the vows with him on the hill of Montmartre. Within months of founding the society Ignatius sent Francis Xavier, his closest friend and most gifted companion, to India. They were never to meet again. Soon others were travelling to China, Japan and the new world of America. When Ignatius died in 1556, a thousand Jesuits were working all over the world. Wherever they went their piety and learning became legendary. They out thought the Chinese in mathematics, geography and astronomy at a time when the Chinese had only contempt for western ideas. They proved themselves more pious than the holy men of India, more industrious than the Japanese and more cunning than the politicians of Europe. They became the confidantes of Europe's royal families and the more confessions they heard the more their influence grew. With ideas ahead of their time they believed that far eastern Christianity had to evolve its own culture so they never insisted on Latin or western practices, in fact Matteo Ricci in China became a Mandarin and Roberto de Nobili in India became a Brahmin. But their very successes provoked hostility and movements began to seek ways of undermining the Society. Inevitably the Jesuits came to Britain, to be used as a counter-reformation thrust, and they settled in pockets of the countryside with recusant families who refused to modify their Catholic faith. The prayer of Ignatius inspired them all:

> *Teach us good Lord, to serve Thee as thou deservest;*
> *To give and not to count the cost;*
> *To fight and not to heed the wounds;*
> *To toil and not to ask for rest;*
> *To labour and not to ask for reward*
> *Save knowing that we do Thy will,*
> *Through Jesus Christ our Lord.*

Francis Xavier (1506–1552)

When Xavier first met Ignatius he was not too impressed but slowly he fell under his spell for Ignatius was offering a challenge and through his spiritual exercises a pathway to deep faith. Ignatius said Xavier was the stiffest clay he ever handled but once the mould was set it was set for life. Along with spiritual exercises went care for the sick and needy in Venice, where his friend Simon Rodriguez said of the work:

> *We made the beds, swept the floors, emptied and scoured winsils, cleaned up the wards generally, carried the bodies of the dead reverently to the graves we had dug for them, and day by day attended hand and foot on the sick, with so much satisfaction and joy that we astonished those living at the hospital.*

Xavier and his colleagues were ordained priests at Venice and by 1540 were waiting in Lisbon ready to set sail on missionary endeavours. The city was teaming with Indians and Africans, some of them slaves. Many were prisoners of the Inquisition and included Muslims and Jews. They were treated as heretics and infidels but already Xavier was asking why these people should be persecution fodder when they might just as easily become disciples. He set sail for Goa in India on his birthday, 7th April, 1541. He was thirty-five years old.

The journey was a terrifying experience in cramped conditions with alternating freezing cold and suffocating heat and with little to eat or drink. People died like flies and when they landed in Mozambique eighty people died instantly. Xavier was ill himself but still managed to preach to townspeople who came out to hear him. His two colleagues stayed in Mozambique but he sailed on and at Malinda on the African coast met a Christian community living in a Muslim city who knew nothing of baptism. Their version of the faith had been passed down through the generations and they had a great reverence for St Thomas, who seems to have been the one who took Christianity to that region. Similarly, in Goa, he found a diocese already established with its own cathedral and bishop. He was offered a smart house but preferred to live with the poor, he worked in a hospital which included lepers, slept on the floor and heard confession. 'Give me a child until he is seven and I will give you the man', is a saying attributed to the Jesuits and Xavier taught the children using simple tunes and stories to open their eyes to Jesus. He met cannibals who happily traded their elderly fathers for eating, where hands and heels were considered a great banquet. His work expanded but he then set his eyes towards Japan and China, he pleaded by letter for Portuguese royals to send out aid and for Ignatius to send out more Jesuits to consolidate the work he had started. He was anxious that the work in India should be consolidated but he himself was eager to move on. 'The journey is our home', he said.

He sailed the three thousand miles to Japan in the company of a man called Yajiro who was Japanese and eager to know the new faith. Xavier christened him and gave him the name Paul. Xavier found the Japanese polite and honourable and dedicated to a peculiar custom of tea drinking (a beverage made with hot water and crushed leaves they called *chaa*). When they showed little appetite for his preaching he decided to dress himself in a Japanese gown and become Japanese. Soon he gained the confidence of people and had baptisms for over five hundred people. In effect, like the apostle Paul, he 'became everything in turn to men of every sort, so that in one way or another he might save some'. China was the next stage of Xavier's travels, he reached Singapore and, to the west of Hong Kong, Sancion, but it proved difficult to get to China and he was struck down with fever before he set foot on the mainland. He never recovered and died on 3rd December, 1552, the very year Matteo Ricci was born. It was left to Ricci to do the work that burned in Xavier's heart, a work destined to be bathed in blood and costing the lives of over a thousand Jesuit priests.

The Jesuit work in England was less spectacular but, in an attempt to win back England to Catholicism, a college was founded at Dovey in Flanders. It instructed English priests, some of whom returned to preach openly in London and elsewhere, thus adding to the ferment during the reigns of Edward VI and Mary. Perhaps if Mary had adopted the subtle approach of the Jesuits to the religious strife in England much rancour could have been avoided. Instead, she seems to have had an instinct for doing the wrong thing. It was during her reign that the 'English Plantations' allowed English settlers onto the Irish lands they renamed 'Queen's County' and 'King's County', after herself and her unpopular husband Philip. It soured relations between England and Ireland, scarcely sweetened since. Mary died a hated woman and hopes for a peaceful solution to disputes turned towards her half-sister Elizabeth.

13 Royals and Puritans

John Foxe	190
Richard Hooker	190
Puritans	191
Anabaptists	192
Baptists in England	194
Huguenots	194
Pilgrim Fathers	195
Civil War	196
Oliver Cromwell	197
John Bunyan	200
John Milton	201
George Fox	202
William Penn	203
Nonconformity	204

*E*lizabeth's accession to the throne put an end to the topsy-turvy world England had become since Henry VIII. The country had lived on a knife-edge with changes taking place with bewildering rapidity, especially on the religious scene. Under Edward VI the language of the Mass had changed from Latin to English, priests had been allowed to marry and even Archbishop Cranmer had appeared in public with a wife. Nuns were encouraged to marry and images disappeared from churches along with gaudy regalia. Then, under Mary, it was all change and attempts were made to return to the status quo. Nuns were ordered to separate from their husbands, Latin-masses returned along with candles and the regalia. With Elizabeth it was all change again but this time it was for keeps and her reign was long enough to consolidate the changes. Protestant practices returned but Catholics were not punished unless it was felt the state was threatened.

A new wave of enthusiasm and hope spread through the nation bringing with it new expectations, which in the main, were about to be fulfilled. Elizabeth herself had religious persuasions which seemed to follow her father's. She leaned towards Rome and disliked extreme reformers but she was free of bigotry and was prepared to tolerate much if it kept the nation free of bloodshed. Her starting position was not good. England was still at war with France. Then, as Anne Boleyn's daughter, she was unacceptable to the pope and there was a Catholic alternative to the throne in the person of Mary of Scotland. Furthermore, three distinct religious groupings had emerged; firstly the old families who clung to the old doctrines and looked towards Rome; secondly, the high-church party, which held that the English church was still part of the 'catholic church' but cleansed of the errors of Rome; and thirdly, the reformers, many of whom had been exiled and had returned totally opposed to any idea of co-operation with Rome at all. The reformers wanted a church free of state interference, a 'pure' church, a Puritan church and this grouping had become a powerful political force for change. Somehow Elizabeth managed to hold these factions together in a coalition even though the papists never rejoined the church, the Puritans eventually left it and the high church was incapable of imposing its wishes upon it. It was a conundrum Elizabeth lived with without solving and nobody has resolved it since.

Despite these problems the nation breathed more freely and a new 'Elizabethan spirit' inspired the country. Francis Drake circumnavigated the globe in the *Golden Hind*, an achievement acknowledged with wild enthusiasm in Plymouth when the battered ship limped into harbour. The Queen knighted him onboard. Later, Drake's brilliant tactics in the defeat of the Spanish Armada secured England's greatest military victory since Henry V at Agincourt and freed the country from the fear of Spain and gave her confidence to assume a commanding position in Europe. When Sir Walter Raleigh named a settlement in America 'Virginia', in honour of the imperious virgin queen, her cup was running over. Such events were accompanied with a great flowering of the English language, expressed most notably by the Stratford playwright William Shakespeare, who caught the spirit of the age and stiffened up the sinews of audiences by the sheer magic of his words. He might portray Henry V as the paragon of all Christian virtue but it was Elizabeth who was reflected in the patriotism of his words:

> *O England!—model to thy inward greatness,*
> *Like little body with a mighty heart—*
> *What mightest thou do, that honour would thee do,*
> *Were all thy children kind and natural!*

Mary of Scotland still presented a problem. Unpopular in Scotland, she fled to England where she was confined while a commission investigated her case. It was a dilemma Elizabeth could well have done without. Her dealings with the Catholic Mary brought her into conflict with her own Catholic subjects, some of whom saw in Mary an opportunity to win back England to Catholicism. It was a problem exacerbated when the pope excommunicated Elizabeth and absolved her subjects from allegiance to her. Catholics true to their church had to be false to their sovereign and there were some plots to assassinate her. It all created great excitement in the country, especially when across the sea ten thousand French reformers, the Huguenots, were massacred in Paris and the Prince of Orange was shot by a papist fanatic. An Association was formed pledged to protect the queen at all costs and even some Catholics joined. It was against this background that Elizabeth signed Mary's death warrant and allowed her to be beheaded at Fotheringay in February, 1587.

Towards the end of her reign Elizabeth put her name to two pieces of legislation that did much to shape the future of England. She signed a Poor Law appointing overseers to every parish and levied a tax on all inhabitants used to help relieve the destitute and provide work. She also granted a charter to the East India Company, giving them a monopoly of trade east of the Cape of Good Hope. Nobody could have foreseen the impetus this would give to the expansion of the

British Empire. In 1603, aged seventy, the queen's health declined rapidly and she died on March 24th expressing a wish that James, already king of Scotland, should succeed to the English throne.

John Foxe (1516–1587)

During Elizabeth's reign a book called *Book of Martyrs* appeared, written by a Protestant clergyman called John Foxe. He was born in Boston, Lincolnshire and educated at Oxford. He had fled the country during Mary's rule but returned to become prebendary at Salisbury cathedral. His book recounts the heroism and suffering of reformers and contends that spiritual war was raging between Christ and the Antichrist, the Antichrist being Catholicism and the Mass. Foxe believed the English people had a unique position in this struggle because their independence had enabled them to withstand perversion within the Church of England, thus preserving true faith. The Anglican Convocation ordered that a copy of the book be placed in all collegiate churches in England, a decision guaranteed to stoke up hostility against Catholics for generations to come. Five bishops feature in Foxe's book but the vast majority were priests and layfolk, including fifty-five women, revealing the importance of women in the church even though they feature sparsely in official church records. The bigotry engendered by the book was considerable, a bigotry fuelled still further, after Elizabeth's death, when a plot was discovered to blow up the Houses of Parliament. The Catholic, Guy Fawkes, was executed for the offence along with others, including a Jesuit called Garnet. Foxe's book, reinforced by this treachery, increased suspicions about Catholic loyalty to the crown.

Richard Hooker (1554–1600)

Thomas Cranmer was the historical founder of English Protestantism but the theological architect of Anglicanism was Richard Hooker. He was raised as a Reformer but converted to Anglicanism, with strong Catholic leanings, while he was a student at Oxford University. The Queen appointed him Master of the Temple in London where he worked with a strict Puritan called Walter Travers. So Hooker used to preach his moderate Catholicism in the morning and Travers contradicted him in the afternoon. It has been said, 'The forenoon spoke Canterbury and the afternoon Geneva'.

Elizabeth favoured Hooker because he leaned towards Catholic traditions without denying the impulses of the Reformers. Through his sermons and writings, he became the exponent of a theology which underpinned the Elizabethan Settlement. It created a kind of half-Protestant, half-Catholic Anglicanism, despised by Puritans and Presbyterians because it neglected the principle of the priesthood of all believers and left a lingering suspicion that he was a closet Catholic. Hooker held fast to Cranmer's Thirty-nine Articles with its affirmation of Scripture as the authority for faith and practice but he did not do away with church traditions. Unlike most Reformers, he did not turn his back on scholasticism and much of his teaching is in the mould of Thomas Aquinas. He was holding a middle ground. Christian truth was not only to be found in the Bible, as Puritans claimed, but neither was the Church of England hidebound by traditions venerated by Roman Catholics. To Hooker the Church had to be seen as an organic institution, which could and should change in new circumstances.

What happened therefore, was that England became home for a unique form of Reform. On the one hand the Thirty Nine Articles of Religion were decidedly Protestant but Anglicanism's *Book of Common Prayer* was overtly Catholic. Some people might call this a fudge, and it certainly did not eradicate theological dispute, but in the end the via media did survive as the characteristic form of broad English Christianity with other expressions of Catholicism and Protestantism living alongside.

Puritans

Radical thinkers inside the church began to ask basic questions about church government as they sought ways and means of ensuring the purity of church-life. Influenced by Calvinism they thought government by synods and elders did away with the need for bishops. Under Elizabeth these Puritans strengthened their position in Parliament and began to press for greater reforms, a pressure resisted by Elizabeth and James. Some remained as a pressure group inside the church but others burned their boats and became independent, no longer recognising the Church of England as their spiritual home. They started independent congregations like one in Norwich under Robert Browne and Robert Harrison. These 'Brownists', as they were called, signal the start of the English Independent or Congregationalist Churches, which were self governing and based on church covenants. They were opposed by successive governments and repressed, harassed and imprisoned. Once again religious persecution drove people from the country and the Netherlands became a refuge for dissenters, amongst whom were the Anabaptists.

Anabaptists

The beginnings of the Anabaptist movement goes back to the 1520s and to Zurich. They held a strong feel for community and a great love for the Bible, which they studied avidly. They concluded from their study that the baptising of infants was meaningless, insisting that baptism in the New Testament sense involved total immersion of believers who testified to their new birth with a symbolic death under the water, rising to newness of life. A group near Zurich, baptised each other and so got the nickname 'Anabaptist' or the 'rebaptisers'. Such independence sent shivers down spines of Catholics and Protestants alike and such radical meetings were forbidden. With macabre irony, Anabaptists in Zurich were threatened by drowning. 'If they want water they shall have it', said the council. Some Anabaptists believed that salvation came to those predestined for salvation, a belief with origins in Calvinism. But there were others who followed the teachings of a man called Jacob Arminius, who belonged to the Reformed Church of Amsterdam. Arminius believed that the grace of God knew no restrictions at all, for all men were open to its persuasion.

Illegal, threatened and persecuted the Anabaptist movement spread through German-speaking Europe, proving once again, that persecution provides yet more seed for faith. They found favour for a time in Czechoslovakia where a Lutheran, Leonhand von Liechtenstein, protected them. They were soon numerous enough to call a synod on the Swiss/German border where an ex-Benedictine prior, called Michael Sattler, was a dominant figure in formulating a document called 'Brotherly Union'. It expressed the view that Christianity was more than a notion of Christendom, it involved discipleship, commitment and a belonging which infused every aspect of life. They believed in giving a tenth of their income back to God (tithing) and sometimes they advocated a complete redistribution of wealth, which led to the primitive communism they traced back to Acts of the Apostles. They refused to repeat oaths because they vowed to speak the truth at all times and often refused to fight because the principle of love forbade aggression. Strangely, these people who did not fight or kill became a threat to the establishment! Their vision of restoring to the church a fellowship of equals uncorrupted by wealth and power, bound together in filial harmony to do the will of God here on earth, provoked a vicious response from those who saw them as heretics and a threat to the stability of Europe. As a result more Anabaptists were martyred for their beliefs than any other Christian group since the apostles. From a jail in Antwerp a young mother wrote to her newly born daughter:

> *My dearest child, the true love of God strengthen you in virtue, you who are yet so young, and whom I must leave in this wicked, evil, perverse world.*
>
> *Oh that it had pleased the Lord that I might have brought you up but it seems that it is not the Lord's will. Even so it has now gone with your father and myself. We were so well joined that we would not have forsaken each other for the whole world, and yet we have had to leave each other for the Lord's sake. We were permitted to live together only half a year, after which we were apprehended because we sought the salvation of our souls. Be not ashamed of us; it is the way which the prophets and the apostles went. Your dear father demonstrated with his blood that it is the genuine truth, and I also hope to attest the same with my blood…*
>
> *Hence, my dear Janneken, do not accustom your mouth to filthy talk, nor to ugly lies…I leave you this letter. Read it when you have understanding and keep it as long as you live in remembrance of me and of your father. Be not ashamed to confess our faith, since it is the true evangelical faith, another than which shall never be found.*
>
> **(Hillerbrand, *Protestant Reformation*)**

The moving story of the Anabaptists was gathered together in an anthology called *The Martyr's Mirror* and is a story of stubborn refusal to be browbeaten by the powerful and of a hope for a better future where there was to be freedom of religion and speech and freedom from fear and from want. Some found their dream in Holland others were soon to search for it in a new world across the Atlantic ocean.

Baptists in England

Links between Anabaptists and English Baptists were strong. A man called John Smyth, a fellow of Christ's College, Cambridge, had fled England and settled in Amsterdam during the reign of James I. Like others before him he had baptised himself and then others as they formed a fellowship. After Smyth's death Thomas Helwys returned to England and formed a church in Spitalfields, London. They followed a theology they had learned from a Dutch theologian called Arminius who could not accept the election ideas of Calvin but preached that Christ had died to save all people not just pre-elected ones. Others of the Calvinist persuasion formed other churches leaving Baptists divided into two camps, Particular Baptists (Calvinists) and General Baptists (Arminian). By 1662 there were about three hundred churches in total, all of them subject at various times to attack from the state.

Many Baptists were to become conspicuous members of Cromwell's army and others were encouraged to become ministers within the established church, a position unthinkable after 1662 when the Act of Uniformity was passed. Their understanding of the church was of a gathered community of faithful dedicated to Christ and baptised into a fellowship of believers. Each church was autonomous though they shared assemblies and there was no place for state interference in their church affairs. This 'divorce' of church from state was a constant source of friction between the Church of England and Separatists.

Huguenots

Another kind of Puritanism showed itself in France but its expression was very different to that of the Anabaptists. Huguenots stemmed mainly from upper and middle-classes and were capable of forming armies, which sometimes scoured the country searching out priests and desecrating Catholic churches. Retaliations followed leading up to the Paris massacre of 1572, already referred to, when ten thousand Huguenots died. They did win a right to freedom of conscience in the Edict of Nantes in 1598 but that did not prevent Richelieu from harrying them thirty years later and besieging their stronghold of La Rochelle. They held out bravely but had to succumb eventually, they lost all their freedoms except freedom of conscience and even that disappeared when Louis XIV revoked the Edict of Nantes and started fresh hostilities against the Huguenots. Within a few years France had lost some 400,000 of her professional and skilled citizens with many of them moving to Switzerland, Germany, England and America where they founded a town called New Rochelle.

Pilgrim Fathers

To persecuted minorities the new world of America beckoned like some distant haven. Buccaneers like the Devonian John Hawkins and his cousin Francis Drake, brought home stories of the new land and others like Sir Walter Raleigh had attempted to root settlements there. When Puritans grew disillusioned with life under James some began to see their future across the Atlantic. In small communities around Yorkshire, Nottinghamshire and Lincolnshire, in villages like Scooby and Austerfield, there were those who prepared to risk a hazardous voyage to find a new way of life. William Bradford from Austerfield was typical of these pilgrims and he led a group to the new world, keeping a record of their adventures. It was illegal to emigrate, so their preparations were all in secret and as a result they were exploited. They tried to sail from Boston in Lincolnshire but were double crossed, handed over to the authorities and imprisoned. Undaunted, they gained a passage to Amsterdam and lived there for some years before taking the plunge and going for 'America or bust'. It was very nearly bust. In 1620 they hired an English ship called *Mayflower* for the crossing. In this little ship, just over 100 feet long, one hundred and two pilgrims crammed together and headed for the promised land. The journey took ten weeks and they arrived in the middle of a harsh winter. They explored the coast, hunting for food and seeking a place to settle. It was life raw and uncompromising and pilgrims began to die with sickening regularity. Bradford wrote:

> *Mr and Mrs Carver died during the first general sickness, Mr Winslow's wife died the first winter...Mrs Bradford died soon after we arrived.*

Within the first six months half of them were dead and only five of the eighteen married women survived. But in the first summer they had a harvest and solemnly gave thanks to God and founded New Plymouth close to present day Boston. The courage and enterprise of the Pilgrim Fathers was the foundation of that American dream epitomised by Emma Lazarus' poem inscribed on the Statue of Liberty in New York harbour:

> *Give me your tired, your poor*
> *Your huddled masses yearning to breathe free,*
> *The wretched refuse of your teeming shore.*
> *Send these, the homeless, tempest-tossed to me*
> *I lift my lamp beside the golden door!*

...they had a harvest and solemnly gave thanks to God!

It was an impossible dream and New England often became oppressive and self-righteous but for all that their achievement was monumental and a great inspiration for those oppressed in their own home lands.

Civil War

The independent spirit of the Puritans persisted and their confidence and influence increased in Parliament. King James, for his part, believed that a king ruled by divine right and had written a book expressing that belief before his accession. James' views were resented by Presbyterians in Scotland and Puritans in England but supported by many Anglicans, so the struggle for liberty became mixed up with religion. The battle between king and Parliament was about to reach a bloody conclusion. James sowed the wind but it was his successor Charles, who was destined to reap the whirlwind. James and Charles both resented interference from Parliament especially when they were seeking to raise taxes. On the other hand, Puritans feared that monarchy could develop into despotism and defended their Parliamentary rights passionately. On the face of it these issues are not religious concerns but in the seventeenth century everything in Britain had religious overtones. High Church clergy preached that resistance to the king could lead to eternal damnation and Puritans were convinced that Charles' marriage to Henrietta, daughter of the king of France, was tantamount to admitting that he was a Catholic.

Charles began to assert himself by dissolving Parliament when it suited him but the House of Commons passed a Petition of Rights, ratified in the Lords, demanding several basic things; (i) no taxes or loans to be levied without consent of Parliament, (ii) no freemen to be imprisoned against the law of the land, (iii) no soldiers to be billeted on private houses, and (iv) in peaceful days martial law to be abolished. So, that meant that when Charles wanted to raise taxes (as he did in 1640 to put down the Scots) he had to convene Parliament to do it. As the trouble in Scotland had been provoked by the king's futile attempt to foist a Catholic looking prayer book on people now largely Calvinistic, he did not get Parliamentary approval. The king was forced into a truce with the Scots at Ripon, conclusively demonstrating where real power now resided. Charles, however, was prepared to push the issue to the limit and in 1642 he raised a Royalist banner to begin Civil War. Cavaliers (Royalists) lined up against Roundheads (Parliamentarians) and battles, sieges and skirmishes began. It was all very indecisive, with neither side able to force any advantage until the emergence of a man called Oliver Cromwell.

Oliver Cromwell (1599–1658)

Cromwell enjoyed a modest family income, which dated back to the dissolution of the monasteries. It had provided him with a small estate in Huntingdon where he had attended school before going to the very puritanical Sussex College at Cambridge. He was the Huntingdon Member of Parliament during 1628–1629. Then in 1636 his wealth increased when he inherited an estate from his wife's family, enabling him to move up-market to Ely where he lived in the shadow of the cathedral. In Ely he experienced a religious conversion, which was to motivate him for the rest of his life. In 1640 he returned to Parliament as a back-bench MP for Cambridge.

When the Civil War began Cromwell discovered, almost by accident, that he was a soldier and a general of genius. He was given the job of organising defences around Cambridge and was successful in recruiting a troop of horse who had 'the fear of God before them and made some conscience of what they did'. His troop was expanded into a regiment renowned for discipline and valour. He proved to be brilliant at picking officers who could inspire men with religious fervour, more than a match for the more flashy Cavalier gentry. Cromwell's star had started to climb. Soon he was general of cavalry for all the counties of East Anglia, a force that played a conspicuous part in epic victories at Edgehill, Marston Moor and Naseby. Cromwell was an astonishingly good commander of troops with cool calculation allied to frenzied action. He fought like a man possessed with righteous fury scattering enemies like Jehovah in the Old Testament. Before and after battle he prayed that the mercy of God would bless his enterprise. The king was 'out on the ropes' and a Parliamentary victory seemed assured but what the king could not achieve by force he tried to achieve by intrigue. Parliament was divided and incapable of seizing the initiative and hesitancy gave Charles the second wind he exploited to the full.

Conservatives wanted the new Model Army to disband immediately but the army refused and mutinied, so Cromwell found himself acting as a bridge between the army and Parliament while trying to work out a solution with the king at the same time. Then the king fled to the Isle of Wight and sought a deal with the Scottish nobility trying to get them to invade England. This was the second stage of the Civil War and once again Cromwell came out on top when he put down a serious revolt in Wales before defeating the Scots. Cromwell was now convinced the king was not a man to be trusted and consented to his execution. It is said that Cromwell went to inspect the body of the king in the dead of night and sadly shook his head as he murmured, 'Cruel necessity'.

Charles I executed, 'Cruel necessity', said Cromwell.

The execution and founding of a Republican Commonwealth did not win popular approval at home or abroad. Undeterred, Cromwell sought to fill the power vacuum with his own certainty of purpose. He quashed mutinies in the army before departing for Ireland, a country riven with struggles between Catholics and Protestants and between Irish, English and Scots. He lay siege to Drogheda in 1649 and ruthlessly suppressed all uprising. He then moved into Scotland and dealt firmly with an attempt to put Charles II onto the Scottish throne. He issued 'Wanted, dead or alive' posters and described the prince as 'a black man, two yards high'. He negotiated with reluctant Scots using the memorable words, 'I beseech you, in the bowels of Christ, think it possible you may be mistaken'. When that appeal failed he routed them at Dunbar and took Edinburgh. He could now breathe and concentrate on building up the power of the British navy until it was the most powerful in Europe.

Cromwell was now at his zenith and John Milton called him 'Our Chief of Men'. He had become disenchanted with the reduced Parliament (Rump Parliament) and started to shape it to his liking by appointing approved individuals who shared his own Puritanical outlook, these included religious enthusiasts like Praise-God Barbon who gave the name to the *Barebones Parliament*. Political stability was sought by making Cromwell the Lord Protector for life, assisted by a Council of State, which could call Parliament as and when required. Not surprisingly, Parliament did not approve the change and the new system could only be enforced by the army. But he did seek one man one vote and felt that the vote should be with property owners because they had a permanent interest in the state. He got rid of corrupt politicians declaring, 'It is time for me to put an end to your sitting in this place...you would sell your country for a mess of pottage. You have no more religion in you than my horse.' The Speaker was dragged from his chair and grasping the mace (that shining bauble), Cromwell commanded them to be gone on peril of their lives. Cromwell refused the crown preferring to be Lord Protector but it was a position difficult to maintain and when Oliver Cromwell died, his eldest son Richard, was not able to keep control. As his father said, he was no good— 'All he wants is a shoulder of mutton and a whore'. A period of anarchy followed until the restoration of the monarchy with Charles II.

Cromwell, with deep Puritanical beliefs, was a great man convinced God was working providentially in his life and he seems to have been sincerely convinced that Charles I had to be resisted if justice was to prevail in Britain. The success he enjoyed was the proof he needed that God was with him and directing his path. His brief five year rule as Protector was one of surprising religious toleration for a fundamentalist. He relaxed laws against Catholics and encouraged Jews to seek refuge in England. There was a consolidation of the three nations within the British Isles. The country prospered and for this brief period was at peace. Further than that it is difficult to pin down this gifted yet isolated man. He was an independent Puritan who never seems to have joined any one religious denomination or been influenced by any particular clergyman, though his daughter was married in a ceremony using the *Book of Common Prayer*. He was suspicious of license and closed theatres because he saw moral danger in them. He was without personal vanity and wanted pictures of himself painted 'warts and all'. Much about him remains a mystery but no other life shows more clearly how religion in Britain had been radically changed since the first steps of Reformation. Perhaps it also demonstrated that the British (certainly the English) do not care for revolutionary change in governments but prefer gradual change.

John Bunyan (1628–1688)

For a time during the Civil War one of Cromwell's soldiers was a tinker's son called John Bunyan. He lived in Bedfordshire and at his wife's leading mixed with a group of Independent Christians in Bedford. He struggled with religious terrors and during a battle the death of a close comrade affected him greatly. The church helped him with his fears and he became a preacher. After the Restoration of the monarchy John found himself locked up in Bedford jail for his refusal to stop preaching and he was in and out of prison for the next twelve years during which time he started to write. His first book, *Grace Abounding to the Chief of Sinners*, is a testimony of his own spiritual experience and his second, *Pilgrim's Progress*, is an allegory of a Christian journey during which he meets other travellers who help or hinder his pilgrimage. He also describes places he visits along the way. Sometimes the journey is tough going and at other times joyous but throughout he is never allowed to forget that though there are pleasant inns along the way only the final destiny is real home:

> *Then Mr Valiant-for-Truth said: I am going to my father's, and though with great difficulty I am got hither, yet now I do not repent*

me of all the trouble I have been at to arrive where I am. My sword I give to him that shall succeed me in my pilgrimage, and my courage and skill, to him that can get it. My marks and scars I carry with me, to be a witness for me that I have fought his battles who will now be my rewarder. When the day that he must go hence was come, many accompanied him to the river side, into which as he went he said, 'Death where is thy sting?' And as he went down deeper he said, 'Grave where is thy victory?'. So he passed over and the trumpets sounded for him on the other side.

Bunyan continued his teaching inside the prison and after his release he returned to his evangelical work around Bedford. His books, especially *Pilgrim's Progress*, with its homely style and mixture of biblical and village education, became popular reading in virtually every Victorian home and is still regarded as the greatest religious allegory ever written in English.

John Milton (1608–1674)

A Puritan writer with a background completely different to that of Bunyan was John Milton, the outstanding writer of the seventeenth century. His father was a musician and lawyer in London and he benefited from education at St Paul's and at Christ's College, Cambridge. He seemed destined for the church but found it impossible to accept the churchmanship of Archbishop Laud, whose liberal views Milton found hard to swallow. Instead he studied the classics and at Cambridge wrote Latin and English verse and moral tales, which demonstrated the triumph of virtue over evil. He published pamphlets in support of the Puritans and fought hard to defend the liberty of the press. He became Latin secretary to the Council of State and held the post until the Restoration despite losing his sight. He vigorously put pen to paper in an attempt to prevent the Restoration for which he was arrested and fined. It was during this period he wrote *Paradise Lost*, followed by the sequel, *Paradise Regained*.

Milton's work does not make for easy reading in our age, not familiar with the Bible or the classics as was the case with his readers. Nevertheless, like Shakespeare, he celebrated the great heroic events of English history, especially the emergence of England from the Civil War, the self-assurance gained from the defeat of the Spanish Armada and the growing independence gained through the Reformation. In

Paradise Lost, his first words announce the subject of his work, just like the great classical poets had done:

> *Of Man's first disobedience, and the fruit*
> *Of that forbidden tree, whose mortal taste*
> *Brought death into the world and all our woe*
> *With loss of Eden.*

George Fox (1625–1690)

I have in my study a picture of Lichfield telling me that the cathedral was founded in 656 as a shrine to St Chad and was rebuilt between 1195 and 1336 and is the only English cathedral with three spires, the central one being a replacement of one destroyed during the Civil War. One day in 1651 those spires must have gazed down in wonder at the sight of a young man walking through the streets crying, 'Woe to the bloody city of Lichfield'. The man was George Fox and he was to write later, '…as I went through the streets crying, there seemed to me to be a channel of blood running down the streets, and the market-place appeared like a pool of blood'.

Years before this incident Fox had climbed Pendle Hill in Lancashire, a place of grey mists and crags where, a few years before, twenty witches had cast spells over the populace, a misdemeanour for which they were hanged publicly at Lancaster in 1612. Fox had a vision of Christ gathering people together in a great victory over Satan, for the people had 'come of age' and accepted that the priesthood of all believers meant that they were indeed priests themselves. Yet, priests remained. Even the reformed churches still had their religious experts, pastors with their pulpits and priests with their vestments. He dismissed 'steeple-houses' arguing that the real church existed in men's hearts and when he started to preach in the open-air it was to claim that 'Christ has been too long locked up in the Mass or in the Book'. He attracted fervent followers who became fellow-evangelists, men and women who became known as 'the valiant sixty'. They spread over the country and sailed the seas seeking converts. Within three years of his experience on Pendle Hill, fifty thousand people were following his vision.

Such enthusiastic Christianity curried no favour in established churches hostile to the Puritans who had killed a king and driven bishops from office. A succession of Acts limited the freedom of the Dissenters including Fox. One day in Derby, Judge Bennett sentenced him to six months in jail for blasphemy and as he was led away Fox cried, 'You should tremble in the fear of God'. The judge laughed at the word 'tremble' and said to Fox, 'It is you are the quakers'. The name stuck and 'Quakers' became the name for them, though they called themselves 'Society of Friends'. Their methods were sometimes very dramatic and Fox would interrupt preachers in mid-sermon and engage them in fierce debate, a tactic once resulting in him being hit on the head with a brass-bound Bible! Samuel Pepys observed a Quaker incident while he was waiting in a crowd for Charles II to arrive at Westminster Hall:

> *One thing extraordinary was this day a man, a Quaker, came naked through the Hall, only very civilly tied about the privities to avoid scandal, and with a chafing dish of fire and brimstone upon his head, did pass through the Hall crying, 'Repent, repent'.*

These dramas were not the be-all and end-all of the Society however, and their meeting-houses were free for everyone to speak as led by the Spirit. Serving girls could take part in worship with aristocrats and they often knew the Scriptures better. They gained a reputation for integrity and Cromwell said they could not be influenced 'either with gifts, honours, offices or places'. They treated kings and judges as fellow men and would not defer to any of them, but they also treated lowly men as though they were kings. It was a religion with appeal to people across the social divide. The dreadful conditions endured by Fox in prison led to him campaigning against prison neglect and other social concerns, revealing a social dimension to the Quakers, which has been to the fore ever since.

William Penn (1644–1718)

Penn, unlike Fox, was an aristocrat, an admiral's son who mixed easily in the company of the king, his mistress Nell Gwyn and the diarist Samuel Pepys. He became a Quaker after hearing one of the wandering preachers and like many others found himself in prison after attending one of their meetings. So when Charles II offered to repay a £16,000 debt owed to Penn's father, with a piece of land in the New World, Penn saw it as a heaven sent opportunity to build an ideal Christian community away from restraints in England. It was a 'holy experiment' and Penn's colony (now State) of Pennsylvania, with its capital of

Philadelphia (City of Brotherly Love) became a haven for the persecuted and oppressed. Even witch hunts like those at Salem, so graphically depicted in Arthur Miller's *The Crucible*, were unheard of in Pennsylvania. When a witch appeared before Penn and said she had ridden on a broomstick, Penn responded by saying that she had a perfect right to do so if she desired as there was no law against it! Witchcraft was never heard of again in Pennsylvania.

Penn's magnanimity extended a welcome across the seas to Huguenots, German Lutherans and all other nonconformists from Europe until Quakers were a minority within their own colony. But the principle of toleration was not diluted, even Indians trusted Quakers and some became Quakers themselves. It was in this tolerant community that the immorality of slavery was first seriously questioned, and in Philadelphia that a law was enshrined making religious freedom a fundamental right of every individual:

> *Congress shall make no law respecting the establishment of religion or prohibiting the free exercise of.*

In later years financial burdens plagued him and for a time he was in a debtor's prison and in 1712, when ill, he almost completed the transfer of the colony to the Crown. His wife rescued him and looked after his affairs until his death.

Nonconformity

With the Restoration of Charles II it was time to clarify the confused state of the church in Britain. Charles himself was a Roman Catholic but restoring Roman Catholicism as the state religion was no longer possible. On the other hand, Puritan control of Parliament began to wane after Cromwell and they were soon in a minority. Bishops returned from exile and prisons and demanded back their churches. The old Prayer Book, with a few alterations, was authorised by Parliament and all clergy were expected to adopt this pattern of worship. This was the 1662 Act of Uniformity and those unwilling to conform were driven from their livings. These 'dissenters' or 'nonconformists', about two thousand in all, were the backbone of the nonconformist conscience, which gave birth to independent churches in Britain like the Baptists, Congregationalists, Quakers and Unitarians. A clause in the Act of Uniformity forbade anybody to teach in a school without a bishop's license and only baptised members of the Church of England were allowed to teach in Universities. To consolidate the position even further, an Act was passed in 1665 forbidding nonconformist ministers to hold meetings within a five mile radius of a town. This 'Five Mile Act' is the reason why so many old chapels are to be found on the hills around places like Huddersfield and Bradford. Like all oppression it never worked and the congregations forced to worship away from towns, spent Sabbath days and festivals in their Tabernacles and Ebenezers in a bond drawing the fellowships closer together and eventually leading to them forming their own institutions and even their own University.

1665 was also the year of the last and most terrible plague to visit England, the Plague of London. It was a plague which illustrated spectacularly how the life of a modest village parson could influence the life of a community. Three hundred miles north of London, in the small Derbyshire village of Eyam, a tailor called George Vicars took delivery of a box of clothes from London. It contained plague germs and soon people started to die. When villagers prepared to leave, the rector, William Mompesson, persuaded them to stay in order to prevent the plague spreading to other villages. The village paid a heavy price and two hundred and fifty of the village population of three hundred and fifty died, including Mompesson's own wife. This ordinary rector and his wife are still honoured in the village today.

One year later, London was again the scene of calamity when the Fire of London raged through the city for five days during September. The inferno destroyed the old St Paul's along with over eighty other medieval churches. Out of the ashes arose Christopher Wren's new St Paul's and fifty other churches all paid for out of taxes.

Acts of Parliament limiting the activities of Nonconformists were also used against Roman Catholics and throughout the reigns of Charles II and James II plots and counter plots were hatched. One of these incidents, which led to many executions, was the 'Popish Plot' claimed by a man called Titus Oates. He came forward with accusations of a supposed Jesuit plot to murder the king and overthrow Protestantism in England. In the volatile atmosphere of distrust the country was stirred to anger and approved several executions. On his death bed Charles did declare himself a Roman Catholic and James never hid his leanings towards Rome but when William of Orange and Mary became joint sovereigns it was deemed necessary for the Commons to draw up a 'Declaration of Rights', which included a clause declaring that no Roman Catholic should henceforth succeed to the throne. That declaration has never been repealed.

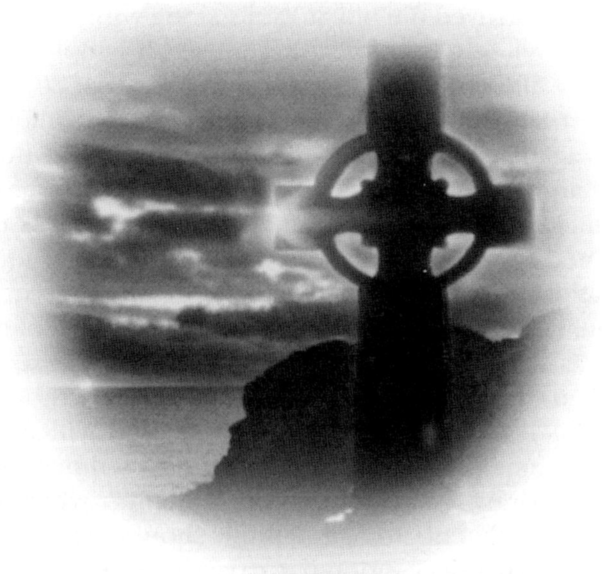

14 Awakening

Joseph Priestley	209
Jonathan Edwards	209
George Whitefield	210
John Wesley	212
Sarah Peters	215

The passions of sectarian religion began to subside during the seventeenth century giving way to a more 'sweet reasonable' way of looking at life. 'For modes of faith let graceless zealots fight', wrote Alexander Pope in *Essay on Man*. It was a time of rationalism epitomised by the French philosopher, Rene Descartes, who claimed that knowledge and certainty could be worked out from pure reason. He went back to basics and the one thing he was certain of was the fact that he was thinking. He could say therefore categorically, 'I think therefore I am'. From this platform of certainty Descartes built a systematic philosophy, which included proofs for the existence of God. Voltaire, another Frenchman, expressed the new spirit of the age of enlightenment by upholding values of reason, toleration and justice. 'If we believe absurdities we shall commit atrocities', he wrote.

Sir Isaac Newton (1642–1727) belongs to this period of enlightenment and is one of the great figures in the history of science. His *Laws of Motion* established the science of mechanics, while his discovery of the laws of gravitation and calculus have been the tools of mathematics and physics ever since. He made the first reflecting telescope and used a prism to split light into colours of the spectrum. Newton's science led him to theological conclusions that the Universe was determined by fixed physical laws, which were further proof that creation was governed by a Mind and a controlling hand. Newton had uncovered the tip of God's great iceberg of wonder.

> *I do not know what I may appear to the world, but to myself I seem to have been like a boy playing on the sea-shore, and diverting myself by now and then finding a smooth pebble, or a prettier shell than ordinary whilst the great ocean of truth lay all undiscovered before me.*
>
> **(Sir Isaac Newton, Memoirs, by Brewster II, XXVII)**

Such rationalisation led to sweet reasonableness in the pulpit where passion and excesses of enthusiasm were frowned on. In dignified worship sermons were read and often went on interminably. Hogarth's engraving of a *Sleeping Congregation* shows a parson droning on while the congregation snores. Only the clerk is awake, casting a lascivious eye over a comely maiden's cleavage. In such a church people knew their place and this is depicted in the seating arrangements where the rich and comfortable sat in the best pews and the poor stood up. Religious observance had become cosy, predictable and unchallenging. Rationalism was affecting nonconformity as well and some ministers adopted ideas difficult to accept within an orthodox Christian framework.

Joseph Priestley (1733–1804)

The 'spirit of the age' is reflected in the life of a Yorkshireman called Joseph Priestley. The son of a Calvinistic minister, he became a Dissenting minister himself and had churches in Suffolk and Cheshire before becoming a tutor at Warrington Academy in Lancashire. Possessing a curiosity which went beyond things theological he was noted for developing practical courses for students in industry. Reports of his work spread to America and Benjamin Franklin encouraged him to conduct experiments in the new science of electricity. Priestley then moved to Leeds to take up an appointment as an Independent minister and became so prominent in the city that a statue of him still presides over the City Square. It was in Leeds his interests turned to gases and in 1774 he discovered oxygen.

Priestley's religious thinking had now led to Unitarianism and he became radical enough to have a book, *History of the Corruptions of Christianity*, officially burned. Unitarianism dates back to the days of the Civil War and to a man called John Biddle (1615–1652) whose preaching reawakened ideas of Arius in the fourth century. He denied Jesus was divine and scoffed at the ideas of a Trinity. Priestley moved to Birmingham after Leeds and when the French Revolution broke out his open support for the revolution led to a mob breaking into his house and destroying his possessions. He was so discouraged by this turn of events that he emigrated to America where he spent the rest of his life writing and experimenting. After his death no fewer than twenty-five volumes of his writings were collected and published.

The modern world had now fully dawned and intellectual ideas and scientific discoveries increased rapidly through Europe and jumped the Atlantic to America. When a new religious awakening sprang up therefore, that too occurred on both sides of the Atlantic.

Jonathan Edwards (1703–1758)

With an amalgam of religious sensitivity and natural curiosity, Jonathan Edwards was something of a prodigy who, by the age of thirteen, had mastered Greek, Latin and Hebrew. He engaged himself in natural science and while still at school worked out a philosophical theory of Being, which predated the work of the British philosopher Berkeley. At twenty-one he was a senior tutor at Yale and in 1727 was appointed associate pastor of an independent church in Northampton, Massachusetts. Edwards' reputation has come down to us as a fire-and-brimstone preacher but this is hardly fair to him because of over six hundred sermons still available to us in manuscript form, very few could be described as hellfire and brimstone in character. Nor was he over emotional in his delivery. Nevertheless, he was a revivalist who stood at the very centre of the Great Awakening that swept through the colonies in the 1740s.

In his *Narrative* Edwards explains how he preached a series of sermons on the theme of justification by faith and how souls came in flocks to Jesus Christ.

> *There was scarcely a person in the town, old or young, left unconcerned about the great things of the eternal world. Those who were wont to be the vainest and the loosest; and those who had been most disposed to think and speak slightly of vital and experimental religion, were now generally subject to great awakenings.*
>
> **(Edwards, *A Faithful Narrative of the Surprising Work of God*)**

The results of this awakening were remarkable. People in the town who had long standing debts paid up in full, enemies became friends and a spirit of love affected the whole community and beyond into Connecticut. The impetus of the movement began to subside after two years only to be revived again a few years later. Edwards was involved but this time the dominant figure was that of an Englishman called George Whitefield.

George Whitefield (1714–1770)

Whitefield was a student at Pembroke College in Oxford when he met the Wesley brothers and joined a 'holy club' frequented by other pious students. He was converted and afterwards sailed to America where he busied himself in church activities and charity work. Returning to Britain he became friendly with a Welsh preacher called Howell Harris who encouraged him to preach at open-air meetings. Afterwards he returned to America for a six-week mission, which took the colonies by storm. Using his great booming voice he moved out into the open-air when the churches became too small to house the 25,000 or so attracted to the meetings. The Awakening was now in full spate and spread to New York, Maryland and Virginia. Benjamin Franklin became interested in Whitefield simply because he found it difficult to believe newspaper reports that one man could be heard at one time by as many as 25,000 people. He conducted his own experiments and concluded that his voice was capable of being heard by 30,000! The actor David Garrick once said he would give a hundred guineas if he could say, 'Oh', like Mr Whitefield.

His preaching reached the neglected classes, including the poor and Negro slaves, who had been overlooked by other preachers. They received the gospel with zeal and translated the message into the heart melting spirituals that have enriched Christianity ever since. It was a preaching dramatic and compelling, delivered in plain language from the heart offering one last opportunity for sinful congregations to repent. Anglicans were often reluctant to let Whitefield loose on their congregations but others were inspired by his example and continued the revival long after he had returned to England. His words were a constant rebuke to them—'Congregations are dead because dead men preach to them'.

Through their ministries, Edwards and Whitefield gave a new impetus to churches and to their responsibilities for each other, and that included Negro slaves and Red Indians. Accompanying the passion and the prayer went the concern for education religious awakening always brings. This led to the founding of Princeton College as well as several new religious societies. It is possible to make out a case that the awakening also provided the confidence needed for Americans to pave the way for their own independence.

Whitefield was not finished with America but after this mission he returned to Britain and set off on an astonishing diary of engagements all over Britain, including campaigns with Howell Harris in Wales and fourteen missions to Scotland. He was chaplain to Selina Hastings, the Countess of Huntingdon (the St Teresa of Methodism) who provided funds for his missions and introduced him to British nobility. He was not interested in the administrative task of maintaining the infant churches formed after his preaching. He passed that responsibility to others, but some churches in the south and west of England were known as the Countess of Huntingdon's Connection. Whitefield compiled a hymn-book and made several more visits to America where he died in 1770.

John Wesley (1703–1790)

The British/American connection followed in the life of John and Charles Wesley though this time the fruit ripened in Britain. The Wesleys were born in Epworth, Lincolnshire, John being the fifteenth child of the rector Samuel Wesley and Susannah his wife. A grandfather had been a Puritan minister turned out of his living after the Act of Uniformity in 1662. In 1709 the rectory was burned down and John was only rescued at the last minute. For the rest of his life he believed he had been saved for a purpose.

Discipline and early education were provided by Susannah and all his life John remained devoted to her and depended much on her judgement. Education continued at Charterhouse school and Christ Church, Oxford, before he went into residence at Lincoln College where he became a fellow. With his brother Charles he joined the 'holy club' and it was there he met George Whitefield. The members adhered methodically to religious practices and beliefs, the name 'Methodist' was given to them by fellow students as a term of derision because of the way they methodically budgeted their time and resources and put aside every penny they could to help the poorest prisoners—they were regular visitors at prisons and hospitals. As Samuel Wesley grew older he wanted John to succeed him as the rector of Epworth but John and brother Charles had sights set elsewhere and determined to go to America as Anglican missionaries.

John's religion was pious and austere rather than joyous and on the ship to Savannah, Georgia, he met some German Moravians who impressed him with their simple, yet joyous faith. On Sunday 25th January he wrote in his *Journal*:

> *The winds roared about us and whistled as distinctly as if it had been a human voice. The ship not only rocked to and fro, but shook and jarred with so unequal, grating motion, that one could not but with difficulty keep one's hold of anything, nor stand a moment without it. Every ten minutes came a shock against the stern or side of the ship, which one should think should dash the planks in pieces...The sea broke over, split the mainsail in pieces, covered the ship and poured in between the decks.*

Passengers were terrified but even the women and children of the Moravians showed no fear but carried on singing their psalms. Wesley had to ask, 'Why had they a faith and assurance he could not match despite all his striving?'

John's rigid views on most things got him into trouble in Georgia where his congregation complained that there were too many services. One man told him bitterly, 'All your sermons are satires upon particular people, therefore I will never hear you more and all the people are of my mind, for we won't hear ourselves abused'. Wesley was unpopular, his brother was unhappy and he had upset a woman who would have given the earth to marry him. Disillusioned, he sailed back to England in some distress. Back home he sought out the Moravians and particularly Peter Bohler, who convinced him that 'justification by faith' was the thing that would give him the certainty he sought, just as it had Paul, Augustine and Martin Luther before him. Charles Wesley had already had a conversion experience when John attended a meeting of a little society of religious folk at Aldersgate and heard a man reading from Luther's preface to the *Epistle to the Romans*. Wesley wrote of the occasion:

> *I felt my heart strangely warmed. I felt that I did trust in Christ, Christ alone, for salvation: and an assurance was given to me, that he had taken away my sins, even mine.*

That experience released a force of dynamic Christianity so great it has continued to shape the world ever since. He went from that meeting at Aldersgate to found societies all over the country, travelling on horseback and preaching four and five times every day. Few pulpits were opened to him but like Whitefield he preached in the open and was received with enthusiasm. Great crowds flocked to hear him, people responded to his preaching in droves and soon groups of his followers formed Methodist societies with leaders committed to regular classes. Lay preachers (like Wyclif's Lollards) took the gospel far and wide.

Like Whitefield he preached in the open air.

Wesley's *Journals* contain many descriptions of abuses he and his followers endured. He was struck in the mouth so that 'blood gushed out immediately' others threw 'dirt, stones and clods in abundance'. On one occasion his house was about to be burned down until 'one of them happened to remember that his own house was next door' and persuaded the mob to refrain. Other mobs broke up his meetings, people were dragged by the hair and others beaten with clubs. A bull was used to terrify a congregation and it was not unheard of for members of congregations to be dragged away as enlisted soldiers. They were the subjects of cartoons and mocking verse while newspapers and books portrayed them as religious fanatics. So they must have seemed to those more used to the comfortable, common-sense religion of an Anglican parson like James Woodforde who noted in his diary on the day the Bastille fell in Paris:

> *I caught a very fine trout this morning about a pound and a half. Mr Du Quesre was out with me a fishing but could not catch a trout. We had for dinner a fine dish of fish, most of my catching, ham and chicken, peas and beans, a leg of mutton roasted, a couple of duck, currant and apricot tarts, barberry tarts and custards.*

While Woodforde ate his fill the poor lived in garrets and cellars, half starved with cold and hunger even though they were in full-employment. One of Wesley's converts found that even his pocket had to be converted and through frugal living managed to save some £20 of his annual income of £47 to give to the poor.

John Wesley's industry was truly incredible. He travelled 250,000 miles on horseback, reading as he went, and preached 40,000 sermons. He wrote books on economics and medicine (*An Easy and Natural Method of Curing Most Diseases*, became a best seller) as well as theological works. There was hardly an issue he did not address from prison reform to hospitals and the abolition of slavery. He provided books at reasonable prices to encourage the reading habit and people in the Methodist classes became some of the most informed in the country.

There were sad things about his life. Romances dated back to his American days but he was always a slow suitor. One woman, Grace Murray, nursed him through sickness and, as a devout Methodist, journeyed with him often and it is quite likely that John would have married her but his brother Charles interfered. He found the interference difficult to forgive but eventually he married Mary Vazeille, a widow with four children. She could not cope with his travels and left him. Perhaps John grew to envy Charles' marriage to Sally Gwynne, who often rode behind her husband on his preaching tours and led the singing with her beautiful Welsh voice. Later unhappiness was caused by the gradual but inevitable separation from the Church of England, though both John and Charles died as members within that church.

John Wesley's ministry had a great effect on the poorer people of Britain. It has often been argued that in a time of social instability the Methodist Revival played a significant part in averting a British revolution similar to that in France. That is speculation of course but what is beyond doubt is that he lived out the faith he preached in spectacular fashion. His practical creed was, 'Earn all you can, save all you can, give all you can'. For all his own endeavour he died a poor man.

Sarah Peters

Women have always been a vital part of Christianity though their true worth has never been recorded as it should. They have been especially important in Methodism, from Susannah Wesley to the present day. Sarah Peters is one unsung hero from Methodism's early days.

Sarah Peters had been impressed by the example of the Wesley brothers who from their 'holy club' had worked with prisoners on the gruesome death row. Charles often stayed with them right to the foot of the scaffold. Sarah shared in that work and took under her wing a prisoner called John Lancaster, who had been to Methodist meetings but had fallen on hard times and was in prison for stealing. The offence carried the death penalty. She never missed her times for visiting even when the prison was rife with fever. She conducted services in the prison attended by many men and women. When Lancaster was taken in a cart to be hanged he called out to the rest, 'Come my dear friends, let us go joyfully, for the Lord is making ready to receive us into everlasting habitations'. A few days later Sarah Peters herself caught the jail fever and died.

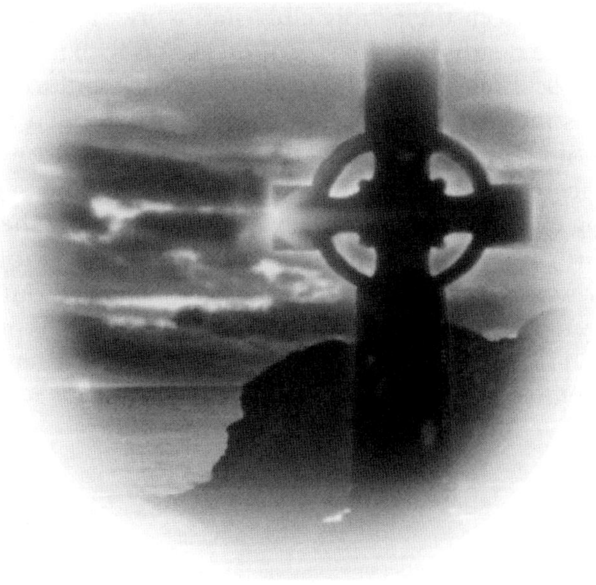

15 Social Gospel

William Wilberforce	218
William Carey	220
David Livingstone	221
Elizabeth Fry	223
Kitty Wilkinson	224
Lord Shaftesbury	224
Sunday Schools and Ragged Schools	226
Dr Barnado	229
Charles Haddon Spurgeon	230
Dwight L. Moody	231
Florence Nightingale	234
William Booth	236
Pentecostalism	238

While Methodism was spreading through Britain, Jean-Jacques Rousseau was using his eloquent pen to spread another message in France. He was a visionary who believed human beings were naturally good but corrupted by false values in society. The sad result was 'man is born free but everywhere he is in chains'. Rousseau's remedy was to uphold and apply virtue. A society of citizens had to be established agreeing to 'do unto others as they would be done by'. His book, *Contract Social*, struck France with the force of a new gospel. Suddenly, rivers of revolutionary sentiment (as in Victor Hugo's memorable *Les Miserables*) broke forth and were not staunched until the Bastille had been stormed, a king and queen guillotined and the Declaration of the Rights of Man established. But what are the rights of man? That is a question.

William Wilberforce (1759–1833)

The opening up of a New World led to a European demand for sugar, tobacco and cotton, all produced in quantity by the labour of African slaves who were herded and coerced by systematic violence. Spain, Portugal, France, Holland and Britain were all involved. Britain was the largest slave trader and between 1680 and 1786 imported well over two million slaves into the British colonies from Africa. Statesman supported the trade as a pillar of national strength. Nelson considered it an essential prop of the mercantile marine and Bristol and Liverpool grew into prosperous cities because of it. The established church in Britain did little to prevent the trade and some clergy thought

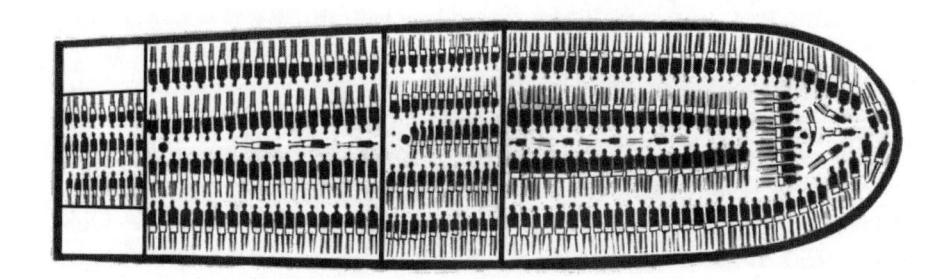

Britain imported over two million slaves into British colonies from Africa, packing them into ships like sardines.

Christianity no more designed for the Negro than for any other brute animal sharing his toil. Yet it was in Britain that a movement arose, which in the end so worked upon the conscience of the world that it abolished official slavery altogether. Lecky in *History of England*, said of Britain's crusade against slavery, 'It may probably be regarded as among the three or four perfectly virtuous pages in the history of nations'. Prominent in those virtuous pages is William Wilberforce.

When he was fourteen Wilberforce had written to a newspaper attacking the evils of slavery. He was a sickly child but within that weak body beat a very passionate heart and a very strong moral conscience. This was to lead him into politics after a university education at Cambridge. He was elected Member of Parliament for his home town of Hull, aged just twenty-one. At twenty-five he travelled to the Continent with a muscular clergyman called Isaac Milner who involved him in endless discussion about religion with frequent references to the Greek New Testament. The upshot was Wilberforce was converted and he resolved 'to live to the glory of God and the good of my fellow creatures'. In Parliament he allied himself with a group of men, none of them in influential positions, who gradually overcame the vested interest of a slave-owning Cabinet and exposed the shamefulness of the slave trade. He knew he was saying farewell to any political ambition but threw himself into the task of collecting evidence of brutality against Africans and making a catalogue of their considerable skills and abilities.

Wilberforce became known as the 'Nightingale of the House' and was the leader of 'the Clapham Sect', a committee of evangelical Christians whose consciences had been quickened by the social implications of John Wesley's preaching. Wilberforce received several death threats but he never wavered from the rightness of his position. He received support from Prime Minister William Pitt but was constantly thwarted by Cabinet until the wheel began to turn and legislation hit the Statute Book. 1772 saw slavery abolished in Britain but it was 1806 before slavery was declared illegal. The vote was 283 votes against 16 and the result led to an ovation never surpassed in the House of Commons. Wilberforce sat with his head in his hands, tears streaming down his face. Even then the struggle was not over, for slave-ships continued to sail illegally and men and women were captured in greater numbers than before. Slaves were often thrown overboard in chains if a British cruiser was sighted. It was 1833 before slavery was finally abolished in the British Dominions and the following year freedom from slavery became actual fact in the West Indies. On the night of July 31st, 1834, thousands of Negroes crowded into their churches to wait for the first stroke of midnight. As it tolled they leaped to their feet with a cheer to raise the roof and from that moment 800,000 slaves held under the British flag were free. It was a famous victory for human rights and it is impossible to overstate the part played by a man whose faith had made him stick to a task until it was certain of success. In the hour of that success Wilberforce was on his death-bed but still able to understand what was happening and give thanks to God for it. A few days later he was buried in Westminster Abbey.

Wilberforce had not worked alone of course and a notable part in the slavery saga belongs to John Newton, who had left school at eleven to work on a slave-ship and had caught natives in West Africa to be sold in the slave-markets. Then, after being frightened for his life in a fearsome storm he read *The Imitation of Christ* by Thomas à Kempis and was dramatically converted. Encouraged by John Wesley and George Whitefield he became an Anglican priest. To add reality to his powerful preaching he introduced heart-felt hymns into his services, often writing them himself. They included 'Amazing Grace':

> *Amazing Grace—how sweet the sound*
> *That saved a wretch like me!*
> *I once was lost but now I'm found,*
> *Was blind but now I see.*

William Carey (1761–1834)

If the abolition of slavery was one spin-off from the Great Awakening, missionary activity was another. William Carey was given the incentive to mission by the theology of Jonathan Edwards. He was an apprentice shoemaker when he was converted as an eighteen year-old, joined the Baptists and was baptised as a believer four years later. He became pastor of a church in Leicester. He was inspired by accounts he read of Captain Cook's voyages to Australia and the South Pacific and became convinced that the gospel was something for everybody, not just a few predestined for heaven. It led him to write, *An Enquiry into the Obligations of Christians to use Means for the Conversion of the Heathen*, which concluded that a command had been given to the apostles to teach all nations and not just some. In a gripping sermon preached in Nottingham, he urged Christians to 'expect great things from God and attempt great things for God'. It was a sermon directly responsible for the founding of the Baptist Missionary Society in 1792. A year later he put his life where his mouth was and sailed to India with his family. As he studied Indian language and literature, this shoemaker discovered he had a great gift for languages and set about translating the New Testament into Bengali. He became a tutor in language at Fort William College and for over twenty years worked on no less than six complete translations of the Bible and twenty-four partial translations.

He was joined in the work by two other Baptists, Joshua Marshman and William Ward and together they formed more mission stations and schools. Serampore College stands today as a monument to Carey's foresight in encouraging Indians to improve their education and take over the running of the churches and missions, 'It is only by means of native preachers we can hope for the universal spread of the gospel through this immense continent'. He was far sighted in other ways too and was interested in botany and how to improve farming methods. He campaigned tirelessly for the abolition of sati, (the burning of widows) and involved himself in many social concerns. Despite his humble beginnings, Carey is now generally acknowledged as 'the Father of Modern Missions' and he was the example of other pioneering missionaries, like Hudson Taylor in China and William Knibb, who joined the fight against slavery in the West Indies. Then there was David Livingstone...

David Livingstone (1813–1873)

Like William Carey, Livingstone came from humble stock. Born to God fearing but poor parents in Blantyre, Scotland, he was working in a cotton mill at ten years of age. It was monotonous work and to pass the hours he propped a book up on his machine and read avidly. Night classes improved his education further and after a conversion experience he began to think of himself as a missionary. He saved enough money to study medicine in Glasgow and London before serving with the London Missionary Society in Southern Africa where he married. Soon he was journeying into uncharted territory and became an intrepid explorer, building up relationships with many Africans and discovering the secrets of the interior. He was the first white man to see the wonder of the Victoria Falls:

> *No one can imagine the beauty of this view from anything witnessed in England. It has never been seen by European eyes but seems so lovely it must have been gazed upon by angels in their flight.*

Livingstone saw at first hand the evils of the slave-trade as he travelled from East to West, a journey memorably recorded in his *Missionary Travels and Researches in South Africa*, a book which made him a household name in Britain. He returned home and addressed students at Cambridge where he ended a speech with an impassioned plea:

> *I beg to direct your attention to Africa. I know in a few years I will be cut off in that country which is now open; do not let it be shut again! I go back to Africa to try to make an open path for commerce and Christianity. Do you carry out the work which I have begun? I leave it with you.*

The speech received volley after volley of cheers and sparked off a wave of missionary endeavour amongst students, which was not always as sensible as it was idealistic and several lives were lost in subsequent missions. Nevertheless, Livingstone's travels cast a spell over Britain and America and news of his exploration of Lake Nyasa and his mapping of the Zambezi river captivated millions. When he disappeared in 1865 there was great concern for his safety and an American journalist called Henry Morton Stanley went to Africa to track him down. He found him six years later near Lake Tanganyika and greeted him with the words, 'Doctor Livingstone, I presume?' When he died in 1873 African companions carried his body to the coast and he was later buried in Westminster Abbey.

Livingstone's achievements were many. He drew attention to an 'open sore of Africa' in his battle against the Arab slave trade and did much to substitute commerce and agriculture for slavery. He cultivated friendships with Africans and, unlike other African adventurers, educated and encouraged them. He gave impetus to the missionary movements within churches and long after his death Scottish missions were formed, which perpetuated his own ideals:

> *I place no value on anything I have or may possess, except in relation to the kingdom of Christ. If anything will advance the interests of the kingdom, it shall be given away or kept, only as by giving and keeping it I shall most promote the glory of him to whom I owe all my hopes in time and eternity.*
>
> **(Livingstone's Journals)**

The work of spreading Christianity through Africa was taken up by Africans themselves, notably by Samuel Adjai Crowther (1806–1891) who survived capture by slave traders when a British warship released them. He was taken to Sierra Leone where he was converted and worked for the Church Missionary Society. He eventually found his long-lost mother and sister who grew to share his faith and work. He visited England where he met Queen Victoria and returned home as the first African, Anglican bishop. During the next fifty years ministers and missionaries poured out of Sierra Leone to cover West Africa.

The stimulation to mission generated by Livingstone struck a chord of challenge and self-sacrifice in many a young heart but there was to be a reaction. As the Industrial Revolution took hold in Britain, men and women were sucked into urban life to man the increasing demand for labour in the factories. Conditions of life in the burgeoning towns and cities deteriorated. This led to a cry to rescue from their plight those trapped in 'Darkest England'. After all, does not charity begin at home?

Elizabeth Fry (1780–1845)

Elizabeth, the daughter of a Quaker banker in Norwich, married a London merchant and had a large family. Not content with a simple family life she put her social concern into action by getting involved in the state of British prisons. She began a welfare programme at Newgate prison where she visited women prisoners, daily teaching them to sew and read the Bible. After a while she began a campaign to separate the sexes within prison and insisted on women warders for women prisoners and different categories for different prisoners. She collected evidence to put before a select committee of the House of Commons. She also became involved in prison after-care and a nightly shelter for the homeless in London. She was a woman before her time and travelled to the continent on many occasions to help reforms there. She produced reports on social conditions in Ireland and prompted the provision of libraries in coastal stations and naval hospitals. Her work was only curbed when her husband went bankrupt in 1828 but even then she kept her evangelical zeal and her book *Texts for every day of the Year*, had a wide circulation. Her favourite maxim was 'Charity to the soul is the soul of charity', a maxim she lived out with her life.

Kitty Wilkinson (1786–1860)

Another woman before her time was Kitty Wilkinson, an Irish girl from Londonderry, who moved to Liverpool when she was nine with a widowed mother who was partially blind and suffering from dementia. When she was older she hired a room and taught sewing and reading to children for 3d a week. She then married and had two children before she too was widowed. Left now with sons and a totally dependent mother she worked in a nail factory and lived in a cellar. The remarkable thing about Kitty was that she never succumbed to the squalor around her and kept her family and home spotlessly clean. Her work was arduous but she remained unfailingly generous and helped countless who were sick. She began to adopt orphaned children and when she married again, to a warehouse porter called Tom Wilkinson, they turned their home into a virtual orphanage where they clothed, fed and educated as many as forty-five children.

When cholera broke out in Britain, Liverpool was hit more than most places and two thousand citizens died within a few months. Kitty nursed and fed victims and, disregarding her own health, fought the cholera with soap, water and fresh-air. Her method was to boil and disinfect clothes in her copper and dry them outside in the yard. In effect, her home became the first public wash-house and as a direct result of her example Liverpool was the first city to open public baths and wash-houses. In 1846 the Wilkinsons were appointed Superintendents. The epitaph on the tombstone of this quietly devout woman reads:

> *For they did cast in of their abundance, but she of her want did cast in all that she had, even all her living.*

The life of Kitty Wilkinson was honoured in the staircase window of noble women in the Lady Chapel of Liverpool Cathedral. Sadly that window was destroyed during the Second World War.

Lord Shaftesbury (1801–1885)

The appalling living, working and dying conditions of thousands in industrial Britain were a scandal. 'Get rich quick' industrialists paid little heed to the anguish of workers who tended looms, scrambled for coal or did any job to earn a crust. Elizabeth Fry and Kitty Wilkinson were providing first-aid against the stream but there was a need to change things at the top. The impetus for change came from the unlikely source of the British aristocracy. Disraeli declared, 'It is the name of Lord Shaftesbury which descends to posterity as the one who worked more than any other individual to alleviate the conditions and raise the status of his countrymen'. He was, without doubt, one of the finest fruits of the evangelical awakening. The seventh earl was born with a silver spoon in his mouth but that did not prevent him from striving throughout his life to get spoons into the mouths of others. What made this aristocrat so passionate for the poor is usually traced back to 1815 when, as a fourteen year old school boy in Harrow, he walked down Harrow Hill beside the school. As he walked he heard bawdy singing coming from a group of drunken louts, some of whom were carrying a rough casket containing the body of one of their fellow workmen. As they staggered along they stumbled and fell into a stupid heap sending the casket crashing to earth. The coffin bearers quarrelled and cursed and accompanying urchins burst into laughter. Finally the drunks managed to pick up the casket and with renewed curses and gin songs continued their funeral march. Shaftesbury said, 'The remains of an immortal being, born and raised in Christian England, were about to be placed in the earth with indignities ill becoming the wildest savages in Central Africa'. Shaftesbury was an evangelical of the Wilberforce school who believed salvation applied to bodies as well as souls:

> *When people say we should think more of the soul and less of the body, my answer is that the same God made body and soul...God is worshipped not only by the spiritual but by the material creation. Our bodies, the temples of the Holy Ghost, ought not to be corrupted by preventable disease, degraded by avoidable filth, and disabled for his service by unnecessary suffering.*

When he entered Parliament as a Conservative member in 1826 he became an important force in early British legislation to improve working conditions. Industrialisation had happened so quickly Britain's system of law was ill equipped to prohibit the human exploitation of factory workers. Bosses trotted out similar clichés to those used to keep slavery, saying that improving regulations and working conditions would raise costs and make goods less saleable, thereby harming the workers themselves. It was nonsense and a factory owner in Scotland called Robert Owen had proved that it was possible to provide good working conditions and still make a profit. Acts of Parliament had little practical effect. A Health and Apprentices Act of 1802 sought to fix apprentices working days to a maximum of twelve hours and forbid night work and a later Act of 1819 tried to prevent children under nine being employed (though only in cotton mills). Both Acts were toothless because there were no inspectors to police the factories and children's ages were concealed.

Shaftesbury's energetic leadership soon changed the inertia of Parliament and by forging a strong coalition of politicians and religious leaders, he assured that the Factories Act of 1833 was effective and workable. No children under nine were to work in a mill, children under thirteen could only work a maximum nine hour day and young people up to eighteen were restricted to a twelve hour day. By today's standards it seems very little indeed but it was a start. The Mine's Act did not follow until 1842 and that prohibited women and boys under ten from working underground. Employers still strove to get round the legislation but Shaftesbury fulfilled his great ambition in 1847 by establishing a statutory ten-hour day for women and young persons and this indirectly helped the cause of shorter working days for men. Greater safety measures were also introduced, greatly reducing the number of accidents in the work place.

Anthony Ashley Cooper, the 7th Earl of Shaftesbury, inspired by his evangelical but practical Christianity, had done much to make life more tolerable for people whose faces were being ground into the dirt by unscrupulous masters. In the mills the chains were loosened, down pit-shafts a little light had percolated and the future was brighter. The influence of Shaftesbury seeped everywhere and his workload included constructing model homes for the deprived, improvements for slum schools, banning sweep boys and improving conditions for milliners and dressmakers. He supported the British and Foreign Bible Society, the London City Mission, the Church Missionary Society, the YMCA and Ragged Schools...

Sunday Schools and Ragged Schools

Shaftesbury remained in the Church of England all his life but often found himself spokesman for the Nonconformist Conscience, which had little representation in Parliament. Without the ethical values flowing from the evangelical awakening, Shaftesbury's victories would not have been possible. There were workers ('consecrated cobblers'

*The influence of Shaftsbury seeped everywhere…
even into the slums.*

they were disparagingly called) who, despite crushing conditions, maintained a belief that things would improve and it was from their ardour and faith that Sunday Schools for the uneducated were born, along with co-operative aid societies for the poor and penny pamphlets for the newly literate.

One man who engaged himself in the education of poor children was Robert Raikes (1735–1811). He promoted the Sunday School idea after meeting with a man called Thomas Stock who had run such a school in Ashbury, Berkshire with some success. As publisher of the *Gloucester Journal* Raikes knew a lot about neglected children and decided to help them. The work immediately took off and schools sprang up all over the place. Within six years, 200,000 children were being taught in Sunday Schools with a simple curriculum, which included writing, arithmetic and reading, with Bible studies to provide the ethical milieu. Some teachers were paid but later the work relied on volunteers. Hannah More (1745–1833) was also prominent in Sunday School work. She had been part of the literary scene of London and was friendly with Samuel Johnson, Sir Joshua Reynolds and the actor David Garrick. Then the ex-slave trader priest, John Newton, attracted her and she joined the evangelical community centred around Clapham. She formed a Sunday School at Cheddar, financed in part by William Wilberforce. This school had an industrial component and provided training in spinning and domestic service. The schools spread through the Mendips and despite some ridicule (William Cobbett described her as the 'Old Bishop in Petticoates') she provided an educational foundation for hundreds of lives.

The same zeal that had given birth to Sunday Schools was also behind the growth of Ragged Schools. John Pounds, the crippled shoemaker from Portsmouth, and workers at the London City Mission were the driving force behind these schools. Pounds befriended and almost fathered some five hundred outcast children. 'That man is an honour to humanity' said Dr Thomas Guthrie, 'He deserves the tallest monument ever raised on British shores.' When a Ragged School Union was formed it was Lord Shaftesbury who became President. The aim became education for all children because it was wrong to leave so much talent and potential untapped and then punish them for crimes not their fault but the outcome of criminal neglect. By 1870 the Ragged Schools boasted 440 paid teachers and thousands of volunteers. Charles Dickens became an advocate for the schools and underlined their value in *A Christmas Story*:

> *There is not one of these children—not one—but sows a harvest mankind must reap. From every seed of evil in this boy a field of ruin is grown that shall be gathered in and garnered up, and sown again in many places of the world, until regions are overspread with wickedness enough to raise the waters of another Deluge.*

An article by Dickens about Ragged Schools was read by the great Victorian preacher Charles Spurgeon and he too became a friend to the organisation. In Sheffield, Roman Catholics opened St Vincent's School attended by hundreds and supported by Protestants and Catholics alike. When Shaftesbury visited the school he said,

> *Here is activity while others sleep. The grand principle of the Ragged School system is that it takes children in rags and turns them out washed. It takes them ignorant and turns them out taught. It takes them heathens and turns them out Christians.*
> **(Sheffield Iris Newspaper, 4th March, 1869)**

Dr Barnado (1845–1905)

Speaking at the Exeter Hall in 1893, Dr Barnado said of Ragged School education:

> *It has been patronised, then ignored, then criticised, then tolerated, but now it is imitated and there are imitations in many ways, even in the statute books of the nation. There are today a thousand activities, a crowd of philanthropic agencies in active operation, but if you ask where they all come from, you will not find them in the House of Lords or the House of Commons; not even from the palaces of wealth and fashion, but from the humble doors of some coach-house or stable, where began the ragged schools.*

Barnado was a Ragged School teacher himself and his own rescue work grew out of it. He was a member of the Plymouth Brethren who left Dublin and went to London in 1866, hoping to become a missionary doctor. Then he visited the Stepney slums and was moved by the plight of a homeless waif called Jim Jarvis. This inspired him to set up his first home for destitute boys in 1870. He was a great organiser with a flair for publicising his concerns. By 1873 he had taken over a public house and transformed it into a church home and coffee palace. Three years later he built a village in Ilford providing homes for girls. Later he sent children to Canada because employment prospects were better there and by the time of his death he had admitted 59,384 children into his homes, arranged emigration for 20,000 and materially assisted another 250,000. Barnado's slogan was, 'No destitute child ever refused admission'. His work goes on to the present day.

Charles Hadden Spurgeon (1834–1892)

Once or twice in a century God hauls off and creates a servant so mighty in gift that the only proper response is 'Wow!' Spurgeon was one of God's special projects in the nineteenth century.

So wrote Haddon Robinson in a foreword to a book of Spurgeon's devotions *Morning and Evening*. Spurgeon was undoubtedly the outstanding British preacher of his day. In an age before microphones, six thousand people crowded into his church twice a day to hear him. He preached at other gatherings during the week, often at ten different venues throughout the country. His Sunday sermons were taken down by stenographers, printed and distributed widely. They were cabled to New York on Monday and reprinted in newspapers all over America. His sermons sold 25,000 copies every week and were translated into over twenty languages. Quoting Haddon Robinson again, 'He preached from the same pulpit for forty years and did not preach himself dry. God created a bush that blazed with fire and yet was not consumed'.

This great Victorian preacher never claimed to be a scholarly theologian or even an original thinker but as a communicator he had few equals. He was born in Kelvedon, Essex and both his father and grandfather were pastors of Independent churches. One Sunday when he was sixteen, he was caught in a snowstorm in Colchester and went inside a Primitive Methodist chapel to shelter. There was a service taking place but the scheduled preacher had not made it through the snow and the service was being led by an untutored layman who harangued the sparse congregation with a text about repentance. It went straight to the heart of Spurgeon and changed his life. He was baptised and almost immediately became a Baptist pastor and in 1854, at the tender age of nineteen, he was invited to London to a Baptist church in Southwark. Soon his preaching was pulling in such crowds that the church was overflowing. In 1859 it was thought necessary to build a new church to house the congregations—the Metropolitan Tabernacle.

By now Spurgeon was a married man and had founded a 'Pastors' College' to train men for the preaching of the gospel. He bore the cost of the college on his own for fifteen years until the Tabernacle shared the work. He helped found the Association of Baptist churches in London and also set up an orphanage in Stockwell, which still operates as Spurgeon's Homes. As well as supporting the Ragged Schools he founded Temperance and Clothing Societies.

His phenomenal endeavour as preacher and philanthropist did not spare him criticism from the press or from other clergy. Nor did he escape the slings and arrows of misfortune, for his wife Susannah was a virtual invalid from the age of thirty-three and Spurgeon himself suffered from gout for the last twenty years of his life. In his final years he sought to counteract radical teaching from fellow ministers in the Baptist Union and felt compelled to resign when they disregarded his advice. The affair affected him deeply but by then his fame and reputation were assured. A friend's testimony could hardly be more warmhearted:

> *I have seen Mr Spurgeon hold thousands in breathless interest. I knew him to be a great man, universally esteemed and beloved. But as he sat by the bed of a dying orphan boy he was grander and greater than when he swayed multitudes.*
> **(Drummond, Lewis, *Spurgeon, Prince of Preachers*; Kregel Publishing, 1992)**

But let the last word be with Lord Shaftesbury:

> *Few men have preached so much and so well, and few have combined so practically their words and their actions.*

Dwight L. Moody (1837–1899)

Sitting in the packed gallery of the Metropolitan Tabernacle one Sunday morning in March 1867 were a thirty year old American and his wife. They were Dwight and Emma Moody, who had longed to hear Spurgeon preach and were entranced by him and stunned by the singing of six thousand voices. Emma wrote home, 'His manner is very simple and he is a very plain looking man but he had the attention of his whole audience'. Moody longed to preach like Spurgeon and see singing in America like that in the Tabernacle. It was an unlikely prospect.

Moody was born in Northfield, Massachusetts, a farming community of about a thousand. His whisky loving father died when he was four leaving behind a wife and nine children. Dwight was the fifth son and his formal education was from five to thirteen. All his life he struggled with his writing, which was completely devoid of punctuation of any kind. But there was great love in the extended Moody family, coupled with a discipline that stood him in good stead throughout his life. He went to Boston where his uncle gave him a job in his store and a room over the shop. He wrote home:

> *I have a room up on the third storey and I can open my winder and there is 3 grat buildings full of girls the handsomest thare is in the city thay will swar like parrets.*

His uncle directed him to the YMCA, which Moody called the 'Christian saciation'. For a dollar a year it gave him all the books he wanted to read free of expense. He was also able to attend lectures and thereby learn from the learned as well as from books. He attended a revival meeting at the Mount Vernon Church and was converted but he was not allowed to join the church because he was too tongue-tied to articulate his faith. But the seed was sown and Moody was on his way.

He decided to move westward seeking his fortune and settled in Chicago, the hub of the west where steamers and trains poured into town bringing immigrants, manufacturers and all the accompanying dirt and stench. He still had difficulty expressing his faith but helped out at a Baptist Sunday School by bringing in the waifs and strays. He met Emma, a teacher and the daughter of a French Huguenot family who had emigrated to America via England. She undertook to improve Moody's education. His son wrote later:

> *To the day of his death, I believe he never ceased to wonder at two things—the use God had made of him despite his handicaps, and the miracle of having won the love of a woman he considered to be completely his superior.*

Moody's preaching really began as Sunday School talks to some of his waifs and strays and at the YMCA prayer meetings. Before long his voluntary missionary work dominated his time, though he paid the bills by selling shoes. He was never ordained but his simple oratory began to arrest listeners and he became a much sought after speaker. Moody wanted to visit Britain and particularly wanted to meet three people; George Williams, the founder of the YMCA, George Muller, the legendary man of faith whose orphanage was provided for by a simple trust in God and Charles Hadden Spurgeon, who, although only three years older than Moody, was already drawing thousands to his services. The urge did not subside, hence the visit to the Metropolitan Tabernacle in 1867.

Three years after visiting the Tabernacle, Moody went to a YMCA International Convention in Indianapolis and met Ira Sankey who was destined to join him in a preaching-singing combination as irresistible as that of the Wesley brothers. Moody was about to become an evangelist but it only happened after a catastrophic fire raged through Chicago leaving fifty churches in ashes, the town a smouldering ruin and Moody free of the ties binding him to Chicago. He was to be a man of the world. For the next twenty-five years he conducted missions continuously; York, Edinburgh and Glasgow, lighting fires left burning long after he had moved on. During the Scotland mission Sankey came into his own and his songs and solos were printed and distributed all over the country. Then they moved on to Ireland, Liverpool, Manchester, Sheffield, Birmingham. All Britain was singing. Then to London, to mass meetings where all kinds of people, dockers to duchesses, came to listen to the straight talking American. Edward Studd and his three sons went to listen and C.T. Studd, the most celebrated England cricketer of his day, gave up cricket to become a missionary in China. An estimated two and a half million people attended meetings on that first mission to Britain. When they returned to America he was a fully fledged evangelist and they took town after town by storm. Overcoming obstacles and prejudice he founded educational establishments like Mount Hermon in his home town of Northfield, which became the centre of his operations. He returned to Britain with a special concern for the young and spoke at both Oxford and Cambridge Universities where the Students' Christian Movement was formed. It still flourishes today.

Moody was a phenomenon. Without any natural advantages, his complete lack of sham, transparent sincerity and downright honesty brought religion out of the clouds and into practical reality. He was a preacher and a doer who travelled more than a million miles and addressed more than 100 million people. The man who could not articulate his faith enough to join the church had become the greatest Christian communicator in nineteenth-century America.

Florence Nightingale (1820–1910)

The 'practical Christianity' of the period was demonstrated in the life of a woman who single-handedly raised the status of nursing from a chore to that of a highly trained and respected medical profession. That woman was, of course, Florence Nightingale who, to quote a hackneyed phrase, 'became a legend in her own time'.

She came from a wealthy family and was actually born in Florence, Italy (hence the name) but was raised mainly in Derbyshire. Her father gave her a sound classical education including Greek, Latin, French, German, Italian, history, philosophy and mathematics. For the rest of her life she read widely in many languages and could certainly have achieved distinction in almost any path she chose. On February 7th, 1837, she believed she heard God speaking to her and became convinced she had a mission. As yet the mission was unclear but it was soon to be revealed. She became an expert on public health and hospitals and in 1846 she heard about the Institute of Protestant Deaconesses in Germany that trained girls of good character to nurse the sick. She completed the course and was subsequently appointed Superintendent of the Hospital for Invalid Gentlewomen in London. When the Crimean War broke out in 1854, Florence read reports of the appalling conditions endured by wounded British soldiers at the large British Barracks Hospital at Uskudar (now part of Istanbul, Turkey). She wrote to the Secretary of State for War offering her services and he proposed forthwith that she should be placed in charge of all nursing operations at the war front. She set off accompanied by thirty-eight nurses.

They arrived on the very day the battle of Inkerman was fought and found conditions even worse than expected. The barracks were flea and rat infested, water was severely rationed and the doctors were hostile. However, the hospital was so greatly overcrowded with sick and wounded that doctors were forced to use all the labour available and asked Miss Nightingale for help. Her first requisition was for two hundred scrubbing brushes and the nurses set to with a will to cleanse the place. Filthy clothes were washed outside the hospital and a schedule was drawn up for care and diets. Hampered by bureaucratic demands for reports she nevertheless soon had control of the hospital. This sometimes meant sending home nurses for drunkenness and immorality. At night she alone walked the wards with her lamp, checking on the soldiers and gaining for herself the title, 'Lady with the Lamp'. Through hard work and good technique

At night she alone walked the wards with her lamp.

at Uskudar and later at Balaklava, the mortality rate amongst the wounded was dramatically reduced.

By the end of the war Florence Nightingale had become a national heroine but she avoided acclaim and sought to permanently improve the lot of the British soldier. She was resisted but after lengthy discussions with Queen Victoria she achieved many of her objectives. Funds raised as a tribute to her services amounted to £45,000 and with the money she opened the Nightingale School for Nurses at St Thomas' Hospital, London and started the first professional education for nurses in Britain. This was followed by training for midwives and for nurses working in workhouses which she helped to reform. For the second half of her life she was an invalid and by 1901 was completely blind yet she kept in touch with every aspect of nursing including that of the British army in India. In 1907 the king conferred on her the Order of Merit, the first woman ever to receive the award. She refused the offer of a state funeral at Westminster Abbey and was buried in the family grave in Hampshire. Throughout her life she had maintained a sense of purpose with simple faith. She wrote:

> *When we speak with God, our power of addressing Him, of holding communion with Him and listening to His still small voice, depends upon our will being one and the same with His.*

William Booth (1829–1912)

As there is a darkest Africa, is there not also a darkest England? The lot of the negress in the Equatorial Forest is not, perhaps a very pretty one, but is it so very much worse than that of many a pretty orphan girl in our Christian Capital?

These were questions asked by William Booth, which probed beneath the facade of Victorian Life in Britain. The population of the country was streaming from the land to man the factories of cities and towns. Soon populations of towns had quadrupled and people were having to adjust to a way of life altogether different to anything they had known before. Candleford was giving way to Coketown. The Britain of peasant, yeoman and craftsman was about to disappear forever. Thousands chased jobs in places where they were unknown, mere work fodder in factories of sweated-labour with only back-to-back housing to go home to. The life expectancy in these 'Coketowns' was as low as twenty-five. In the countryside the church had been part of the pattern of their life, in the towns they left their churchgoing behind and teeming populations often surrounded half-empty churches. Booth's answer was to dress Christianity in new garb to make it attractive and relevant to the changing nation.

William Booth had been at various times a Weslyan preacher and an ordained Methodist minister but he never sat comfortably as a minister and preferred to be an itinerant evangelist. By 1865, William and his wife Catherine (also a gifted preacher) had begun their own missionary tent in Whitechapel, London. It was from this Mission that the Salvation Army grew. Not surprisingly it raised opposition. Some thought the antics of Booth and his followers made Christianity seem ridiculous, others objected to the military overtones and the uniforms. Brewers objected to the teetotal aspects of the Mission which affected their trade. The members suffered serious abuse with hundreds of men and women assaulted and meeting-houses damaged. Booth was authoritarian, discipline was rigid and as his control over the Mission strengthened so it became even more military in nature with groups called corps, meeting in citadels and going out in uniforms to sell their newspaper *The War Cry*. His logic was simple, he was engaged in a war, not simply against principalities and powers but against exploitation and vice. If sinners were to find salvation their bellies had to be fed, their children had to be secure, fed and warm, then and only then, could they be taught. Thus, the gospel and the soup kitchen worked in tandem. By 1872 they were running five 'Food-for-the-Million' shops and Elijah Cadman was advertising meetings of 'The

Hallelujah Army Fighting for God' in Whitby. Booth began to be labelled 'General'. In 1878 the Salvation Army had evolved, 127 evangelists were manning mission stations all over the country and conducting services backed by bands and rollicking music. 'Why should the devil have all the best tunes?' asked Booth. The uniforms became official and the first volume of 'Orders and Regulations for the Salvation Army' appeared with Booth as commander-in-chief. He embarked on a bewildering number of welfare schemes, which provided cheap food, night shelters, an unemployment exchange, a missing-person's bureau, legal aid for the poor and a poor-man's bank. He also wrote *In Darkest England— and the Way Out*, which was an immediate best seller and caused great controversy. Catherine died at this juncture after a prolonged illness but Booth continued the work, travelling all over the world organising the Army into an international evangelical and aid concern. Millions responded to the General's fight against evil with the power of the gospel:

> *The Army is coming—amen, amen!*
> *To conquer this city for Jesus— amen!*
> *We'll shout, 'Hallelujah' and praise his dear name,*
> *Who redeemed us to God through the blood of the lamb.*
> *The sound of his footsteps is rolling along;*
> *The kingdom of Satan, triumphant so long,*
> *Is shaking and tottering, and downward shall fall*
> *For Jesus the Saviour, shall reign over all.*

Many of William Booth's ideas are now welcomed into main stream Christianity and have been incorporated into the welfare systems of Britain and other countries. He was a man before his time. When he died 150,000 people filed past his coffin and 40,000 attended his funeral. Only posthumously was he accepted by the establishment but now he is renowned and the Salvation Army, though changed, still bears testimony to the vision of William Booth and his wife Catherine.

Booth was engaged in a war against exploitation and vice.

Pentecostalism

During the life of Dwight L. Moody an American holiness movement put down roots in some American churches. This movement tried to preserve a Methodist teaching claiming that people could be totally sanctified in this life and attain a Christian perfection. Some members left Methodism as a protest against a lack of discipline and another man called Orange Scott left because he felt Methodism had become comfortable with slavery. Two sisters, Sarah Lankford and Phoebe Palmer, formed a Tuesday meeting that did much to spread the idea of achieving total holiness here and now. The Church of the Nazarene was probably the largest of these independent holiness groups.

Then in 1906, on Azusa Street, Los Angeles, William J. Seymour, a black man with one eye, founded a mission. He was a shy man, certainly no orator, but his mission started a wave of revival soon attracting national attention. Meetings at the mission lasted for three years and featured charismatic events like speaking in tongues, considered to be a proof of God's blessing. An Anglican clergyman called Alexander A. Boddy, promoted a Pentecostal awakening in England and soon it was a movement with world-wide associations. A Cornishman called Thomas Ball Barratt became a Pentecostal evangelist in Norway and other parts of Scandinavia. Today, Latin America boasts some 15 million Pentecostalists and there has been growth in Africa, Russia, China and Indonesia. In many of these places they have done much to loosen political oppression. Initially, Pentecostalists were anti-intellectual and fundamentalist but over the years this has become less pronounced. Along with speaking in tongues there is a strong healing aspect to meetings. Spontaneity and joy feature large in worship particularly in black congregations like those in the Church of God in Christ.

Initially, established denominations resisted the waves of Pentecostalism but 'spirit filled' worship has now penetrated into all churches including Roman Catholic. There can be no doubt that the growth of Pentecostalism was a major feature of church life in the twentieth-century. The lack of a priestly hierarchy has released the laity from the strictures of conformity and congregations have become less middle class. Dance and expression have returned to worship and a veritable orchestra of instruments can now be found leading a worship that can be quite 'poppish' and very attractive to younger people. Charismatic leadership can be undisciplined and a lack of history and structure has led to divisiveness within the Pentecostal movement but the new life breathed into old bones is now generally welcomed.

16 Seeds of Doubt

Charles Darwin	240
Karl Marx	242
Existentialism	246
Soren Kierkegaard	246
Friedrich Nietzsche	248
Sigmund Freud	249
Carl Gustav Jung	251

*I*f the nineteenth century was a time of social and industrial progress it was also a time when accepted ways of thinking were challenged in dramatic ways. Immanuel Kant (1724–1804) had sought to weaken theological argument by denying the old proofs for the existence of God. All man could hope to do, he thought, was to make sense of his own existence and the world around him, any speculation about God was without value. But even Kant had to acknowledge that two things left him speechless with wonder—the starry sky above him and the deep moral law within him. Like Blaise Pascal (1623–1662) he seems to have accepted that the heart has reasons the mind knows nothing of. Philosophical thought from Kant, Hegel and Schleirmacher caused sensations inside the classrooms and studies of intellectuals but hardly troubled the waters of Mr Everyman in the street. Biology and geology were about to do so.

Charles Darwin (1809–1882)

When Darwin was twenty-four years old he joined a surveying voyage round the world on HMS *Beagle*. One day in a forest outside Rio de Janeiro he collected sixty-eight different species of small beetle. He had not been looking for beetles particularly but the variety in such small insects astounded and puzzled him. Why should there be such a bewildering variety of forms? The conventional wisdom was that all species were immutable, unchangeable and each separately created by God. But why such variety? Darwin was not an atheist, indeed he had studied for a divinity degree at Cambridge, but his mind wanted an answer to the vast multiplicity around him. For a further three years he sailed with the *Beagle* until they arrived at the lonely archipelago of the Galapagos where his puzzlement increased. He was intrigued to discover animals there quite like animals on the mainland yet differing from them in significant ways. Tortoises, for instance, were similar to those on the mainland yet many times larger. Moreover, the giant tortoises on each of the islands differed from each other as well. On arid islands they fed from leaves on trees and had longer necks than those on well watered islands where they cropped vegetation on the ground. Darwin began to wonder if perhaps species were not fixed at all but had in fact changed over time to adapt more successfully to their surroundings. The idea took hold and he began to push it further. Perhaps over millions of years animals could change quite substantially?

The theory of evolution took a long time to arrange itself in Darwin's mind.

Perhaps fish had also evolved? Had they gradually developed muscular fins enabling them to crawl from the sea to become amphibians? Perhaps amphibians became reptiles? Could ape-like creatures have been ancestors of man? Philosophically the idea was not entirely new but Darwin was about to provide geological evidence capable of being tested and analysed. The theory of evolution had itself evolved. It was a concept that took a long time to arrange itself in Darwin's own mind and for twenty-five years he amassed painstaking evidence before actually publishing *The Origin of Species*. In essence his argument was that all life evolves to fit new circumstances. If it does not evolve it runs a danger of extinction. Surviving life forms pass on their survival genes to their offspring until the adaptations necessary for survival become assured. When that happens a new species will have grown out of another.

Theological implications in Darwin's theories were picked up quickly. The Bible said that God had created the world in six days, now Darwin was saying it had taken millions of years and was, in effect, a natural selection or, as social theorist Herbert Spencer was to call it, 'a survival of the fittest'. The implications were obvious. If living things had evolved by natural process then humankind was not a special creation but was on the same plane as animals. This was a serious challenge to orthodox theological opinion. Furthermore, perhaps evolution was still going on? Perhaps species are in constant states of change?

Darwin was anxious that his theory would not be accepted and being a very shy man he declined to get involved in public discussion. So T.H. Huxley became his most ardent advocate and he got the nickname, 'Darwin's Bulldog'. In 1860 he became involved in a famous tussle with Samuel Wilberforce, the bishop of Oxford and son of William Wilberforce. In an Oxford debate the bishop intervened to ask T.H. Huxley if he traced his descent from apes back through his grandfather's side or his grandmother's? Huxley replied by saying he would rather be descended from an ape than from a man of intelligence who used his eloquence to obscure real issues. These exchanges were attempts at point scoring and the superficial part of the debate but they helped to harden theological and scientific positions and drive a wedge between the two disciplines in the public mind. Huxley introduced the word 'agnostic' to describe his own theistic position because did not know whether there was a God or not. Darwin seemed to favour this position in his later book, *The Descent of Man*. Nevertheless, he still struggled with Christianity. When his daughter Annie died, he said, 'In my most extreme fluctuations I have never been an atheist in the sense of denying the existence of a God'.

In 1925 the evolution debate became very important for biblical fundamentalism during the famous 'Scopes monkey trial' in Dayton, Tennessee. The trial was immortalised in the play *Inherit the Wind*, later made into a brilliant Spencer Tracy film. John Scopes was a high-school biology teacher arrested for teaching evolution against state law. The case was turned into a media circus before the court convicted Scopes. But the trial was a withering exposé of naïve theological thinking.

As evolutionary ideas became an accepted feature of the modern world-view, few areas of human activity escaped some kind of evolutionary analysis, often exaggerated or misapplied. Was there an evolutionary view of history for example? Were poor people caught up in an evolutionary purpose as they marched towards progress, casting off feudal and capitalist principles in favour of a communist society? Would the upshot be a new ruling class, a working class, loosed from its chains? Were they about to drive the bourgeoisie into extinction? A man, impeccably middle-class himself, was about to dedicate his life to such a belief.

Karl Marx (1818–1880)

In his formative years Karl Marx was exposed to both Judaism and Christianity. He was the son of a Jewish lawyer from the Rhineland town of Trier who had converted to Lutheranism. The culture he breathed was that of a town that had been Christian since the time of Constantine. It was a Christianity well laced with Judaism and Jewish rabbis were liberally sprinkled through his family tree. By the time he went to university he had ostensibly thrown off this middle-class influence though he was fond of boasting that his wife was the former Baroness von Westphalen. Somewhat ironically, his school leaving certificate described him as, 'Being of evangelical faith with a well grounded knowledge of Christianity but with a poor grasp of history!'

The world Marx was born into was still suffering acutely from the effects of the Industrial Revolution. Obviously, there were great benefits from industrialisation but the social injustices following were unspeakable. The means of production were owned (and still are) by a class dominated by a desire to secure maximum private gain, while the actual work done was performed by another class who were grievously underpaid for their labour. In this matrix, Marx raged against injustice. His was the same desire for social justice that had dominated the thinking of the great Eighth Century prophets of Israel. However, unable to see his kinship with the prophets, he dismissed religion as a device by which labour-slaves are kept in subjection to their masters. It is clearly wrong that the capital of a few people should dominate the lives of millions of workers but whether he should have been the one to write, 'Capital comes into the world soiled with mire from top to toe, and oozing blood from every pore', when Capitalism enabled him to lead the life of an eternal student, is questionable. Marx worked out a theory that history was a class struggle leading to an inevitable end, namely, the rise of workers and the establishment of a communist society without private property with the state controlling all means of production. A Communist Manifesto he shared with Engels, called upon the downtrodden to unite in revolution to overthrow the existing order and force in a new society:

Marx worked out a theory that history was a class struggle leading to an inevitable end...

Let the ruling classes tremble at the communist revolution. The proletarians have nothing to lose but their chains. They have a world to win. Working man of all countries, unite!
(Marx and Engels, *Manifesto of the Communist Party*; 1848)

The year of the Manifesto saw Marx expelled from Germany and he moved to London as a refugee. He used his time in student agitation and gathering material from the British Museum for a book. The book became *Das Kapital*. He lived in two squalid rooms in Soho, though he still managed to keep a maidservant. He and his wife buried three children from those rooms but he had an illegitimate son to one of his maidservants. Apart from very occasional journalism he never had a job but he was known to speculate on the stock market. He had strong opinions about most things but was fiercely intolerant of those who disagreed with him, on one occasion denouncing a friend as a 'pettifogging bourgeois Philistine'. In short, Marx was a riddle wrapped inside an enigma.

Revolution was in the air bringing with it fear and suspicion and in Paris communists shot six hostages, including four priests and the archbishop of Paris. This seemed to establish the anti-clerical nature of the revolution early on. Religion was the opium of the people and therefore it had to go in the flames about to burn. Marx believed when the revolution broke it would be in one of the industrialised nations where workers were being exploited the most severely. As everybody now knows, it eventually happened in the most backward country in Europe—Holy Russia.

The Orthodox Church of Russia with its long tradition of subservience to the state stretching back to Constantine and Constantinople in the East, was shell-shocked when the full might of the state was turned against it. Some eight thousand priests, monks and nuns were murdered when Marx's theories became practicalities within a communist state. Propaganda against all forms of religion began, the League of Militant Atheists was set up and exhibitions were held in the Museum of Atheism in Leningrad (now St Petersburg). Sometimes it was crude propaganda, as in Georgia where hungry children were told to pray to God for their daily bread. Three times they prayed and nothing came. Then they were told to pray to Lenin and, lo and behold, bread arrived by the truck load! Even the heroic cosmonaut, Yuri Gagarin, was reported as saying he saw no sign of a deity as he circled the world in space! Evangelical meetings were banned by order of the state and Orthodox churches were closed, many becoming museums. But faith was not to be removed by propaganda or state decree and congregations met secretly in woods and homes. Baptists and Pentecostalists even flourished under persecution and Tertullian's words from the third century rang true again—'The blood of the martyrs is the seed of the church'. Strangely, on the steps of churches used as museums, people went to offer their prayers. Religious artefacts continued to be made, even in state factories:

> *A. Galichansky, a worker of this factory has been welding in the firm's time crosses at 25 roubles a time. He also paints crosses with the state's paint in the required colour. Other workers have been casting little statues reflecting the likeness of a citizen called Christ, who, according to rumours, has been dead since AD 33.*
> **(Sunday Times; Feb 2nd, 1976)**

As with Darwin and evolution, so with Marx and socialism. A false either/or debate drove people into hostile camps leading to strenuous vilification. In fact, there is no reason at all why Christianity and Socialism should be incompatible as eighty priests declared in Chile when they expounded their views of Liberation Theology:

> *There are more evangelical values in socialism than there are in capitalism. The fact is that socialism offers new hope that man can be more complete and hence more evangelical; i.e. more conformed to Jesus Christ, who came to liberate us from any and every sort of bondage. Thus, it is necessary to destroy the prejudice and mistrust that exists between Christians and Marxists.*
> **(Eagleson, John and Knoll, Mary, *Christians and Socialism*; Orbis Books, 1975)**

Clearly Christianity by its very nature recognises the personal worth of individuals and is in sympathy with the under-dog and therefore would be in complete accord with Communism on that score. However, the Communist idea that Christianity is a reactionary force making people submissive and subject to capitalist bosses is absurd, as nearly every page of this book demonstrates. Yet this is the string upon which Communism has constantly harped. Where Christianity most clearly disagrees with Communism is in the Marxist faith that economic factors are the decisive features of history and that some *process of history* is leading to an inexorable progress towards a higher level of Society. The nightmares of the twentieth century, some of which we will consider soon, have shown such beliefs to be utter foolishness.

Existentialism

While Karl Marx was working out historical theories on the anvil of his own experience, two philosophers were moving philosophy away from its traditional standpoint of objective spectator to that of actively struggling in the world of experience and suffering. This 'experiential philosophy' has become known in the twentieth century as existentialism. Descartes had declared, 'I think therefore I am', the existentialist declared, 'I feel and I struggle, therefore I am'. It is a protest against the serenity of Mount Olympus and conventional morality. Man faces an unpredictable world and at any moment connections (like those in Hegel's philosophy of an Ideal World) can break down revealing public order as no more than a veneer. At any moment human beings can be brought face to face with pure contingency.

> *Let us now be on our guard against the hallowed philosophers' myth of a 'pure, will-less, painless, timeless knower', let us beware of the tentacles of such contradictory notions as 'pure reason', 'absolute knowledge', 'absolute intelligence'. All these concepts presuppose an eye such as no living being can imagine, an eye having no direction...*
> **(Nietzsche, F., *The Genealogy of Morals*; Anchor Books, 1956)**

Existentialism says people stand alone. You are. You exist. That is where philosophy must begin with your own existence and is therefore essentially subjective.

> *Let him do what he will, he philosophises not with the reason only, but with the will, with the feelings, with the flesh and with the bones, with the whole soul and the whole body.*
> **(Unamuno, M., *The Tragic Sense of Life*; Fontana, 1962)**

Whether we like it or not we have been dumped in the world to make sense of it as we will, creating value and determining our existence as we proceed. This is existentialism.

Soren Kierkegaard (1813–1855)

Kierkegaard was born in Copenhagen, the son of a prosperous Lutheran merchant who had prospered through hard work but never managed to throw off a guilt complex, which he passed on to his son. There were seven children in the family, all of whom suffered physical frailty and mental instability, possibly from in-breeding. Soren regarded himself as an *extraordinarus* from school days to the grave and he found it hard to make definite decisions. He was extremely fond of a young woman called Regina Olsen but after a long courtship he eventually broke off the engagement. He took ten years to finish a degree course after which he prepared for ordination in the Danish Lutheran Church but he was never ordained.

Instead he became a thinker and writer. At the heart of his thinking is the idea that there is a profound difference between time and eternity and between the finite and the infinite. Man and his world belong to the former, God to the latter. There is no continuity between the two, if a bridge is to be built it must come from God's side and this is what happened with the Incarnation of Christ. However, even here Christ comes incognito and can only be known through faith, which alone can transcend limits of time and space. The faith-man gambles his life on the existence of God. It is the premise motivating all his decisions.

> *Think of the captain of his ship at the instant when it has to come about. He will perhaps be able to say, 'I can either do this or that', but, unless he is a pretty poor navigator, he will be aware at the same time that the ship is all the while making its usual headway and therefore it is only an instant when it is indifferent whether he does this or that. So it is with man. If he forgets to take account of the headway, there comes at last an instant when there is no longer any question of an either/or, not because he has chosen but because he has neglected to choose, which is the equivalent to saying, because others have chosen for him, because he has lost himself.*
>
> **(Kierkegaard, S., translated by D. & L. Swansom, *Either/Or*; Anchor Books, 1959)**

Individuals matter, freedom matters, choices matter, others matter, facing up to one's own finiteness matters. The unique individual, who makes himself through his own choices is at the last expendable and it is this which gives life its tragedy and loneliness. The cosmos does not require our presence in the slightest—look around you, funerals every day! Yet man journeys on, a pilgrim pressing towards his inevitable end. Kierkegaard's own journey is one of faith and hope because believing in God is to long for his existence and to act as though he existed. To live by this longing gives an inner spring to action. The longing begets hope and hope begets faith. From this divine longing is born the sense of beauty and goodness.

On his death-bed this strange introverted man, refused the ministrations of the official church saying, 'Parsons are royal functionaries and royal functionaries are not related to Christianity'. According to a companion, he died with the assurance of grace, with 'a sublime and blessed splendour' of appearance. Kierkegaard may have been an *extraordinarus* but, with uncanny prescience, he foresaw the bankruptcy towards which Europe was heading with a full head of steam. The moral order was breaking down and standing at a profound junction in history, with the sparks flying upward, Kierkegaard saw it as his destiny to sound a cry of alarm. Sadly, his voice drifted into an empty wilderness.

Friedrich Nietzsche (1844–1900)

Nietzsche was another existentialist but, unlike Kierkegaard, his thought led him to atheism and, some believe, to the kind of philosophy preparing a way for the rise of the Nazis during the 1930s. Like Kierkegaard he came from a Lutheran family, the son and grandson of Lutheran ministers. He was christened Friedrech Wilhelm after the King of Prussia but he dropped the Wilhelm deliberately, possibly because the king went mad. Nietzsche himself was to lose his reason when he was forty-five.

Even though he suffered from poor eyesight and migraines, he was a brilliant student and was appointed Professor of Classical Philology at the University of Basle at the age of twenty-four. He left the University briefly to serve as a medical orderly in the Franco-Prussian war but returned to teach until ill health forced him into permanent retirement with a small pension. He was greatly influenced by Darwin's theories of evolution, by the philosophy of Schopenhauer and by his friendship with the composer Richard Wagner, (later Wagner's hatred of the French and the Jews drove a wedge between them). Nietzsche had the notion that traditional values, represented by Christianity, no longer held any power to shape the lives of individuals. The impotence of Christianity he summed up in the phrase, 'God is dead'. He offered mankind a bleak nihilism, a belief in nothing, an extreme scepticism and a denial of value. His alternative was to hold aloft a tragic hero who affirms life in the face of meaninglessness. The masses might still cling to traditional crutches but the tragic hero, the *Superman*, replaces gentleness and kindness (a slave morality) with independent and highly individualistic courage. Concentrating on the world as it is now, *Superman* disdains rewards in the next world to do battle with the suffering and pain that accompany present existence. He creates his own values and affirms a 'master morality' liberating him from the values of the past. Others who had taken up this lonely superman role in previous stages of history included Socrates, Jesus Christ, Michelangelo, Shakespeare and Napoleon.

It has been argued that Nietzsche's *Superman* provides the philosophical idea taken up by dictators like Hitler, Stalin and Mao Tse-Tung. After all, if you accept the benign indifference of creation and substitute men who create their own morality the green light is on for gas-chambers, gulags and ethnic cleansing. Others say he has been much misrepresented and that his sister did him a disservice by releasing unedited notes of his, which unlike his other work, had not been polished for publication. Nietzsche spent the last eleven years of his life in asylums or in his family's care. He wrote nothing and was incapable of conversation. But his earlier work lived on and he was the first to pose most cogently implications to be drawn from Darwin's evolutionary theories. If Darwin's new view of evolved man had destroyed the traditional Christian view of human kind where was the place for Christian morality?

Sigmund Freud (1856–1939)

Another seminal thinker affected by Darwin was Sigmund Freud. An Austrian physician and the founder of psychoanalysis, he opened new windows into the understanding of human personality. Like Marx, his family was Jewish. When he was three years old the family had to flee their home in Freiberg, Moravia because of anti-Semitic riots. They moved to Vienna where Freud went to school and became fascinated by Darwin and the developing science of the day.

A brilliant student, he began his medical education when he was seventeen and specialised early in the central nervous system and psychiatry. He observed the technique of the French neurologist Jean Charcate and was impressed with the apparent success of his treatments. When he married he needed an income and so started his own practice, where he closely observed his patients and began to understand there were unconscious forces working in people that sometimes surfaced in physical ways often inducing physical illness. Alfred Hitchcock popularised Freud's theories in films like *Marnie*. Marnie is a young woman who suffers from chronic hysteria, revealed in abnormal reactions to thunder, the colour red and sexual advances. During a painful investigation into her repressed childhood a psychiatrist uses free-association of ideas to dig deep into her unconscious mind, she eventually realises that her behaviour has its origins in her traumatic childhood. The story unfolds. Marnie's mother, a prostitute, had savagely beaten a client to death when he had transferred his sexual interest to the child. This murder was witnessed by the child and the horrors of the event including, for Hollywood effect, thunder and much blood, were so dreadful they were repressed in Marnie's unconscious mind. This 'self protection' was so successful that to all intents and purposes she forgot the incident. But in sleep and relaxed conditions the recollection does seep back into the memory. Once the reason for Marnie's irrational behaviour is known and faced up to it ceases to effect her life. The ending is neat, it includes a romantic interest between patient and doctor and everybody lives happily ever after. Freud's cases are never as neat as that but the film does illustrate some of his ideas, namely — (i) childhood trauma affects adult life, (ii) it is usually of a sexual nature and (iii) it often involves parents.

In 1897 Freud started to analyse himself (some analysts consider this impossible) and this work was to offer him a solution to child sexuality. Many of his patients claimed they had been sexually seduced by one of their parents. Freud came to believe this was fantasy rather than fact. In other words, incestuous impulses do arise and might sometimes be fulfilled by parents. But much more likely is a kind of wishful desire a child has to sleep with a parent of the opposite sex. This concept, we now know as the *Oedipus Complex*, began to take form. Also in 1897, Freud began to stress the importance of dreams in finding a way into a patient's mind. Dreams were the 'royal road' into the unconscious mind, where deep layers of repressed memory lay untouched by conscious thought. In relaxed conditions, like sleep or hypnosis, these repressed memories could leak into the conscious mind giving a glimpse of what lies beneath. Thus, the mind is like an iceberg with only a small part accessible but with far greater areas hidden below. This is the theory explored in his book, *Interpretation of Dreams*, published in 1900.

About two years after *Dreams* the Vienna Psycho-Analytical Society was formed. Freud invited four young men to join him on Wednesdays to discuss psychological matters. They turned into casual but regular meetings and by 1908 twenty-two earnest young men were thrashing out ideas. Freud was seeking to put his own ideas through the filter of other lively minds in an effort to arrive at an agreement of basic psychological concepts everybody could adhere to. This did not prove possible and prolonged quarrels led to defections from the Society and to the forming of other schools. Adler and Jung later became almost as famous as Freud himself. Towards the end of his life Freud began to speculate philosophically about the nature of man, religion and God, much to the displeasure of those who said his erudition in psychology did not qualify him for philosophy. To Freud belief in an after-life seemed unlikely and he was once described as a 'cheerful pessimist'. Later, when the Nazis burst into his Jewish home he became more of a pessimistic realist.

As Darwin's evolution challenged contemporary Judeo-Christian belief, so Freud challenged religions by intimating that human beings were less in control of their minds than they thought. He contended that conscience and action arose from within people rather than from God. Therefore, religion was illusory and God was a device of the mind conjured up to cope with inner tension. 'The face smiling down on us in the cradle, was magnified to infinity to smile down on us from heaven'.

In 1938, Freud's life ended as it began, with flight from anti-Semitism. Germany annexed Austria and he escaped with his family to England. He was by this time very ill, stricken with cancer of the jaw, exacerbated by heavy smoking. When he died his place as an original thinker was assured even though his basic concepts were not as immutable as he claimed. Nevertheless, his work radically altered views about human nature and his main ideas have stood the test of time.

Carl Gustav Jung (1875–1961)

The Swiss psychologist Jung was part of the inner circle that worked closely with Freud but he broke with him to develop his own work. He was a poor pastor's son who knew what it was to be isolated as a child because of his poverty. It has been suggested that an incident in his childhood did much to direct him to a life in psychiatry. He was knocked down by a schoolchild and he banged his head on a curbstone. He subsequently disliked school and so fainting fits got him away from school and the source of his pain. He only returned because of the distress he was causing to his family. So Jung had a young and personal awareness of the way neurosis can affect physical illness.

Jung coined words like 'extrovert', 'introvert', 'persona' and 'archetype', now part of the English language. Like Freud, he used word association and dream interpretation to get into the unconscious mind. Unlike Freud, he had a sympathetic interest in religion and on journeys around the world he was astonished to discover religious motifs shared by people of all races. He worked out the conclusion that there was a common substratum in human beings that transcends differences of culture and development. He saw it as a 'collective unconscious' providing symbols, myths and images, that are a common fabric of all religions. It led him to believe man possesses a natural religious function, as much a motivating force for human action as the sexuality central to Freud's thinking. Once asked in public if he believed in God, Jung replied, 'I don't believe. I know'. Above the door of his house he carved the words, 'Called or not called, God will be present'.

17 Sects

Mormons	254
Joseph Smith	254
Brigham Young	255
Christian Science	256
Mary Baker Eddy	256
The Baha'is	257
Baha Allah	257
Jehovah's Witnesses	259
Charles Taze Russell	259

'Times are changing', Adam is reputed to have said to Eve as they left the Garden of Eden. So it has always been. The history of religion is one of change and reformation as movements spring up, that try to restore a primitive purity to a faith fossilised in tradition and practice. Spurgeon realised this when he said, 'Every generation needs re-generation'. More recently John Stott wrote:

> *Every church should be engaged in continuous self-reformation, scrutinising its traditions in the light of Scripture and where necessary modifying them.*

But where does reformation end? Sometimes in the process of reformation, changes take place which are so radical, so different to the norm, they can no longer be regarded as branches from the old tree. Instead they become new religions, or sects, sub-divisions of mainstream belief disapproved of by the orthodox. The nineteenth century gave birth to several of these sects.

The Mormons

Mormonism, dating back to 1830, stems from Christianity and was fundamentally a protest against a faith in need of restoration. It was claimed that a new revelation restored that purity and came through a man called Joseph Smith.

Joseph Smith (1805–1844)

Smith was born in Sharon, Vermont. His background was poor but pious and from the age of fourteen he reported seeing visions, which called him to revive the Christian religion. Further claims recount how he was led by an angel to a collection of golden plates containing a narrative written in hieroglyphic script. This he was miraculously able to translate. Smith claimed *The Book of Mormon* to be a record of the religion of ancient peoples of North America. In 1830 the Church of Jesus Christ of Latter Day Saints was formed and quickly attracted a following. It also stirred up violent opposition especially against Smith himself. The headquarters of the movement were set up in Illinois where the Mormons began to practice polygamy stirring up opposition even more. Smith is believed to have had about thirty wives but he acknowledged only one. Unpopular though he was, he declared his candidature for the United States Presidency. He got thrown into jail instead to face a charge of treason and conspiracy. Assurance of safe custody proved to be unfounded when, on the night of June 27th, 1844, a mob broke into the jail and murdered Joseph and his brother Hyrum. The main group of Mormons then moved towards Utah where they settled. Joseph Smith's son, Joseph III, was the official leader of the reorganised church but Brigham Young was elected acting president of the Mormons.

Brigham Young (1801–1877)

Young was also born in Vermont and had very little formal schooling. He was a Methodist but was drawn into the new fellowship by a brother of Joseph Smith's and before long was one of the new movement's leading lights. He spent time in England where he worked with a Mormon mission in Liverpool and arranged the emigration of 70,000 converts to America.

The antipathy, which had led to the murder of Joseph Smith, continued and in 1846 Brigham Young organised the migration of five thousand Mormons across the Rocky Mountains and Plains to the Great Salt Lake Valley. There Young founded Salt Lake City and was formally elected head of the Mormon Church. The region prospered and the US Congress officially made Young the governor of the territory of Utah. By 1852 he had publicly endorsed the doctrine of polygamy and this so upset non-Mormons in the region that his appointment was terminated. Young, however, refused to accept the decision and for a time armed rebellion was threatened, a situation averted largely through Young's statesmanship. No longer governor, he continued to exert great influence over affairs in Utah even though he was indicted but not convicted on polygamy charges. He had at least twenty-seven wives and fifty-seven children. Seventeen wives survived him when he died in 1877.

Mormons regard their church as the one true and living church on earth, a belief which underpins their desire to evangelise the world and win adherents from more orthodox churches. They differ from mainstream Christianity in believing the Trinity to be three separate individuals and they believe in a prenatal existence for human souls. They also hold that if they fulfil God's commandments fully they will attain the status of godhood in future lives. Leadership of the church is by laypeople and worship is simple with prayers, hymns and a Lord's Supper and sermons delivered by lay members. Every member is expected to be a missionary and they organise a large welfare programme for the needy. Tea, coffee, alcohol and tobacco are prohibited. The church supports temples, a Brigham Young University and the world famous Mormon Tabernacle Choir. In modern times the polygamy issue has been played down and most Mormons now have only one spouse.

Christian Science

Christian science is based on the life of Christ but emphasises the healings mentioned in the Gospels. The founder of the movement was Mary Baker Eddy.

Mary Baker Eddy (1821–1910)

She was born in New Hampshire in the United States and was mainly educated at home by her brother. The Bible was an important part of that education and she studied it all her life. She married at twenty-two but was widowed shortly afterwards when her husband died of yellow fever, leaving her with a baby son. The child's welfare was left largely to members of the family rather than to Mary herself. A second marriage was to a dentist and lasted for twenty years before ending in divorce. Husband number three followed four years later, he was Asa Eddy, a follower of the new religion.

In middle-age, Mary suffered from severe injuries after a fall and when she recovered quickly the recovery was attributed to the operation of God's power through spiritual law. She believed she had discovered the power of Jesus to heal and thought it could be applied to all people. She taught that prayer could unlock spiritual resources and was more powerful than conventional medicine, hence the publication of her textbook, *Science and Health*. Two years after founding a church she moved to Boston where membership grew quickly and led to extensions and the forming of new churches. By the time of her death there were 1,190 churches and societies in the United States and others overseas. The management of the church was left in the hands of a board of directors who govern according to guidelines in Eddy's book, *Manual of the Mother Church*.

Freud and Jung would probably have had a field-day if Mary Eddy had ever been on their consultation couches. She was an hysterical child who often had convulsions, leaving the family in no doubt that death would come any day. But she always recovered rapidly from her spasms and her doctor sometimes impatiently diagnosed 'hysteria mingled with bad temper'. He occasionally treated her by mesmerism or mental suggestion, much in vogue in New England, and such treatment probably coloured her later beliefs. The healing work of a man called Phineas Quimby interested her greatly and he treated her on several occasions—though she later accused him of mesmerism. After forming her own church she had a confident ease on the rostrum, contrary to her behaviour in earlier life, but she could still be sharp and usually got annoyed when people asked her why she used eye-glasses instead of overcoming her deficient sight with the power of her mind. She got involved in several long and expensive lawsuits, that brought discredit on the church she had founded and many members left as a result. There was also some internal bickering before she moved her church from Lynn to Boston in 1822.

Yet, despite all Mary Eddy's oddities, Christian Science became firmly established as a Christian sect and the movement still has members counted in millions.

The Baha'is

The Baha'i faith is not really a sect but the youngest of the world's independent religions. It is the successor to Babism, named after Bab—martyred in 1850 by the Persians who massacred some 20,000 of his followers. Bab had foretold the appearance of a divine figure soon to come and in 1863, in Baghdad, Baha Allah declared himself to be that figure.

Baha Allah (1817–1892)

Baha'is regard Baha as the most recent in the line of messengers of God who stretch back to the beginning of time and include Abraham,

Baha'is have a world headquarters on the slopes of Mount Carmel.

Moses, Buddha, Zoroaster, Christ and Muhammed. He strove to establish a religion free of nationalism and narrow culture, universal in its appeal. His teaching called for a moral revolution which would abolish injustice and bring relief for the underprivileged. 'Humanity is one' he said, 'and the time has come to inaugurate one global society'. Barriers of race, class, creed and nation will have to give way to a universal civilisation. Baha'is work to make that dream a reality and at the present time form a world-wide community of some six million adherents. Other aims include equality of the sexes, universal education and an international language. They have a core of sacred literature, which includes the writings of Bab, Baha Allah and his son Abd al-Baha. There is no other institutional authority but wherever nine or more Baha'is meet a 'spiritual assembly' may be formed. Baha'is have a world headquarters on the slopes of Mount Carmel in Israel where there is also a shrine to Bab.

Universal brotherhood is the theme of Baha'is but that has not prevented them being at the receiving end of much persecution since the martyrdom of Bab, especially in Iran since the formation of the Islamic Republic of Iran in 1979. Meetings for the spiritual and moral education of Baha'i children have been a particular source of irritation for Islamic fundamentalists in Iran.

Jehovah's Witnesses

Another sect derived from Christianity is that of the Jehovah's Witnesses whose members believe in the second coming of Christ and claim to be the guardians of primitive Christianity. The sect was founded in 1872 in Pennsylvania by an American clergyman, Charles Taze Russell.

Charles Taze Russell (1852–1916)

Russell rejected orthodox Protestantism believing he had been given a special revelation. When only twenty he organised a Bible study group and published a book stating that Christ was about to return, albeit invisibly. The year was to be 1874 and then in 1914 the world would end. He gathered followers, established a church in Pittsburgh and began publishing *Watchtower*, which sets out his views. Initially called Russellites, congregations sprang up and became filled with missionary zeal, each witness regarded himself as a minister. Selective in Bible teaching, they adopted the familiar policy of door-step evangelism and they also hold services in Kingdom Halls.

Historically, witnesses have testified their allegiance to Christ by refusing to salute any flag, refusing to exercise their right to vote, refusing to perform military service and refusing to accept blood transfusions, claiming that all are contrary to biblical teaching. Conflicts with authorities have resulted from their actions especially when they have refused blood transfusions for their children. They have been lampooned for Russell's predictions about the end of the world. 'Not quite the conflagration I'd expected', says a character from *Beyond the Fringe*, when a group gathered on a mountain to witness the end of the world. Nevertheless, Russell's views have not disappeared and some 3.8 million still believe in the imminent return of Christ who will defeat the forces of evil at the last battle of Armageddon. After this decisive battle Christ will reign on earth for a thousand years, during which time the dead will rise again and everybody will have a second chance to achieve salvation. At the close of this thousand years evil will be finally destroyed.

Russell was involved in several scandals during his life, his wife left him in 1897 and obtained a legal separation in 1906. He advertised so-called 'miracle wheat' in his magazine, to be sold for church funds but the *Brooklyn Eagle* challenged the validity of the product and

Russell sued for libel. He lost the case. He also lost a libel case against the Reverend J.J. Ross who had attacked his doctrines and questioned his scholarship. During this case he committed perjury by asserting under oath that he knew Greek but then could not name Greek letters when asked to do so in court. Nevertheless, his reputation survived the bruising and his bizarre biblical interpretation has lived on.

18 The World at War

Geoffrey Studdert Kennedy	263
Edith Cavell	267
Albert Schweitzer	268
Martin Buber	271
Theodor Herzl	272
Zionism	273
Hitler	273
Kindertransport	275
Dietrich Bonhoeffer	276
The Holocaust (Shoah)	277
David Ben-Gurion	278
Frank Buchman	279
Facing Adversity	280
Gladys Aylward	281
Kagawa	283
Russian Communism	284
Valeri Barinov	285
Irina Ratushinskaya	287
Mother Teresa	289
Second Vatican Council	292
Billy Graham	292
Martin Luther King	294
Modern Martyrs	297

The European Renaissance of the fourteenth and fifteenth centuries pushed civilisation in a direction destined to affect the world for good and evil. From 1300 we can trace an incredible stream of invention and skill quite mind-blowing in its achievement. On the ethical and spiritual side however, there has been no corresponding progress. Consequently, the possibility of a golden future continues to be blighted by our inability to rub along with our neighbours, whether they be next door or in the next country. Peace and stability continue to elude us.

It might have seemed during the reign of Britain's Queen Victoria (1837–1901) that the stability needed for the world was being provided by the British Empire. Social inequalities there were but Britain was the most powerful industrial and military nation in the world. With Napoleon defeated Britain's position of strength seemed unassailable. Germany was not united into a nation, Russia looked only eastwards, China was weak and confused and the United States was obsessed by the move westwards at the expense of the Red Indians. India, Australia, New Zealand, Canada, most of Africa and much of the West Indies were British. A necklace of naval bases stretched around the world ensuring that Britain ruled the waves and maintained a stranglehold on the sea routes of the world. The Industrial Revolution increased the nation's power and wealth and Britain developed into the workshop of the world and its banker as well. Queen Victoria ruled over more people than any ruler ever before. It was a wide variety of people, speaking more languages and practising more religions than could be imagined. One in every five of the world's population owed allegiance to her and the British Empire. Coloured red on the map it covered a quarter of the surface of the earth. Unchallenged by others, the world enjoyed something of a British peace and the confidence of Mr Birling in J.B. Priestley's, *An Inspector Calls*, would have been shared by many.

> *Look at the progress we are making. In a year or two we'll have aeroplanes that will be able to go anywhere. And look at the way the automobile is making headway—bigger, faster all the time. And then ships. Why a friend of mine went over this new liner last week— the Titanic—she sails next week—forty-six thousand, eight hundred tons—New York in five days and every luxury—and unsinkable, absolutely unsinkable. That's what you've got to keep your eye on, facts like that, progress like that.*

Few would have understood the warning of the Inspector:

We don't live alone. We are members of one body. We are responsible for each other. And I tell you that the time will soon come when, if men will not learn that lesson, then they will be taught it in fire and blood and anguish.

When a pistol shot rang out in the streets of Sarejevo in the summer of 1914, killing Archduke Ferdinand, heir to the throne of the Austro-Hungarian Empire, the fire, the blood and the anguish began in earnest. The world was about to experience a war for which there was no precedent, and Britain, whose wars had been maritime in character for centuries, was forced to conscript an enormous army for service in all parts of the world. As the impetus of the war ground to a halt in the mud of Flanders a new chaplain arrived in France during the bitter winter of 1915–1916. Soldiers called him Woodbine Willie.

G.A. Studdert Kennedy M.C. (1883–1929)

It was difficult to be a successful chaplain in the horrors of that Great War. When asked by a new chaplain how best he should work, Kennedy said, 'Live with the men; go everywhere they go. Make up your mind you will share all their risks and more if you can do any good. The line is the key to the whole business. Work in the very front, and they will listen to you; but if you stay behind, you're wasting your time. Men will forgive you anything but lack of courage and devotion.' Asked about spiritual work he said, 'There is very little; it is all muddled and mixed. Take a box of fags in your haversack and a great deal of love in your heart and go up to them; laugh with them, joke with them. You can pray with them sometimes; but pray for them always'. The chaplain asking the questions was T.B. Hardy MC, DSO, VC, whose war record ends briefly:

Died of wounds (gunshot) received in action.

Kennedy was born in the slums of Quarry Hill in Leeds to an Anglican vicar and his second wife. His father's background was Irish though he served St Mary's Church in Leeds for thirty-seven years. He was a bright lad, passionate, eloquent and sincere. He was undisciplined about small matters and cared little for money or things, which he often gave away. After curateships in Rugby and Leeds he was offered a job at St Paul's, Worcester and said to his wife, 'St Paul's has the smallest income and the poorest people—go and look at the house, and if you think you can manage it I will accept'. At Worcester his services became intense experiences during which his preaching riveted growing congregations and led to dozens of supplicants seeking his help and advice. Three months after his arrival at Worcester the First World War began. By the autumn a hundred thousand Russian dead sank into the ooze of the Pripet Marshes. One hundred and twenty thousand Germans died alongside the old British regular army after the battle of Ypres. Opposing armies dug themselves into trenches from the Channel to the Alps. By Christmas 1915, Kennedy was in a little French village leading four hundred troops in the carol 'O Come All Ye Faithful'. He wrote to his church in Worcester, 'Then the glorious point came—I went to a shed in the farmyard and the communicants came to me. There were not many; but they meant it. No lights, no ritual, nothing to help but the rain and the far-off roll of the guns, and Christ was born in a cattle shed on Christmas Day'.

This experience was in sharp contrast to one in Rouen where three hundred men stood in a queue, mere lads waiting their turn with a prostitute, before going West. Such extremes of life needed more than Woodbines and geniality to reach men living on borrowed time but Studdert Kennedy did it with his mix of bonhomie and intense faith. He sang 'Mother Machrie' for the sons, 'Little Grey Home in the West' for the husbands, 'The Sunshine of Your Smile' for the lovers and he wrote home for the soldiers. Before the trains pulled out from the station heading for the front, he walked down the train distributing Woodbines from one haversack and New Testaments from another.

As the war went on and he moved to the front-line himself, he wrote back home as padre with the 157th Brigade of the 46th Division. He wrote *Rough Rhymes*, often in dialect, to express the horrors they were living through:

> *We'll soon ave ye tucked in bed, lad,*
> *'Opes ye gets to my old ward*
> *No more war for you, my 'earty*
> *This'll get ye well away,*
> *Twelve good months in dear old Blighty,*
> *Twelve good months if you're a day,*
> *MO's got a bit of something*
> *What'll stop that blasted pain.*
> *'Ere's a rotten bit of ground mate,*
> *Lift up 'igher up again,*
> *Wish 'e'd stop his blasted shellin'*

Makes it rotten for the lad
When a feller's been and got it
It affec's 'im twice as bad.
Ow's it goin' now then sonny?
'Ere's that narrow bit o' trench,
Careful mate, there's some dead Jerries,
Lawd Almighty, what a stench!
'Ere we are now, stretcher-case boys
Bring him aht a cup o' tea!
Inasmuch as ye have done it
Ye have done it unto me.

The waste of war affected Kennedy deeply and made him question much about his own faith. Before the summer battle on the Somme in 1916, Geoffrey noticed a strong young corporal as he offered him communion with the words, 'Preserve thy body and soul unto everlasting life'. Three days later on one of his post-battle wanderings, he found the corporal's mutilated body in a shell-hole. Faced with such horrors

The waste of war affected Kennedy deeply.

he identified ever closer with the ordinary man, part of that great tide of restless, vigorous life that swept past the doors of churches finding outlets for their energies in a thousand other ways. He longed to capture the bravery and courage of the ordinary Tommy and harness it in the service of Christ who had been locked away in stained-glass windows.

> *I was crucified in Cambrai*
> *And again outside Bapaume;*
> *I was scourged for miles along the Albert Road,*
> *I was driven pierced and bleeding*
> *With a million maggots feeding*
> *On the body that I carried as my load.*
>
> *Yet my heart was still unbroken*
> *And my hope was still unquenched,*
> *Till I bore my cross to Paris through the crowd*
> *Soldiers pierced me on the Aisne,*
> *But twas by the river Seine,*
> *That the statesmen brake my legs and made my shroud.*
>
> *There they wrapped my mangled body*
> *In fine linen of fair words,*
> *With the perfume of a sweetly scented lie,*
> *And they laid it in the tomb*
> *of a golden-mirrored room,*
> *Mid the many fountained garden of Versailles.*

The years after the war were difficult years for the church. The whole world was reeling in the aftermath of the slaughter, men were tired of discipline and angry and raw from the carnage they had been a part of. But they listened to Studdert Kennedy who had been where they had been, was as full of rage as they were, yet, who seemed to know, really know, what they needed. He was as hungry as anybody but he knew where to find bread. This insignificant looking man with big eyes and huge dog-collar had recognised through all the blood-letting, that God was involved with the suffering of mankind. Tubby Clayton, the founder of Toc H paid tribute to the padres of the First World War with these words:

> *They were true priests, true men. The church scarce knew she had them. Their names are now forgotten; but many hands welcomed them into Paradise.*

Prominent amongst them was Woodbine Willie.

Edith Cavell (1865–1915)

Casualties in the First World War were counted in millions and the waste of human life was appalling. Woodbine Willie summarised it in a poem.

> *Waste of Muscle, waste of Brain,*
> *Waste of Patience, waste of Pain,*
> *Waste of Manhood, waste of Health,*
> *Waste of Beauty, waste of Wealth,*
> *Waste of Blood and waste of Tears,*
> *Waste of Youth's most precious years,*
> *Waste of ways the saints have trod,*
> *Waste of Glory, waste of God,*
> *War!*

Not all was waste of manhood, women suffered too and amongst the most senseless of deaths was that of Edith Cavell.

The daughter of a vicar, she spent her earliest years in Norfolk but when she was twenty-two she inherited a small legacy and spent it travelling through the Rhineland. She loved Bavaria and helped fund a Free Hospital there. She worked as a teacher and governess in Essex and Norfolk before moving to Brussels, just as Charlotte Brontë (another clergyman's daughter) had done fifty years previously. When her father became ill she returned to Norfolk, decided to train as a nurse and she worked in hospitals in London, Manchester and Maidstone where she was awarded a silver medal for 'loving services' to the people during a typhoid epidemic. Yet she had grown fond of Brussels and returned to take on the responsibility of converting a private hospital in Ixelles into a teaching hospital, a task for which she won widespread recognition.

She was on holiday in Norfolk during the summer of 1914 when Germany started to mobilise for war but she immediately returned to Brussels. Three days later German troops crossed the Belgian frontier and Britain declared war on the invader. Edith's sense of Christian service had prompted her return to Brussels and it was that which induced her to stay when German troops entered the Belgian capital. Proud of nursing traditions the nurses prepared to nurse sick and wounded of all sides but fate intervened and in the winter of 1914 two seriously wounded soldiers, disguised as civilians, arrived at the hospital and sought the matron's help. She nursed them back to health before sending them by secret couriers to the frontier with neutral Holland. It was the beginning of a succession of hundreds of allied soldiers who were treated and sent back to Britain via Holland. She knew it was only a matter of time before they would be discovered and on August 5th 1915, she was arrested and imprisoned. She never lost her composure during imprisonment and like others before read Thomas à Kempis' *Imitation of Christ*. On October 11th she learned that she was to be executed by firing-squad. Diplomats made strenuous efforts to have the judgement overturned but she herself refused to beg for mercy. Her final message was to her English chaplain, the Reverend Stirling Graham, 'Standing as I do in view of God and Eternity, I realise that patriotism is not enough. I must have no hatred or bitterness towards anyone'. Next morning she was shot dead.

Great crowds attended her memorial service at Westminster Abbey and a statue of her was erected in St Martin's Place, Trafalgar Square. The bishop of London declared that her 'cold blooded murder' was one of the greatest crimes in history.

Albert Schweitzer (1875–1965)

Nineteenth-century children of the parsonage, Jews and Christians, have featured prominently in our faith odyssey. Marx, Nietzsche, Kierkegaard, Jung, Studdert-Kennedy and Edith Cavell were all raised in clergy homes. Albert Schweitzer was yet another. He was a man so gifted he could have achieved distinction in almost any avenue of life. He was born in Alsace, in the borderland between Germany and France, a confused no-man's land where it was difficult to determine whether people were German or French. In 1875, Alsace was a district of farms and vineyards where people bought their food direct from farmers who sold their wares in local markets. Albert's father raised him in a frugal life-style customary in Protestant homes there. Only three years before Albert's birth, Alsace and Lorraine had been taken from France as part settlement of the Franco-Prussian War. Being bilingual and international in outlook therefore went with the territory.

Schweitzer's childhood was studded with incidents, which seemed to do much to form his character. On one occasion he saw a wretched old horse being cruelly treated by two men as it was dragged towards the local glue factory. It affected him deeply. On another occasion he became aware of cruelty deep within himself when he was given the job of controlling the family dog Phylax, who always became excited when uniformed postmen arrived at the house. Schweitzer controlled the dog with a whip, though he knew a stroke of the dog's head would have been just as effective. He was filled with remorse when the dog snuggled close to him after the incident. Once he was out shooting birds with friends when a distant church bell rang out for lent and the bell seemed to compel him to shout and wave until the startled birds had flown off.

> *...ever since, when the Passiontide bell rings out to the leafless trees and the sunshine, I reflect with a rush of grateful emotion how on that day their music drove deep into my heart the commandment: 'Thou shalt not kill'.*
> **(Schweitzer, *Memoirs of Childhood and Youth*; MacMillan, New York, 1961)**

Albert Schweitzer was a brilliant student who prepared himself for careers in music and the church. He was an organist and organ builder, as well as a great interpreter of Johann Sebastian Bach. He was also a theologian and philosopher, which led him to preaching, teaching and writing. He was ordained curate of the Church of St Nicholas in Strasbourg and he continued his studies there, the Sorbonne in Paris and the University of Berlin. When he turned to writing he wrote a masterpiece with the book *Johann Sebastian Bach* and a theological bombshell with *The Quest of the Historical Jesus*. His reputation in both music and theology were assured and the world was ready to award him all its accolades.

Then, Schweitzer did an about turn. In 1905, aged thirty, he decided to study medicine and surgery at the University of Strasbourg. He made his intentions clear—he was going to leave Europe and build a hospital in Africa. This would be his life's work. He was answering some call deep within, which made him want to do something positive to repay all the benefits he had received. He was about to turn his back on the academic life and make his own life his argument. He would advocate the things he believed in terms of the life he lived and the things he did. Not surprisingly, his family was appalled that their brilliant son should be about to bury himself in the jungle. For his part, Schweitzer was surprised that they should chide him for taking Jesus' words seriously.

> *The more I understood Jesus, the more I was impressed by the way he combined faith and simple common sense. The more I studied the history of Christianity, the more I realised the extent of the errors and disagreements which started because men from the first generation to this day played up faith and piety at the expense of reason and so put asunder what God had joined harmoniously'.*
> **(*Reverence for Life, Sermons of Schweitzer*; Harper Row, New York, 1969)**

It is clear Schweitzer saw Christianity as a liberation movement and he grew dissatisfied with the way western civilisation was using large sections of the human-race as raw material, rather than regarding them as children of God. He wrote, 'The demoralisation of the individual is in full swing'.

As Albert planned his future, so his friendship with a young Jewish woman called Helene Bresslau blossomed. She trained to be a nurse so that she could usefully accompany him to Africa. Amazingly, when he had completed his medical training, the Paris Missionary Society rejected his application to serve in Africa because they believed his religious beliefs to be too liberal. He applied again later having raised enough money to cover the expenses of Helen, himself and hospital running costs for two years. On Good Friday, 1913, the town of Gunsbach turned out in force to say farewell at the railway station. With tears in his eyes Schweitzer was off to Lamborene in French Equatorial Africa.

With indefatigable energy he set up his hospital and cared for two thousand patients in the first year. But the war was reaching its bloody hand into Africa and, in 1917–1918, Schweitzer found himself interned in France as a German national. When he returned to Lamborene his hospital was in ruins and needed rebuilding and re-equipping. Characteristically, he set to with zest and was soon back to treating thousands every year, including hundreds of lepers. He funded much of the work with money raised through organ recitals, which involved return visits to Europe. Sometimes he was criticised for his idiosyncratic and paternal attitude to the management of his hospital but for the most part he was revered as a modern saint, a twentieth-century Francis of Assisi who worked out his philosophy of reverence for life in the toughest of environments. In his last years he was much honoured and was awarded the Nobel Peace Prize in 1952. As musician, ethical philosopher and humanitarian he excelled and was acclaimed but his greatest epitaph is in an African prayer:

> *We thank God that he sent Dr Schweitzer*
> *to us and that he was our good shepherd who*
> *gave his life for us, stayed with us, was*
> *buried in our soil and under our palm trees.*

Martin Buber (1878-1965)

Albert Schweitzer's deep sensitivity for life was shared by a Jew called Martin Buber. The two men exchanged letters for many years and Buber was welcomed by many Christian friends who shared his love and knowledge of both Old and New Testaments. He did not accept Jesus as a Messiah because he thought God revealed himself through people rather than in people and held, therefore, that each person had a part to play in redeeming the world. Neither did he believe in Zionism, which advocated a homeland for the Jews. He looked for a Zionism of inner renewal, which welcomed both Jews and Christians.

> *...the idea of a Jewish State with flag and canon and so forth, I will have nothing to do with—not even in my dreams.*
> (***Martin Buber***, Beck and Weiland; 1968)

Buber was of the existentialist school who, in his best known work, I and Thou, distinguished between mutual relationships of an *I/Thou* nature and indirect relationships of the I/It variety. He stressed the worth of each individual and believed that, in religious matters, dialogue between equals was the way to brotherhood rather than in the monologue of stated creeds. Dialogue, he believed to be the essence of biblical Judaism.

Martin Buber was professor of Jewish religion and ethics from 1923-1933 and then of the history of religions from 1933-1938 at Frankfurt University. He was forced out of Germany by the Nazis, went to Israel and became a professor at the Hebrew University. He was leader of the Ichud, an association seeking Jewish-Arab reconciliation and supported the renewal of Hasidism, a mystical movement, which had swept through east European Jewry in the eighteenth and nineteenth centuries. He gained many peace awards in later life and was a consultant to Kibbutz members offering guidance with community problems. Like Schweitzer, Buber often found himself in a minority of one but his vision never wavered.

> *Our voice calls the Jewish people...to be always loyal to the Spirit and not revert to dogma.*
> (Buber, Martin, ***Between Man and Man***; MacMillan, New York, 1965)

Not everybody shared Buber's view of an all embracing, spiritual Zionism. Others despaired of ever finding equality for Jews and dreamed of a future political Zionism cast in their biblical homeland of Palestine.

Theodor Herzl (1860–1904)

Herzl was a playwright who also worked for the New Free Press in Vienna where he studied law. He was appointed Paris correspondent in 1891 and was close at hand to witness waves of violent anti-Semitism, which bubbled to the surface during the Dreyfus affair. Captain Alfred Dreyfus was the only Jewish member of the French army general staff and he was accused of handing secrets to the Germans. He was found guilty and Herzl was present when Dreyfus was publicly degraded by having his badges and buttons cut off and his sword broken. 'Soldiers! An innocent man is being degraded!' cried Dreyfus, 'Soldiers! An innocent is dishonoured! Long live France—long live the Army!' Herzl was appalled as the crowd began to scream, 'Death to Dreyfus! Death to the Jews!'

Before this incident, Herzl had been one of those who assumed that the acceptance of Jews in Europe was virtually achieved. George Eliot's novel *Daniel Deroda* had made out a passionate case for Jewish Zionism, a novel which also influenced Arthur Balfour. After Dreyfus, Herzl's eyes were opened and within six months he had drafted the booklet, *Der Judenstaat* (*The Jewish State*). The instinct of Jews in Europe had long been to keep a low profile and wait for storms to blow over but after Dreyfus voices were raised in anger. A man called Bernard Lazare wrote:

> *He (Dreyfus) incarnates in himself, not only the centuries old sufferings of the people of martyrs, but their present agonies. Through him I see Jews languishing in Russian prisons...Romanian Jews refused the rights of man, Galilean Jews starved by financial trusts and ravaged by peasants made fanatics by their priests...Algerian Jews, beaten and pillaged, unhappy immigrants dying of hunger in the ghettos of New York and London, all of those whom desperation drives to seek some haven in the far corners of the inhabited world where they will at last find that justice which the best of them have claimed for all humanity!*
> **(Johnson, Paul, L'Aurore, quoted in *A History of the Jews*; Phoenix, 1995)**

Herzl pleaded for justice. A Jewish state should be established large enough to accommodate a sovereign people. Argentina and Palestine were suggested as possible places. He called for a Zionist congress, which met in Basle, Switzerland, and it was here, because of its historical associations, that Palestine was chosen as the site of a Jewish state. Herzl never saw his dream realised but in 1949 the remains of his body were transferred to a mountain west of Jerusalem, now called Mount Herzl.

Zionism

By the beginning of the First World War a large number of Jews were already in Palestine, mostly working as agriculturists in organisations known as Kibbutzim. These are self contained co-operative organisations, which remain a part of Israel's life today. In 1917 Zionism received a great boost when Balfour, the British philosopher statesman declared:

> *His Majesty's Government view with favour the establishment in Palestine of a national home for the Jewish people, and will use their best endeavours to facilitate the achievement of this object, it being clearly understood that nothing shall be done which may prejudice the civil and religious rights of non-Jewish communities in Palestine.*

Clearly, as far as the British were concerned, a Jewish homeland was a good thing. But what of people already in Palestine? What about the Arabs who viewed with alarm the presumed arrival of thousands of energetic Jews? When the British took control of Palestine after a mandate in 1920, troubles began in earnest. Emigration started with a trickle in the 1920s. Then in 1931, 4,000 settled. By 1934 the figure had risen to 38,000 and Arabs became really alarmed. When Hitler stepped up his persecution of Jews the trickle became a flood. Land was bought up from impoverished Arabs and Jews started to build new towns like Tel Aviv and establish industries, which increased Jewish wealth even further. Arabs went on strike, called for an end to all Jewish immigration and demanded an Arab national state. Murders became common place and Britain found herself in the middle of a hornet's nest. But there was a larger nest stirring in Europe.

Hitler (1889–1945)

In 1934 Adolf Hitler succeeded to the German Presidential title along with that of Chancellor. He preferred the title Fuhrer. Whatever the title, he controlled the political strings and was also commander of

Hitler…preferred the title Fuhrer.

the armed forces. A plebiscite of the German people approved of the new regime with a 'yes' vote of ninety per cent. Any Jew who had read Hitler's, *Mein Kampf* (*My Struggle*), knew with deep foreboding, difficult times were ahead.

By ordinary standards there were something like half a million Jews in Germany but the Nazis insisted that anybody with a Jewish grandparent should be reckoned a Jew. For most of them Germany was their home and German their natural language. By 1935 laws were passed that forbade the marriage of Jews to Aryan Germans. Jewish businessmen, owners of factories, banks, stores, or any prosperous enterprise, were compelled to dispose of them for a pittance. In 1938 mob violence against Jews broke out all over Germany, synagogues were burnt to the ground, shops and homes were looted and Jews murdered. Many Jews abandoned their homes at this point and leaving their possessions behind fled Germany, some to Palestine, some to America others to Britain. On November 9th, 1938, the bile of anti-Semitism overflowed on the infamous *Kristallnacht*. In Germany and Austria, two hundred and sixty-five synagogues were torched and Jewish properties were smashed up:

The usual procedure was to smash any articles of value with axes, and often, anything breakable, down to the last tea-cup, was broken. The men were allowed to dress and then taken straight away, carrying nothing with them. In Erfurt, the men arrested were gathered into the hall of a school and there beaten before being taken off to the camp. In Chemnitz, one man was shot dead in his own house and the rabbi was beaten and severely wounded while trying to save the sacred books from the synagogue.
(*The Long Horizon*, CBF World Jewish Relief page 20)

Kindertransport

Like people waking from a ghastly nightmare some people began to realise that something must be done and Kindertransport was an attempt to do something. Britain offered visas to ten thousand children in an effort to save them from Hitler. Chief Rabbi Lord Jacobovits wrote:

If there were any, even remote, silver linings on the cloud of disaster which overwhelmed Europe and its wealth of Jewish life and culture, It consisted in the wonderful rescue efforts of people with exceptional hearts, culminating in the Kindertransport.
(Leventon and Lowensohn, *I Came Alone*; Book Guild, 1990)

Infants to teenagers arrived in England, destitute but spared the horror and certain death of concentration camps. Jews and Gentiles welcomed the gaggle of pathetic life into their homes and did what they could for the young refugees. Most never saw their parents again. Voluntary organisations, spearheaded by Jews and Christians alike, moved mountains to provide homes, some even buying houses to convert into hostel accommodation. Schools provided education, tradesmen provided food and clothing and the American entertainer Eddie Cantor raised £100,000 with a sixteen-day tour of Britain. As the world now knows, it wasn't enough but as Archbishop Robert Runcie said:

It is heartening to remember that in those dark days of division in Europe, the Christian churches co-operated with Jewish groups in giving these young Jewish children new homes and fresh hope. Lives were saved as a result of Kindertransport.

The Nazis tried to bring the churches under state control and a Concordat of 1933 guaranteed freedom of worship for the Roman Catholic Church if it withdrew from politics. The uneasy truce was destroyed when Hitler Youth Organisations became compulsory and church schools were closed. In 1937 a Papal declaration was read from all Roman Catholic pulpits condemning Nazi racial and religious doctrines. Acts were passed to force Protestants into one Reich Church but a strong minority refused to join and outspoken preachers like Martin Niemoller were sent to concentration camps. Large congregations gathered together as a form of protest, often the only protest against the regime.

Dietrich Bonhoeffer (1906–1945)

Before the outbreak of war, Bonhoeffer, a German Lutheran pastor, had explored ideas of a 'religionless Christianity'. He argued that Christianity was all about Christ and following him meant a discipleship, which cost something. Discipleship was more than a crutch for a time of need or a comfort in times of stress. Man had to 'come of age' and shake off childish ideas of God and recognise God's presence in his creation and his reality in the way Christians serve their fellow human beings. Jesus was 'a man for others' and Christians must be too. Such discipleship was costly but it was the only kind that mattered. Bonhoeffer's beliefs were about to undergo the ultimate litmus test.

   The son of a famous neurologist, Dietrich studied philosophy and theology at Tubingen and Berlin. After ordination he ministered to Germans in Barcelona and London and then back in Germany resisted all attempts of the Nazis to control the confessing church, even though a training seminary he had founded for training pastors, was closed down by command of Himmler in 1937. In 1939 he turned down an invitation to work in America because he felt his place was at home where Christians were facing real difficulties. He was forbidden to preach or publish but through a friendship with Bishop George Bell of Chichester, his appeals for an anti-Hitler conspiracy reached Britain. As part of a Hitler Resistance movement he smuggled fourteen Jews into Switzerland and was arrested in 1943. In prison he was an inspiration to fellow prisoners and continued to write down his thoughts for his fiancée and friends, which were then leaked out of prison. These *Letters and Papers from Prison*, published after the war, have proved inspirational to many.

> *It is infinitely easier to suffer with others than to suffer alone. It is infinitely easier to suffer as public heroes than to suffer apart and in ignominy. It is infinitely easier to suffer physical death than to endure spiritual suffering. Christ suffered as a free man alone, apart and in ignominy, in body and in spirit, and since that day many Christians have suffered with him.*

Bonhoeffer almost survived the war but on April 9th, 1945, he was executed at Flossenburg on the charge of treason. A tablet in the village church says:

> *Dietrich Bonhoeffer, a witness of Jesus Christ among his brethren!*

The Holocaust (Shoah)

Stocktaking after the fall of the Third Reich was staggering. A third of world Jewry had perished in concentration camps. The Chief Rabbi of the United Hebrew Congregations of the Commonwealth said on the BBC:

> *Entire worlds—bustling Jewish townships of Eastern Europe, the Talmudic academies, the courts of the Jewish mystics, the Yiddish speaking masses, the urbane Jews of Germany, the Jews of Poland who had lived among their Gentile neighbours for eight hundred years, the legendary synagogues and houses of study—all were erased. A guard at Auschwitz, testifying at the Nuremberg trial, explained that at the height of the genocide, when the camps were turning ten thousand Jews a day into ashes, children were thrown into the furnaces alive. When the destruction was over a pillar of cloud marked the place where Europe's Jews had once been; and there was a silence that consumed all words.*
> **(Jonathan Sacks, BBC Radio, 22nd Dec. 1988)**

In secular terms the incredible gifts, which had flowed from Jewish European ghettos for centuries, dried up. For Jews who had lost friends and family in the flames there was a great question—why? A suffocating anger which 'murdered God in the soul' was not assuaged by the execution of Nazi war criminals like Adolf Eichmann. 'Never again' became a prayer of determination and a demand for a Jewish homeland, which became irresistible. On 14th May, 1948, with the

A third of world Jewry had perished in concentration camps.

full horrors of the Holocaust still not appreciated, Israel declared itself an independent state and President Truman accorded it recognition.

David Ben-Gurion *(1886–1973)*

Ben-Gurion's roots were in European Jewry. He was born in Plonsk, then part of Russia, and was the son of an active Zionist lawyer. As a youngster he himself established a Zionist youth society and when twenty he went to work on a farm in Palestine, then under the control of the Turks. He went on to edit a Hebrew newspaper for workers, which led to his expulsion from Palestine. At the beginning of World War I he went to New York. Following the Balfour Declaration of 1917, he helped to organise a Jewish Legion for the British war effort but by the time he reached Palestine in 1918, the war was over and the British were in control.

His Zionist convictions never wavered and he firmly believed that Jews must make returning to the land a priority. He thought a socialist state should be introduced along with a firm commitment to Hebrew culture and the Hebrew language. During World War II Ben-Gurion supported co-operation with Britain but afterwards he was behind sabotage and terrorist attacks. When the new state was proclaimed in 1948 Ben-Gurion was chosen as prime-minister and had the job of unifying terrorist groups into an army strong enough to defeat invading Arabs. He led the country for fifteen years promoting immigration and the development of desert lands. He never left Israel again and spent the last years of his life in a Negev Kibbutz where he continued to study and write until his death in 1973. Of Israel, the embryo nation, Ben-Gurion said:

> *It is an exiled people still in the desert longing for the flesh-pots of Egypt. It cannot be considered a nation until the Negev and Galilee are settled, until millions of Jews emigrate to Israel. This is neither a mob nor a nation. It is a people still chained to their exilic past redeemed but not fulfilled!*
> **(Quoted Johnson, P., *A History of the Jews*; Phoenix, 1995)**

Frank Buchman (1878–1961)

Amid the soul searching that followed World War II some people turned their attention to the aspirations of Frank Buchman, the initiator of a movement called Moral Re-Armament. It had been launched in 1938 when the world was re-arming and Europe was lurching dizzily towards disaster.

Buchman was born in Pennsylvania and ordained as a Lutheran clergyman. He worked with students without any great success but then, aged thirty, went through a conversion experience at Keswick in England and was soon looking for new methods of evangelism to spark off a world change. He organised a programme of moral and spiritual recharge, which addressed the root causes of conflict hoping to introduce a hate-free, fear-free, greed-free world. It caught the imagination of people from every continent and every religion. A better world was the general aim but the starting point was with individuals, who make changes in their own lives they wish to see in society. Four absolute moral standards are called for, honesty, purity, unselfishness and love.

Conferences amongst business people are now a regular feature of Moral Re-Armament and at a meeting in Newcastle in 1998, Chief Rabbi Jonathan Sacks outlined a vision of a 'republic of hope', which repeated Buchman's own vision of high morality within families, communities, schools and public 'shared places'. He stressed the need for social regeneration, which means accepting a spiritual regeneration. 'Not by power, nor by might, but by my Spirit', says the Lord. Today, Moral Re-Armament is active in a hundred nations with a world headquarters in Caux, Switzerland.

Facing Adversity

One of the early features of Nazi anti-Semitism had been the boycott of Jewish businesses. To overcome this injustice a gathering in the City of London, instigated by Lionel de Rothchild and Simon Marks, sought to help German Jews with a central fund sufficient to bring aid to the sufferers. *The Central British Fund for World Jewish Relief* was set up. It was conceived for the purpose of helping Jews fleeing Nazi Germany, but in the sixty years since, the fund has stayed open to respond to later needs. World Jewish relief has been described as 'a ship sailing into the distance, changing direction according to the needs of the day but aware that the horizon comes no closer'.

In the mid 1940s *Christian Aid* was born and became the relief agency for most of the Christian churches in the United Kingdom and Ireland. It works closely with other aid agencies, like the Catholic agency CAFOD, and began by helping refugees to recover from the aftermath of war. From that basis it has moved into over seventy countries where it works with overseas partners, regardless of race or creed. The aim, whenever possible, is to help the poor find solutions to their own problems, and as well as providing aid it produces educational material and campaigns on world poverty issues. Now fifty years old its aims (and those of other Christian agencies like *Tearfund*) are summed up in this prayer:

> *O God, you promise a world*
> *Where those who now weep shall laugh,*
> *those who are hungry shall feast,*
> *those who are poor now, and excluded,*
> *shall have your kingdom for their own.*

I want this world too.
I renounce despair.
I will act for change.
I choose to be included
in your great feast of life.

Gladys Aylward (1902–1970)

A London parlour-maid wanted to be a missionary in China but was turned down by several missionary societies because of her lack of education. Undaunted, she put away her earnings until she had saved enough money for a ticket to Tienstin via Berlin, Moscow and the Trans-Siberian route to China. Somewhere deep within she had a compulsion to take Christianity to the millions of peasants who believed in ancestral worship and the teachings of Confucius. Missionaries had worked in China since 1552, often in extreme danger and even while Gladys was saving her money in 1930, news broke that two missionaries, Edith Nettleton from Yorkshire and Eleanor Harrison from Worcester, had been murdered by Chinese bandits. Rather than put her off, she became even more determined to make it to China.

Her journey started in 1932 and when the train stopped in Berlin, this somewhat naïve girl, who had never been further from London than Swansea, commented on the order and cleanliness of the city streets. That very day 100,000 German youths were marching past Hitler in an election rally. She passed through a tense Moscow, noticing the 'anti God' campaign which was to claim the Russian church for over seventy years. She journeyed on to Japan via Vladivostok and liked what she first saw of Japanese life. After four weeks of non-stop travel she arrived at the mountain town of Yangcheng, where she met Mrs Jeannie Lawson, a Scottish widow, who had been in China fifty-years. Mrs Lawson needed a young, keen helper. In 1932 Chiang Kai-shek, a recently baptised Methodist, was President of the Chinese National Republic but his government was weakened by the Soviet Republic, established by Mao Tse-Tung. Mrs Lawson and Gladys opened an inn where they told Bible Stories and when Jeannie died Gladys expanded the work with the help of a local mandarin. She was appalled to discover that criminals were still beheaded publicly and that the feet of baby girls were bound tight simply because small feet were highly prized by would-be husbands. She became Inspector of Feet and travelled the surrounding countryside with authority to forbid foot binding. It gave her position and respect and within four years she was granted naturalisation as a Chinese citizen.

When the Japanese invaded Yangcheng in 1938, the mission was badly damaged but Gladys Aylward, now known as Ai Weh Teh (The Virtuous One), cared for the wounded and the orphans. She moved through the countryside encouraging her Christian communities and seeing at first hand the dreadful atrocities committed by the Japanese. A 'Wanted, Dead or Alive' notice on Gladys, was posted by the Japanese, along with a reward of one hundred dollars. In 1940 she led a hundred children to safety on an epic journey away from the battle zone across the mountains of Siam. It was a journey that made great demands on her and when it was over she collapsed with typhus fever and pneumonia.

She returned home in 1949 where a BBC producer called Alan Burgess was so captivated by her story that he followed up a radio programme about her with a book called *The Small Woman*, and soon this lone pioneer was in great demand as a public speaker. Up and down the country she thrilled audiences with the story of her life and indomitable faith. But her heart was still in China and in 1957 she got as close to communist China as she could by sailing to Hong Kong and Formosa (Taiwan), where she built up an orphanage and went on evangelical missions. She did this until her death in 1970. The Hollywood film, *Inn of the Sixth Happiness*, made Gladys Aylward well known all over the world. The weakness of the rejected London parlour maid had been turned into remarkable strength.

A 'Wanted Dead or Alive' notice on Gladys, was posted by the Japanese.

Kagawa (1888–1960)

Gladys Aylward had been appalled by the cruelty of the Japanese in their war against China and had passed on to the Chinese authorities all she had seen of Japanese troop movements through the mountains. Not all Japanese approved of the war however, and one man, Toyohiko Kagawa, was firm in his denunciation and went to prison for his pacifist stand during World War II.

Kagawa was the illegitimate child of a wealthy cabinet minister and his geisha, who took a liking to the boy and officially adopted him. Alas, both his parents died when he was four and he was brought up in the ancestral home. He was lonely and unhappy as a child until a Japanese teacher and two missionaries befriended him. He turned from Shintoism to Christianity, even though this led to him being disinherited by the family. He went to a Presbyterian College in Tokyo where the dreadful conditions of the destitute made him dedicate his life to the poor. It was nearly a very short life because he was stricken with tuberculosis and came close to death. His poor health continued but when he went to Kobe Theological Seminary he exchanged his living quarters for the city slums where 10,000 people squashed together in cell-like houses six feet square. He attempted to tackle the root causes of poverty by organising the first labour and peasant unions, campaigning for voting rights for all, men and women. Then the union moved towards Marxism and Kagawa started the Kingdom of God movement, a mission closely allied to the church.

In 1925 trade-unions were granted legal status and a year later the slums were knocked down. Kagawa was appointed to Japan's National Reconstruction Commission and pursued a plan to build a thousand small churches and community centres in farmlands and fishing villages. He stated an aim as 'the salvation of 100,000 poor and the emancipation of 9,430,000 labourers and the liberation of 20 million tenant farmers'.

His imprisonment during the war interrupted his work but afterwards he was appointed to the House of Peers and had an important part to play in Japan's reconstruction. His main concern was always the poor and all the royalties from his many books went to his relief work. To the end he was Japan's apostle of love.

Russian Communism

If it were possible to tabulate a register of infamy for twentieth-century dictators, Adolf Hitler would be at the top of most lists. But if the tabulation were done on the basis of lives lost then Joseph Stalin would outstrip Hitler by some distance. The communist 'experiment' based on the Karl Marx theories of dialectical materialism never progressed beyond the material. The fatal consequence was that millions of human beings lost their rights as people and, if they bucked the system, they lost their lives as well. Zbigniew Brzezinski, National Security Adviser to President Carter, calculated that fifty million people were killed during Stalin's reign, either through direct persecution or bad economic decisions. The church endured savage persecution more sustained than anything in the previous 1900 years. In 1914 there were 163 bishops in office, by 1939 just four! Brzezinski revealed in his book, *The Grand Failure*, how every human and religious value was overturned by communism. What remained was a people who distrusted one another and ceased to function as responsible individuals with a personal destiny. History was rewritten and Russia was robbed of her past, especially her religious past. Systematically, churches were closed, destroyed or reappropriated for secular purposes. Yet people still prayed on church steps or held secret services deep in the woods. The sheer depth of faith was completely misunderstood by the authorities even though one might have expected Stalin, an ex novitiate for the priesthood, to know something of religious passion. Solzhenitsyn understood better:

> *When you travel the by-roads of central Russia you begin to understand the secret of the pacifying Russian countryside, it is in the churches. They trip up the slopes, ascend the high hills, come down the broad rivers, like princesses in white and red, they lift their bell-towers graceful, shapely, variegated high over mundane timber and thatch, they nod to each other from afar, from villages that are cut-off and invisible to each other. They soar to the same heaven. And wherever you wander in the fields or meadows, however far from habitation, you are never alone: from over the hayricks, the wall of trees, and even the curve of the earth's surface, the head of some bell-tower will beckon you.*
>
> *People were always selfish and often unkind but the evening chimes would ring out, floating over villages, fields and woods reminding people to abandon the trivial concerns of this world*

and give time and thought to eternity...our forefathers put all that was finest in ourselves, all their understanding of life into these stones, into these bell-towers.

(Bordeaux, Michael, quoted in *Patriarch and Prophets*, pp 154–55; 1970)

There was a brief let-up of persecution during the war years when Stalin cynically sought the support of Christians by opening some churches for worship, but it was an interlude and subsequent attacks from Krushchev on 'the enemy in the midst' re-introduced anti-Christian legislation with a vengeance. The Russian Orthodox Church, with its history of subservience to the state, was partly neutered and monasticism almost ceased to exist. But total subservience never came near success and individual voices did eventually join in chorus to keep faith alive despite the odds. Baptists Gennadi Kryuchkov and Georgi Vins cried out against injustice and their words reached British ears via Keston College, the Kent based centre for the study of religion under communism. Then Father Gleb, who had returned to faith after a period of committed communism, began to speak out for those Christians and Jews whose faith made them second-class citizens. He was dragged before the courts and sentenced to five years in a labour camp, followed by five years exile. Solzhentsyn's, *One Day in the Life of Ivan Denisovich* went inside the Russian Gulag to tell a harrowing tale of life behind the wire but he also portrayed two Christians, Alyosha, the Baptist, and the nameless priest who worshipped when he ate by making every meal into a Eucharist. Millions did die but others survived to tell a tale of faith flying in the face of injustice and cruelty. Valeri Barinov and Irina Ratushinskaya are two voices to speak for the many.

Valeri Barinov (1944–)

One evening in 1977 a rock group performed at a communist youth club in Lunokhod. They sang western songs including a Paul McCartney number they had been rehearsing all week. Their dated instruments included drums, amplifiers, electric guitars, electric organ and all the paraphernalia necessary for a rock concert. This was disco Russian style, and the group was popular and capable of providing the beat for a good enthusiastic dance session. The leader of the group was Valeri Barinov, who could belt out a full repertoire of Beatles numbers in English and Russian. That was the first half of the show. The second half included new numbers from Valeri himself and an interlude where he read from a small, well used New Testament and then explained the passage. Then it was thumbs up to the rest of the group and on with the show.

Valeri Barinov was from Leningrad, raised by a single mother until her death when he was eleven. He had attended the Rimsky-Korsakov Conservatoire and played the violin but he had to leave and live with an uncle who was a heavy drinker and violence was never far away. Like all Russian youths, Valeri was subjected to atheist propaganda and the smiling face of 'Uncle Lenin' on every street corner. Yet before he went away to do national service, the idea of a living God was implemented in his mind by an aunt who enjoyed a lively Christian faith. He was a searcher who could see blatant inconsistencies in communism but whose heavy binges with the vodka bottle interrupted his Christian enquiries. Christian literature was a rare commodity and Bibles were a luxury. Lorna Bourdeaux describes how biblical knowledge was passed on:

> *Many believers compile their own 'Bible Notebooks'. They are beautifully produced, hand-written compilations of bible passages. The verses of scripture are jotted down during sermons and arranged according to themes, often with a written testimony of the compiler. And so each person who sang or read explained why the verse or passage or poem was important and what could be learned from it. These testimonies were interspersed with joyful outbursts of singing, affirming the great truths of the Christian faith and times of individual fervent prayer.*
> **(Bourdeaux, Lorna, *The Trumpet Call*; Marshal Pickering, 1985)**

In such ways was Valeri suckled in the faith until he himself believed. He became a passionate, uninhibited Christian and something of an embarrassment to the Baptist Church in Leningrad, where they approved of him but were wary lest his forthrightness should attract unwanted attention from communist authorities. Circumspection was not something Barinov had much of. Then he heard a pop group singing Christian songs on a Ukranian radio-station and felt this was something he had to do. He bought an old guitar and formed a rock band, which drew a large following during the 1970s. The lyrics for an Andrew Lloyd Webber style rock musical began to form in his mind (he was familiar with *Jesus Christ Superstar*) and this eventually became *The Trumpet Call*. Cliff Richard heard the music and praised it during a broadcast on the BBC Russian Service:

> *It is a great thrill to find there is a band which enjoys the kind of music I like. But even more than that, the joy for me is that the band is a Christian one and that in the words of their songs they are presenting God and their faith in Jesus.*

Valeri's music was recorded but by this time the KGB were onto him. He found himself in a psychiatric hospital facing people who were gathering evidence about his mental instability. He was denied access to visitors, books, letters or even the proximity of a window. Forced injections were included in his treatment. Nevertheless, *The Trumpet Call* was broadcast on the BBC Russian Service and caused a terrific stir amongst young Russians, who wanted the music for themselves. The reaction of communist reared youngsters to Barinov's words can be imagined:

> *Brothers and sisters make
> ready, make sure that your
> lamps are lit.
> Christ is coming. Go and meet Him
> In Glory the bridegroom arrives…
> O Lord, O Lord come near
> We need you Lord, come near
> To you O Lord we plead
> We're waiting. Come for us.'*

His prison life was eventful and included a hunger strike and a heart attack but he kept in touch with the outside world and pleaded with people to help his wife and children with material things while he was in prison. Eventually he was released and allowed to leave Russia but not before he had stood on the steps of Kazan Cathedral in the middle of Leningrad and preached the gospel. For two generations it had been the chief atheistic museum of the Soviet Union and now Valeri was symbolically reclaiming the building for Christ. Two years later, seven hundred Baptist's gathered inside the building for a service of praise—Baptists reclaiming a classic Orthodox Cathedral! Christian unity in practical action!

Irina Ratushinskaya (1955–)

The religious literature of Russia containing the genius of Tolstoy, Dostoevsky and Solztenitsyn, also found expression in a young poet called Irina Ratushinskaya. Born after the death of Stalin, she was raised under the anti-religious pressure of his successors but she still expressed herself in her poetry of hope. It did however contain elements of protest against oppression, enough to attract the attention of the KGB. She was sentenced to seven years imprisonment in a labour camp, followed by five years exile. In 1986 an Anglican priest called David Rogers caged himself up in his home-town of Birmingham to draw attention to her plight. By then Michail Gorbachev was introducing restructuring policies to Russian life (perestroika) and Irina was released. Two months later the Jewish academic Andrei Sakharov was freed from exile.

Irina's story of life in a Soviet labour camp was written shortly after her release and describes in gripping detail the brutal conditions detainees endured daily. Her book *Grey is the Colour of Hope*, relates her story from the time of arrest as a twenty-eight year old and reveals a deep personal faith, which sustained her through dark days in the 'Small Zone' of the Morduvian camp where 'dangerous' political prisoners were kept. Irena describes her arrival in the 'Small Zone' and how auntie Vera explains the philosophy of the inmates:

> *We may be crammed into a small house, we may be dressed in rags, they can carry out searches and lightening raids in our quarters, but we retain our human dignity. We shall not get down on all fours to them, try though they may to make us. We will not carry out demeaning or senseless commands, because we have not surrendered our freedom. Yes, we are behind barbed wire. They have stripped us of everything they could, they have torn us away from our friends and families, but unless we acknowledge this as their right, we remain free.*
>
> **(Ratushinskaya, *Grey is the Colour of Hope*; Hodder & Stoughton, 1988)**

Locked away Irina remained free. Poems buzzed around in her head that she longed to pass on to her husband Igor when he was allowed a visit. But visits could be cancelled for 'a violation of camp regulations' and what constituted a violation was left to the interpretation of the administration. Her refusal to wear an identity tag (the Small Zone only housed between five and ten inmates) could lead to a ban on Igor's visit for the next seven years. Furthermore, there was always the threat of *shizo*, which meant cold, hunger, filth and total deprivation. From inmates there was the extreme courage of those prepared to endure starvation and solitary confinement rather than lose the pleasure of having a Bible to read in their cell.

Irina was unexpectedly released in 1986, as perestroika spread through the Soviet Union and remarkable changes took place. Baptists from Moscow were allowed to visit and work in the Kashchenko Psychiatric Hospital where Christians like Valeri Barinov had been subjected to brain washing under the KGB. A hundred Baptists helped at the hospital and were allowed to read the Bible to patients. The work was so well received that a communist doctor went to the Baptist Church in Moscow and preached the first 'sermon' ever given by an atheist there:

> *Had I been told several years ago that I, the chief physician of a major hospital, a communist, would stand here before you in a Baptist church, I would never have believed it...Pierre Dusson, a famous psychotherapist, in his book* Fighting Insanity, *drew a formula for curing these unfortunate persons. The formula was chemistry plus love! And although we as doctors and scientists are able to fulfil the first part of this formula to some extent, we are virtually incapable of fulfilling the second part, which is love.*
> **(Bourdeaux, M., *Gorbachov, Glasnost and the Gospel*;**
> **Hodder & Stoughton, 1990)**

So, in the Soviet Union at least, the cold, debilitating hand of oppression was relaxed. But how many lives had been wasted by the merciless years of tyranny stemming from Stalinism? Could the sacrifice of so much blood eradicate the dismal stupidity and self-glorification of twentieth century dictators?

Mother Teresa (1910–1997)

During perestroika Mother Teresa was allowed to visit the Soviet Union. Three visits in seven months ensured that her work of mercy was established with warm official blessing. Such official enthusiasm led some to question why hundreds of nuns from the Orthodox Church were not allowed to practice their vocation openly, but she was welcomed nevertheless, as an outstanding example of Christian love in action.

Mother Teresa was born in Skopje, Serbia in 1910 when Skopje was still part of the Turkish Ottoman Empire. Her parents were Albanian and gave her the names Agnes, Gonxhe, Bojaxhiu. The home was pleasantly well off, pious and dedicatedly Christian in a region dominated by Muslims. Agnes' father was a campaigner for Albanian independence and one day he was invited to a political dinner in Belgrade, one hundred and sixty miles away. When he returned he was a dying man. The suspicion was that he had been poisoned. His subsequent death led to straightened circumstances in the family household but it never lost its welcoming generosity and good books and conversation were a constant feature of her childhood. The local priest was a regular visitor to the house and he read letters from Yugoslavian missionaries in India, which captivated Agnes and prompted her dreams to become a missionary too. The Sisters of Loreto, founded by a Yorkshire woman called Mary Ward, were well established in India and nuns received their training in Dublin. When she was eighteen she said goodbye to her family and friends and boarded a train into the future. She was inspired by the lives of saints and particularly by a girl called Therese who had become a nun at fifteen, served the poor in Vietnam and died of tuberculosis at twenty-four. Her guiding principle had been to perform acts of kindness and service every day and it was this practical expression of faith, which appealed to Agnes. On May 21st, 1931, she took her first vows of poverty, chastity and obedience, taking the name Sister Teresa, spelt the Spanish way because there was already a Theresa in the order. In a closed order she taught in an Indian school.

Teresa was a teacher locked inside a school while outside India was in ferment, first as Gandhi led a non-violent rebellion against Britain, then through the war years, followed by the bloodshed of partition when Hindus and Muslims failed to agree on a new government. Teresa left the school, desperate to find food for three hundred girls who had nothing to eat. She saw bodies on the streets lying in pools of blood, a sight that convinced her she had to leave Loreto and return to those streets. From now on she had to serve the poorest of the poor. With difficulty she received permission to begin her new work and, after training as a nurse, she arrived on the streets of Calcutta with just five rupees (30p). She was thirty-eight.

Calcutta was packed with refugees fleeing from the new Muslim country of East Pakistan. They lived on the streets, anywhere they could find a space. Teresa joined them and started to teach the children who flocked to her. She taught hygiene and gave out bars of soap as prizes. Other nuns joined her, sharing a great concern for the poor who were dying on the streets completely alone without sympathy or hope. Hospitals would not take them so she decided to do something herself. 'We cannot let a child of God die like an animal in the gutter.' She rented rooms and carried people there so they could spend their last few hours surrounded by love. A permanent building was then named, *The Place of the Pure Heart* and her new Order was called Missionaries of Charity. After two years the sisters numbered twenty-eight.

Five years later, eight thousand people had been cared for. At first most died, by 1955 half lived and by 1957 more lived than died. 'These people are our treasures' she said. 'They are Jesus'. Helpers came from all over the world to work with the poor and though authorities sometimes obstructed the work, it continued to grow. Christians, Hindus, Muslims, Atheists—all were welcomed and when people began to show an interest in the rescued children, adoptions were arranged with Indian families in Sweden, Switzerland, France, Ireland, Germany, Canada and the United States. By 1965 over three hundred sisters had joined the Order and on one occasion Pope Paul VI presented his ceremonial car (the Pope mobile) to Mother Teresa. It was a gift from an American University and she raffled it off for £37,500, enough to build a new hospital for leprosy sufferers. Appeals for similar hospitals began to arrive for Mother Teresa and sisters left India to work in other countries. The work had become international and when Malcolm Muggeridge made the TV documentary, *Something Beautiful for God*, the response from viewers raised thousands of pounds and Muggeridge himself had taken the first steps towards personal faith. Honours poured upon her, including the Nobel Peace Prize and for the first time ever Nobel's celebrated audience was invited to pray. She led them in the prayer of St Francis:

> *Lord, make me an instrument of your peace,*
> *Where there is hatred let me sow love…*
> *Grant that I may not so much seek to be*
> *Consoled as to console…*
> *To be loved as to love,*
> *For it is in giving that we receive;*
> *It is in pardoning that we are pardoned;*
> *And it is in dying that we are born to eternal life!*

The heart of St Francis had bridged the years. Once, when asked by a journalist how she felt about herself, Mother Teresa said, 'By blood and origin I am Albanian. My citizenship is Indian. I am a Catholic nun. As to my calling, I belong to the whole world. As to my heart, I belong entirely to the heart of Jesus'.

Second Vatican Council (1962–1965)

When John XXIII (1881–1963) was elected pope in 1958, aged 76, it was generally believed he would be a 'caretaker pope' until stronger candidates became available. In fact he ushered in a new age for the Roman Catholic Church, which achieved closer relationships with other Christian denominations, including Eastern Orthodoxy, and elevated clergy from many developing countries. The most important achievement was to call the Second Vatican Council in a serious attempt to drag Catholics, sometimes 'kicking and screaming', into the modern world. The most obvious result was a rewriting of the Mass, which was to be celebrated in the vernacular rather than Latin. Another result was to recognise more obviously laity in the church and their contribution to the work of evangelism. Study of Scripture was also encouraged along with the commentaries of the early Church Fathers.

Vatican II also led to modern theologians speaking out against the old order of the church with its 'fortress mentality'. They advocated the right of married men to become priests and for the ordination of women and they touched on the untouchable when they proposed the use of contraception and a more sympathetic understanding of homosexuality. Since then there seems to have been a reaction to such liberalisation and theologians like Hans Kung have had their mandate to teach theology in the name of the church withdrawn. The charismatic Polish pope, John Paul II, is often accused of leading this reaction, but this is an open question. Ecclesiastical wheels turn slowly and it is quite possible for seeds planted during Vatican II to bring forth fruit long after the dawn of a new Millennium.

Billy Graham (1918–)

A major influence on the twentieth century has been the American evangelist Billy Graham. In a ministry similar to that of Dwight L. Moody, Billy Graham has preached to 200 million people face to face. Add to that numbers who have seen and heard him via television, radio and satellite links and he has probably preached to more people than any other person ever before. The sheer stamina involved in this workload is impressive, as is his resistance to continuous media attempts to undermine his achievements.

His religious awakening came in Charlotte, North Carolina, when a fiery evangelist called Mordecai Fowler Ham led an eleven week mission. Ham was not universally welcomed in the town but for Graham it was a spellbinding experience, which led to 'a kind of stirring in my breast that was both pleasant and scary'. From that moment, nothing could keep him from Ham's meetings. Slowly, the conviction grew deep within him that he should be a preacher and he went to a Bible Institute in Florida where he became a popular visitor to little churches and chapels. As war came to far-off Europe, Billy Graham was ordained as a Southern Baptist. At his graduation a girl called Vera Resue rose to speak with a mind full of foreboding about a world heading for a new Dark Age:

> *At each critical epoch of the church, God has chosen a human instrument to shine forth His light in the darkness. Men like Luther, John Wesley, Moody and others...There is room for another name in this list.*

Billy Graham learned his trade well. Through Youth for Christ Missions he gained experience and met soul mates like George Beverley Shea, Cliff Barrows and a young woman called Ruth Bell who became his wife. In 1949 a mission to Los Angeles received massive media coverage when dramatic conversions took place during meetings. A Texas cowboy and broadcaster Stuart Hamblen, a criminal Jim Vans, an Olympic runner and war hero Louis Zamparini, all went public about their conversions. *Time* and *Newsweek* wrote feature articles about the new evangelist and the mission stretched from three weeks to eight. His voice became well known across America when the *Hour of Decision* went out on 150 radio stations on the ABC network with the highest listening figures of any religious programme in the country. It was the beginning of an extraordinary workload demanding fresh and interesting material to feed the programme. The formation of the Billy Graham Evangelistic Association followed, which allowed team members freedom to accept missions further afield.

World recognition came in 1954 through the Greater London Crusade. It lasted for three weeks and shook the English capital more than any religious event since Moody and Sankey. Huge crowds at Harringay Arena were followed by a meeting at Wembley Stadium where 120,000 filed through the turnstiles. The Archbishop of Canterbury joined him and Sir Winston Churchill greeted him afterwards in the Cabinet Room. The Mission's outreach was aided when the Post Office provided telephone lines to other parts of the country and newspapers carried bizarre stories, like that of a pickpocket who gave a wallet back to its owner as they both went forward in response to the invitation to 'get up out of your seats' and accept Christ.

After London, missions followed thick and fast; Berlin, where he preached in Hitler's stadium on the text 'I am the Way, the Truth, the Life', then Paris, then Glasgow for a six-week campaign and back to Wembley for another. On and on, India, New York, Australia, Rio de Janeiro. Then Alabama, where he refused to preach to segregated audiences, 'There is no racial distinction here', he said, 'the ground is level at the foot of the cross'. Onward to South Africa, Lausanne, Hungary, Poland (at the time Rome elected Crocow Wojtyla to become Pope John Paul II), Japan, Mexico and, in 1982, Moscow, where the state newspaper *Pravda* reported the phenomenon of a Christian Mission in an atheist state.

As a young man, Billy Graham had listened to Vera Resue plead for another voice to be added to the list of great Christian preachers. Heading the list had been Martin Luther and in 1982, Graham preached from Luther's pulpit in Wittenberg, East Germany. The packed congregation, predominantly young, raised on forty years of atheist teaching, were just as eager to hear the gospel as anybody in Luther's day. Billy Graham wrote:

> *I used the text made famous by Luther himself, "The just shall live by faith'... we visited Wittenberg's Castle Church where Luther had nailed his Ninety-five theses to the door in 1517, thus beginning the Protestant Reformation...In the evening, we drove to Dresden's Lutheran Church of the Cross, largest in Saxony, where 7,000 people, mostly under the age of twenty-five, jammed every space.*

Vera Resue's list had grown longer...Luther, John Wesley, Moody and...Billy Graham.

Martin Luther King (1929–1968)

Another Baptist from the southern states of America to write his own chapter of faith was Martin Luther King Junior. He was named after his father, a Baptist preacher from Atlanta, Georgia. He was a bright lad who briefly toyed with the idea of a career in law before deciding to follow his father into the ministry. He married Coretta Scott in 1953 and by 1955 was a Doctor of Philosophy. That same year he accepted the pastorate of the Dexter Avenue Baptist Church in Montgomery, Alabama, a city strictly segregated by state laws. Almost immediately he was plunged into racial conflict. When a Negro seamstress called Rosa Parks refused to give up her seat on a bus to a white man, she was arrested and jailed. It was one humiliation amongst thousands every year but the injustice to Rosa Parks was the spark lighting the revolutionary fire inside Martin Luther King, which ultimately consumed him.

If Billy Graham preached for conversions, King preached two basic Christian principles of brotherhood and non-violence. The passive resistance of Gandhi in India's struggle for independence was his example and became a weapon in the struggle against segregation. He formed the Montgomery Improvement Association that organised a boycott of the city's buses. The boycott lasted 382 days until the Supreme Court of Washington compelled Alabama to desegregate its transport system. During those 382 days Dr King was arrested, his family was terrorised and his home wrecked by a bomb. The provocation was intense but the Association refused to retaliate and by the end of the boycott he was the recognised spokesman for the Southern Negroes. He then organised 'sit-ins' at exclusive restaurants and in 1960 he was sentenced to four months hard labour in a Georgia penitentiary. By now civil rights had moved to the top of the political agenda as John Kennedy and Richard Nixon fought for the Presidency and King was released.

To speed up legislation his next move was towards Birmingham, Alabama, the largest segregated city in the United States. He persuaded his Southern Christian Leadership Conference to hold a prayer pilgrimage to the Birmingham City Hall during Easter, 1963. The pilgrimage stirred up a frenzy amongst the Ku Klux Klan and a police force notorious for its brutality. Again he was arrested, this time sharing cells with 3,000 of his supporters. The prisons could not cope and millions of comfortable Americans saw on their televisions the distressing sight of peaceful demonstrators, including women and children, being set upon by police using dogs, batons and high pressure hoses. Naked racial hatred had shocked America and most approved when President Kennedy moved the US Army into the region to ensure public order. Birmingham was a news headline for the world and token concessions were granted before a new Civil Rights bill went before Congress.

The accumulated hatred of white extremists contrasted strongly with Martin Luther King's reasonable plea for justice. His stature was enhanced even further by his articulate sermons, which traced with pride his forebear's struggle against injustice. 'We will win our freedom' he wrote from prison, 'because the sacred heritage of our nation and the eternal will of God are embodied in our echoing demands.' His speech from the foot of the Lincoln Memorial in Washington to civil rights campaigners is unforgettable.

> *I have a dream that my four little children will one day live in a nation where they will not be judged by the colour of their skin but by the content of their character. I have a dream that one day in the red hills of Georgia, sons of former slaves and sons of former slave-owners will be able to sit down together at the table of brotherhood.*

Dr King became *Time* magazine's man of the year for 1963 and a year later he was awarded the Nobel Peace Prize.

'Segregation is on its deathbed' King told university students, 'The question now is, how costly will the segregationists make the funeral?' Sadly the answer was, 'Very costly'. Before the Civil Rights bill was passed by the Senate, President Kennedy was assassinated. Then a white civil rights worker was murdered in Selma, leading to a four thousand strong procession marching from Selma to Montgomery. King was assaulted and arrested and the Ku Klux Klan shot a woman civil rights worker. The possibility of murder must have been with him constantly and an apocalyptic tone entered King's speeches. They were heading for the Promised Land but 'I may not get there with you' he said. He was preparing a poor-peoples march on Washington in 1968 and intended to support the garbage workers of Memphis in a struggle to improve their status. It was there on April 4th, 1968 a gunman's long-range rifle shot him dead.

Mourners from across the world attended his funeral in Atlanta. Rich and powerful came in hordes and witnessed one final sermon from this preacher of passive resistance—his coffin was carried along by a mule-train.

Modern Martyrs

Martin Luther King is one of ten modern martyrs whose statues were unveiled at a service in Westminster Abbey on July 9th, 1998. The statues, set in prominent niches above the great west door of the Abbey, are designed to symbolise the plight of persecuted Christians everywhere in the twentieth century. Alongside Dr King are the **Grand Duchess Elizabeth of Russia**, Queen Victoria's granddaughter, who despite her virtuous life was killed along with the Russian Royal family by the Bolsheviks; **Manche Masemola**, a fifteen-year-old South African girl killed by her parents in 1928 for following an Anglican preacher; **Maximilian Kolbe**, a Polish monk sent to Auschwitz by the Nazis and killed in 1941 by lethal injection when he took the place of another prisoner who had been selected for death in retaliation for an escape; **Lucian Tapiedi**, killed by tribesmen in 1942 when he helped missionaries escape from Japanese invaders in Papua New Guinnea; **Dietrich Bonhoeffer**, whose execution by the Nazis we have already considered; **Esther John**, a Pakistani Muslim who converted to Christianity, refused family demands to return home and was murdered in 1960; **Wang Zhiming**, a Chinese Christian pastor who defied orders from Chairman Mao to humiliate landlords or denounce foreign powers and was arrested by Red Guards and shot at a mass rally in 1973; **Janani Luwum**, the Anglican Archbishop of Uganda who protested to Idi Amin about the violence of his security services and subsequently disappeared never to be seen again; and **Oscar Romero**, Archbishop of San Salvador, who condemned the death squads roaming his country and the rich people behind them. He was assassinated as he celebrated mass in 1980.

So much bloodshed, so much heartache. The twentieth century, born in the midst of so much hope, ended with the knowledge that it has seen more people die for their faith than any other century in the history of the human race. As the calendar turned up virgin white pages of a new millennium the auguries for a new age, hate free, fear free, greed free, are not good. The astonishing material progress of the modern world grows ever faster yet still cannot hide the flawed nature of human beings, which continues to keep the wheel of our existence red hot. Perhaps the penny will drop and the discovery of selfless living, exemplified by the saints of the past 2,000 years, will be discovered as the pearl of greatest worth. Theirs is the torch to grasp lest all we know to be true in our deep selves sinks into the abyss of a new dark age made more sinister by the lights of perverted science. Now where have we heard that before?

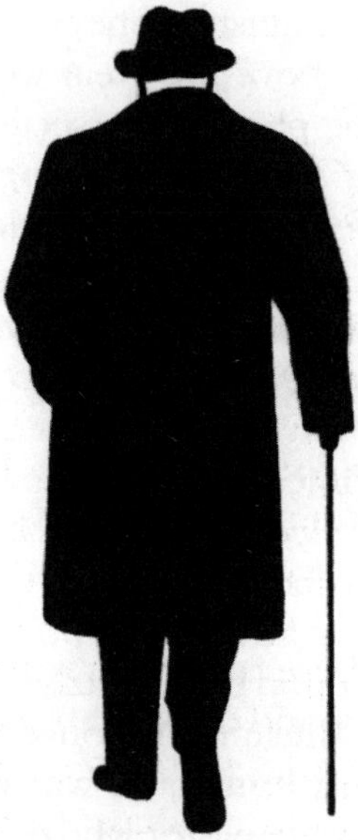

19 Postscript

So I draw this faith odyssey to a close. I am very much aware of many other stories which could have been written and have been written by others. But '…if it were all to be recorded in detail, I suppose the whole world could not hold the books that could be written' (John 21:25). These have been written so that we might trace the thread of our ancestry and understand something of the faith that has made the modern world. For, make no mistake, the past is not dead. Omar Khayyam could not have been more wrong when he observed:

> *How time is slipping under our feet,*
> *Unborn Tomorrow, and dead Yesterday…*

Yesterday is not dead; it lives on in lives made richer and braver by others who have gone before. Is Tertullian dead? Why, he breathes afresh every time brave men resist oppression. Is Francis dead, he whose love for the unloved set his heart on fire? Why, his love is rekindled every time a heart is touched with compassion. Does Nero still live? Why, I see his rebirth in every news bulletin on every day of every week. Is Martin Luther dead when I can hear his voice crying yet, 'Here I stand, God help me, I can do no other'. If these people are dead then we are all dead for there is no health in us.

When I was a boy I was the proud owner of a big red book of stories about heroic men and women who had done extraordinary things and made amazing sacrifices for their fellow men. One story was of Captain Oates, a member of Scott's ill-fated expedition to the South Pole. When his frostbitten feet turned gangrenous he sought death rather than deny his companions the chance of survival, 'We knew it was the act of a brave man and an English gentleman' wrote Scott in his journal and, as a boy, I knew it was the right thing and a wonderful thing to do. I believe such stories should be passed on with a child's milk just as Jewish children learn lessons from their ancestry.

> *Teach them to your children, and speak of them indoors and out of doors, when you lie down and when you rise. Write them upon the door posts of your houses and on your gates.*
> **(Deuteronomy 11:19)**

We will not forget the dreadful things of course but we will refuse to wallow in them, for inspiration begets inspiration and we will need inspired people to face the dangers waiting to ambush us in the new millennium. Sooner, rather than later, we will have to ignore people who have given up God for the Lottery. We will have to vote for people who promise more than a well feathered nest. We will have to shout a resounding, 'No!' to cynical people who sell arms to Africans so they might kill each other by the million. We will shout, 'Yes!' to those who want to rip the yolk of debt from the necks of the poor. We will look at the drug addicted children on city streets in every country of the world as though they were our own children. We will not be told what to do by people who do not know what they ought to do. And that is just for a start. Nietzsche's Superman will need to be a real hero. As D.H. Lawrence once pleaded,

> *For God's sake, let us be men not monkeys minding machines or sitting with our tails curled while the machine amuses us, the radio or film or gramophone...*

Lawrence's words sound so very like the words of Benedict of Nursia from the fifth century :

> *However late it may seem, let us rouse ourselves from lethargy...Let us open our eyes to the light that shows us the way to God. Let our ears be alert to the stirring call of his voice crying to us every day: TODAY IF YOU SHOULD HEAR HIS VOICE, DO NOT HARDEN YOUR HEARTS.*
> **(Rule, Prologue 8-9)**

Perhaps the call has been the same for 2000 years. It is the response that can change the world.

Appendix

Roman Emperors mentioned in the book from Augustus (Octavius) to the fall of Rome in AD 476.

Augustus	27 BC–AD 14
Tiberius	14–37
Caligula (Gaius)	37–41
Claudius	41–54
Nero	54–68
Vespasian	69–79
Titus	79–81
Domitian	81–96
Trojan	98–117
Hadrian	117–138
Antoninus Pius	138–161
Marcus Aurelius	161–192
Commodus	180–192
Septimus Severus	193–211
Alexander Severus	222–235
Decius	251–253
Valerian	253–259
Diocletian	284–305
Constantius I	305–306
Constantine I	311–337
Julian the Apostate	361–363
Theodosius the Great	379–395 (in the East)
	394–395 (in the West)
Leo I	457–474 (in the East)
Romulus Augustulus	475–476 (in the West)

Some Byzantine Rulers from the fall of Rome to the fall of Constantinople in 1453.

Zeno	474–491
Justinian the Great	527–565
Constans II	641–668
Leo III (the Isaurian)	717–741

Constantine V	741–775
Irene (empress)	797–802
Leo VI (the Wise)	886–912
Zoe (empress)	1028–1050
Alexius I (Komnenos)	1081–1118
Andronicus II (the Elder)	1282–1328
Constantine XI	1448–1453

Some Holy Roman Emperors 800–1806

Charlemagne	800–814
Louis I (the Pious)	814–840
Charles II (the Bald)	875–877
Charles III (the Fat)	881–887
Otto I (the Great)	936–973
Wenceslas	1378–1400
Karl VII of Bavaria	1742–1745
Franz I of Lorraine	1745–1765

Some Popes of the Roman Church

Xystus	257–258
Damasus I	366–383
Innocent I	401–417
Boniface I	418–422
Leo I	440–461
Gregory I	590–604
Sergius I	687–701
Leo III	795–816
Urban II	1088–1099
Clement V	1305–1314
Gregory XI	1370–1378
Urban VI	1378–1389
Martin V	1417–1431
Callistus III	1455–1458
Alexander VI (Rodrigo Borgia)	1492–1503
Julius II	1503–1513
Leo X	1513–1521
Puis XII	1939–1958
John XXIII	1958–1963
Paul VI	1963–1978
John Paul II	1978–

(first non-Italian pope since 1523)

Index

abbey 83, 101, 109, 111, 220, 222, 235, 268, 297
abbot 64–66, 81, 98, 109, 112–113
Abd al–Baha 258
Abd el Malik 115
Abelard, Peter 110–114
abolition of slavery 214, 220
Abraham 9, 90, 125, 257
abstinence from alcohol 43
Abu Bakr 89, 92
Acre 126, 129–133
Act of Supremacy 168
Act of Uniformity 12, 194, 204, 212
Acts of Parliament 205, 225
Acts of the Apostles 43, 193
Adages 159
Adam 11, 23, 27, 61–62, 254
Adams, John 183
Adler, Alfred 251
Admonitions 140
Adrianople 38
Adriatic 71
Aeolia Capitolina 11
Africa 23–25, 29–30, 40–41, 59–62, 70, 93, 96, 120, 182, 185, 218–219, 220–223, 225, 236, 238, 262, 269–270, 294, 297, 300
Agincourt 189
agnostic 42, 242
agriculture 222
Aidan 77, 81–82
Aisha 89, 92
Aix–la–Chapelle 98–100
al–Aqsa Mosque 128
al–Hakim 120
Alabama 294–295
Alaric 70–71
Alban 78
Albanian 289–291
Albergensians 141
Albertus Magnus 142
Alcuin 99–100
Aldersgate 213
Alexander III 138
Alexander VI 153, 155–156
Alexandria 26, 30–33, 44–46, 53, 63, 66–67, 73
Alexandria, Clement of 26, 30–32, 67
Alexandria, Cyril of 66, 73
Alexius 121, 123–125, 127
Algeria 23, 59–60
Ali ibn Abi Talib 92–93, 120
Allah 89–91, 257–258
allegory 144, 200–201
Alps 162, 180, 264
Alsace 268
altar 48, 102, 105, 115–116, 137–138
Alyosha 285
ambassador 74, 170
Ambrose 51, 55–57, 59–60, 63, 72, 75, 111
America 167, 176, 184, 189, 195, 209–212, 214, 222, 230–233, 238, 254–255, 259, 274–276, 291–295
Amiens 55, 117
Amin, Idi 297
Amsterdam 192, 194–195
An Inspector Calls 262
Anabaptists 192–194
Anachorets 65–66

Ancient World 21, 30, 67, 74
Anglican 12, 190–191, 196, 211–212, 214, 220, 223, 238, 263, 288, 297
Anglo–Saxon 75, 78, 81, 83, 97, 99, 117
Anicetus 18
Annobius 35
Anogni 146
Anselm 108–110
Anthusa 63
anti–Semitism 14, 251, 272, 274, 280
Antichrist 190
Antioch 10, 17–18, 28, 33, 57–58, 63, 124–125, 127, 129
Antioch, Ignatius of 17–18
Antony 47, 51–54, 79
Antwerp 172, 193
Apollinarius 21
Apologies 16, 19–20, 22, 25–26
apostles 10–11, 17–18, 22–23, 25, 27, 30, 36, 41–43, 46–48, 71, 73–74, 97, 159–160, 163, 186, 193, 220, 283
Apostles' Creed 27
Aquinas, Thomas 142–144, 182, 191
Aquitaine 127, 130
Arabia 86, 89–90
Arabs 86–88, 91, 96, 133, 222, 273, 279
Aragon, Katherine of 165, 167–170
Arch of Titus 10
Archbishop 81, 98, 109, 136–138, 146–147, 149, 160, 166, 168–170, 180, 188, 201, 244, 275, 294, 297
Archduke Ferdinand 263
architects 114, 160
Ardennes 127
Argentina 272
Arianism 44, 46–47, 54–56, 70, 74–75
Aristotle 19, 109, 142–143
Armageddon 259
Armagh 79
Armenia 38, 120
Armenian 12, 127
Arminius, Jacob 192, 194
Ascalon 130
Asceticism 21, 26, 43–44, 52–53, 55, 57, 64, 75, 79, 161
Ashbury 228
Ashkanazi 96
Asia 14, 21, 38, 100, 120, 124, 134
Assisi, Francis of 138, 141, 144, 270, 291
Association of Baptist churches 231
Assyria 89
Astrolabe 111
astronomy 46, 96, 108, 155, 184
Athanasius 32, 45–47, 52–53
atheism 20, 52, 240, 242, 244, 248, 286, 289, 291, 294
Athenagoras 21
Athens 26, 54
Atlanta 295–296
Atlantic 93, 193, 195, 209
Attalus 21
Attila the Hun 70
Auden, W.H. 11
Augsburg Confession 172
Augustine 41, 51, 59–62, 73, 75, 78, 80–81, 86, 96–97, 99, 111, 142–143, 213
Augustinian 141, 158, 161
Augustus 14, 16, 33, 99, 120
Aurelius, Marcus 21, 24, 44
Auschwitz 277, 297
Austerfield 195
Australia 220, 262, 294
Austria 251, 274
Austro–Hungarian Empire 263
Auxentius 55
avarice 71, 144, 181
Averroes 142–143
Avignon 146, 149
Awakening 81, 209–211, 220, 225–226, 238, 293
Aylward, Gladys 281–283
Azusa 238

Bab 257–258
Babylas 28
Babylonia 89
Bacchus 157
Bach, Johann Sebastian 269
Baghdad 120, 257
Baha 257–258
Baha'is 257–258
Baha-ad Din–Shaddad 132
Balaklava 235
Balfour Declaration 278
Balfour, Arthur 272–273
Balkans 105
Bamburgh 82
Bapaume 266
baptism 26, 29–30, 35, 38, 40, 45–46, 53, 55, 59–60, 63, 74, 81, 83, 102, 164, 175, 185–186, 192, 194, 205, 220, 230, 281
Baptists 52, 63–64, 194, 204, 220–221, 230–232, 245, 285–287, 289, 293–295
Bar Kokhba 10, 14
Barbarians 33
Barcelona 183, 276
Barebones Parliament 199
Barinov, Valeri 285–286, 289
Barnado, Dr 217, 229–230
barons 110, 137
Barrows, Cliff 293
Basil the Great 51, 54, 62
basilica 38, 43, 81, 124, 157, 160
Basle 160, 173–174, 248, 272
Basque 183
Bastille 214, 218
Battle of Edington 102
Bavaria 98, 267
BBC 277, 282, 286–287
Beagle 240
Beatrice 144
Bec 109
Becket, Thomas 110, 136–136, 159
Bede 81–82
Bedford 200–201
Beirut 217
Belgrade 123, 290
Ben Hur 16
Ben–Gurion 278–279
Benedictines 65, 75, 109, 111, 113
Bengali 221
Beninicasa, Catherine 148
Berkeley 209
Berlin 269, 276, 281, 294

303

Bernadone, Pietro 139
Berne 173
Bertha 80
Berwick 176
Bethlehem 11, 38, 58, 116
Beverley Shea, George 293
Beverley 117
Beyond the Fringe 259
Beza, Theodore 175
Bible 9, 11, 27, 31, 54, 57–59, 64, 86, 90, 102, 108, 142, 147, 149, 151–152, 159, 161–163, 165, 169–175, 177, 191–192, 201, 203, 221, 223, 226, 228, 241, 256, 259, 281, 286, 288–289, 293
biblical Judaism 271
biblical 26, 31, 52–53, 93, 99, 118, 121, 147, 158–159, 161–162, 172–175, 201, 242, 259–260, 286
Biddle, John 209
bigotry 188, 190
Birmingham 209, 233, 288, 295
bishop 7, 17–18, 21–22, 28–30, 32, 35, 41, 44, 46, 53–57, 59–60, 62–63, 67, 70–75, 78, 81–83, 97, 109–110, 117, 122, 129–130, 139, 141, 147, 158, 163, 169, 171, 173, 176, 180, 185, 190–191, 202, 204, 223, 228, 242, 268, 276, 284
Bismark 183
Bithynia 16, 44
Black Book 169
Black Death 146, 148
Black Friars 142
Blandina 22
Blantyre 221
Blois, Stephen of 121
Boddy, Alexander A. 238
Bohemia 149, 182
Bohler, Peter 213
Boleyn, Anne 168–170, 188
Bologna 108, 157, 160
Bolsheviks 297
Bonhoeffer, Dietrich 276–277, 297
Boniface 97–98, 146
Book of Common Prayer 171, 173, 191, 200
Book of Kells 80
Book of Martyrs 190
Booth, Catherine 148–150, 169, 236–237
Booth, William 236–237
Bordeaux 49, 146, 285
Borgia, Cesare 155–156, 167
Borgias 153, 155–156–157, 167
Bosphorus 73, 124
Boston 190, 195, 232, 256–257
Bouillon, Godfrey of 121, 127
Boulogne, Baldwin of 121
Bourdeaux, Lorna 286
Bourges 174
Bradford, William 195
Brahmin 184
Bramonte, Donato 157
Bresslau, Helene 270
Britain 4–5, 11, 19, 75, 78, 80, 82, 86, 97, 100, 102, 115, 117, 126, 134, 160, 177, 182, 184, 197, 199–200, 204, 210–212, 215, 218–219, 222–225, 232–233, 235–237, 262–263, 267–268, 273–276, 279, 290
British and Foreign Bible Society 226
British Empire 190, 262
British soldier 235, 264
Brittany 111, 130
Brontë, Charlotte 267
Brooklyn Eagle 259
brotherhood 91, 258, 271, 295–296
Brotherly Union 192
Browne, Robert 192
Brownists 192
Bruges 152
Brussels 127, 267
Brzezinski 284
Buber, Martin 271
bubonic plague 146
Bucer, Martin 173–174

Buddha 258
Bunyan, John 144, 187, 200–201
Burgess, Alan 282
Burgundy 126, 131, 133, 151
Burgundy, Duke of 131
Bury St Edmunds 101
Byron 144
Byzantia 38, 72, 75, 86, 89, 96–97, 99, 104–105, 115, 120–121, 123–124, 130, 144, 152

Cadman, Elijah 236
Caecilian 60
Caedmon 83
Caesar, Julius 14, 23
Caesarea 32, 44–46, 54, 124, 127
Caeserea, Eusebius of 34, 38, 43–46, 57
caesars 33, 72
CAFOD 280
Cairo 128
caliphs 88–90, 92, 96, 120, 128, 132
Callistus III 156
Calpurnius 78
Calvary 112, 164
Calvin, John 174–176, 194
Calvinism 191–192, 197, 209
Cambridge 108, 159, 170, 172, 194, 197–198, 201, 219, 222, 233, 240
Canada 230, 262, 291
Candleford 236
Canon Law 27, 110–111, 141, 155, 168, 271
Canterbury Tales 138, 153
Canterbury 80–83, 109–110, 136, 138, 147, 153, 166, 168, 170, 191, 294
Cantor, Eddie 275
Cape of Good Hope 189
capitalism 175, 242–243, 245
Capone, Al 163
Cappadocean Fathers 54, 58
cardinals 105, 160, 180–181
Carey, William 220–221
Carman 81
Carolingians 98, 102
Carra de Vaux, Baron 96
Carthage 23–25, 28–29, 59–60, 70–71
Cassiodorus 64, 67
Castile 141
Castle of San Angelo 19
catacombs 28, 62
catechism 175
catechumen 9
cathedral schools 108
cathedrals 54–55, 57, 63–64, 74, 79, 82, 101, 108, 110–111, 114, 117–118, 138, 141, 151, 174, 185, 190, 197, 202, 224, 287
Catholic Christianity 75, 102
Catholic Church 17, 73, 75, 150, 161, 177, 188, 194, 276, 292
Catholic faith 181, 184
Catholic orthodoxy 181
Catholic tradition 55
Catholic 12, 17, 40, 45–46, 55, 73, 75, 96, 102, 133–134, 150, 154, 160–161, 171, 173–177, 180–181, 183–184, 188–192, 194, 197, 199–200, 204–205, 229, 238, 276, 280, 291–292
Catholicism 62, 170–171, 174, 186, 189–191, 204
Cathori 29
Caux 280
Cavaliers 197
Cavell, Edith 267–268
Caxton's 152–153
celibacy 43, 53, 56, 67, 100, 109, 169–170, 173, 181
Celsus 31–32
Celtic Christianity 78–83, 97, 103
Cerinthus 43
Cerularius 105
Chalcedon 72–73, 175
Chancellor 136, 147, 159, 167, 169, 273

Charcate, Jean 249
charity 29, 63, 91, 166, 210, 223, 291
Charlemagne 98–100, 103, 105, 121
Charles I 196–199
Charles II 199, 203–205
Charles V 164, 170
Charles VII 151
Charterhouse 212
Chartres 117
chastity 126, 183, 290
Chatillon, Reynold of 129–130
Cheddar 228
Cheshire 209
Chesterton, G.K. 140
Chiang Kai-shek 281
Chicago 232–233
Chief Rabbi 275, 277, 280
Children's Crusade 133
Chile 245
China 134, 152, 184, 186, 221, 233, 238, 262, 281–283
Chinese 184, 281–283, 297
chivalry 113–114, 122, 138, 183
Chorney, Daniel 104
Christ 7, 16, 18–23, 25–28, 30–32, 38–41, 45–46, 56, 59, 61, 73, 78, 81, 99, 102, 104, 110, 112, 127, 140, 149, 159, 163–164, 175, 180, 183–184, 190, 194, 199, 201–202, 210, 212–213, 220, 222, 238, 245, 247, 249, 254, 256, 258–259, 264, 266, 268, 276–277
Christ's College 194, 201
Christendom 49, 75–76, 192
Christian 7, 10–12, 17–20, 22–31, 34–36, 38, 40–43, 47–48, 52–54, 56, 58, 61, 63–64, 66–67, 71–72, 74, 78, 80, 83, 86, 91, 93, 97–99, 101–103, 108, 111, 113–114, 122, 129–130, 134, 138, 153, 157, 161, 163–166, 185, 189, 191, 193, 200, 203, 208, 225, 232–233, 236, 238, 243, 249, 253–254, 256–257, 267, 271, 275, 280, 282, 286–287, 289, 292, 294–295, 297
Christian Aid 280
Christian belief 19, 22, 31, 42–43, 91, 161, 286
Christian church 29, 35
Christian communicator 233
Christian Europe 93
Christian Fathers 108
Christian humanism 166
Christian morality 157, 249
Christian orthodoxy 26, 43
Christian scholars 54, 58
Christian Science 256–257
Christianity 7, 9–12, 14–22, 25, 17–36, 38–43, 47–48, 52–67, 70–72, 74–75, 78–79, 81, 83, 86–88, 91, 93, 96–99, 101–104, 108, 110–111, 113–114, 120–126, 129–130, 133–134, 138, 140, 142–143, 146, 152–153, 157, 159, 161–166, 180, 182, 184–185, 189, 191–193, 200, 202–203, 206–209, 211, 213, 219–220, 225, 229, 232–233, 245, 268, 271, 275, 285, 289, 291, 297
Christmas Day 99, 137, 264
Christmas 48, 99, 116, 137, 228, 264
Chrysopolis 38
Chrysostom, John 51, 62–64, 72, 120
Church Fathers 10, 54, 71, 75, 100, 108, 110–111, 158, 175, 292
Church Missionary Society 223, 226
Church of England 170–171, 190–191, 194, 205, 215, 226
Church of God in Christ 238
Church of the Nazarene 238
church 9–10, 12, 14, 16–19, 21–31, 33–36, 38–46, 48–49, 54–64, 66, 71–75, 79–82, 86, 96–100, 103–105, 109–112, 114–118, 120, 124, 126, 130, 133–134, 136–139, 141, 143, 147, 149–152–154, 156, 158–165, 168, 170–171, 173–175, 177,

304

180–182, 188–194, 197, 200, 202, 204–205, 209–211, 220–222, 230–231, 233, 236, 238, 244–245, 255–25
church and state   56, 63–64, 98, 100, 109, 136, 182
Churchill, Sir Winston   294
Cicero   59
Cimabue   144
Cinque Ports   130
Circumcellions   41
circumcision, male   91
Circus Maximus   16
Cistercians   113
Citeau   113
City of God   62, 99
Civil War   14, 196–198, 200–202, 209
civil courts   136
civil rights   295–296
civil rulers   174
civilisation   24, 258, 262, 270
Clairvaux, Bernard of   113, 126, 128, 180
Clapham   219, 228
Clayton, Tubby   266
Clement V   146
Clement VII   155
clergy   28–29, 36, 40–41, 44, 46, 52, 56–58, 60, 63, 72, 100, 133, 137, 146–147, 150, 169–170, 172, 180–181, 197, 204, 218, 231, 268, 292
clerical celibacy   173, 181
clerics   108–109
Cleves, Anne of   169
Clovis   74
Cloyes   133
Cobbett, William   228
Coenibites   65
Coketown   236
Colchester   230
Colet, John   159
Cologne   117, 133, 172
Colosseum   10, 15, 17
Colt, Jane   166
Columba   77, 79–80
Commodus   24
Common Law   168
Commons   167, 197, 205, 219, 223, 229
commonwealth   153, 167, 199, 277
Communion (see also Eucharist and Lord's Supper)   23, 27, 30, 47, 57, 60, 64, 149–150, 164, 175, 235, 265
communism   39, 101, 157, 193, 242–245, 282–289
Communist Manifesto   243
Communist Revolution   101
community   29, 35, 55, 60, 65, 89, 92, 104, 113, 117, 164, 185, 192, 194, 203–205, 210, 228, 232, 258, 271, 283
Comnena, Anna   123
Compiegne   151
concentration camps   275–278
confession   59, 60–61, 103, 158, 163, 169, 172, 181–182, 184–185
confessors   28, 53
conformity   48, 238
Confucius   281
Congregationalist   192
Congress   204, 255, 272, 296
Conservative   173, 198, 225
Conservatoire   286
Constans   47
Constantine V   104
Constantine   35–41, 44, 47, 71, 74, 97, 120, 152, 243–244
Constantinople   10, 38–40, 54, 57–58, 63, 71–75, 97–99, 104–105, 114, 120, 122–124, 126, 132, 134, 244
Constantius   33–35, 47
Continent   110, 176, 219, 221, 223, 279
contraception   292
Contract Social   218
convent   83, 141

conversion   11, 19, 25, 27, 29, 35, 38–39, 57, 58, 61, 66, 74, 78, 81, 83, 98, 102, 140, 174, 176, 182, 190, 197, 210, 213–214, 219–221, 223, 232, 242, 279, 297
Cook, Captain   220
Copenhagen   246
Copernicus   155–156
Coptic   12, 52
Cordoba   96
Corsica   62
Council of Aix–la–Chappelle   111
Council of Arles   78
Council of Carthage   29
Council of Chalons   111
Council of Constance   148, 150
Council of Constantinople   104
Council of Egyptian bishops   44
Council of Ephesus   66, 73
Council of Nicaea   27, 46–47, 53, 70, 72
Council of State   199, 201
Council of Trent   154, 160, 180
council   27, 29–30, 44–47, 53, 66, 70, 72–74, 78, 103–104, 111, 113, 121, 137, 141, 148, 150, 154, 160, 167, 180–181, 192, 199, 201, 292
counter–reformation   184
County of Edessa   127
Coverdale's English translation   170
Cowther, Samuel Adjai   223
Cranmer, Thomas   168–171, 173, 188, 190–191
creation   10, 20, 22–23, 42–44, 48, 61, 139, 144, 189, 191, 208, 225, 230, 240–241, 249, 276
Creeds of Nicaea   45, 73, 175
creeds   22, 27, 40, 45–48, 73, 105, 114, 170, 175, 215, 258, 271, 280
Crescens   20
Crimean War   234
Crispus   36
Croesus   161
Cromwell, Oliver   176, 194, 197–200, 203–204
Cromwell, Thomas   169
crucifixion   38, 125
crusade   123, 125, 127–130, 133, 140, 149–150, 219, 293
Crusaders   103, 115, 121–125, 127–129, 131–132, 134, 136
Crusades   122, 132–133, 140
Cuthbert   83, 100
Cyprian   27, 29–30, 60, 96
Cyrene   89
Cyrillic   134
Czechoslovakia   149, 163, 192

da Vinci, Leonardo   153–155
Dacia   16
Dalmatia   57
Dalriada   80
Damascus   58, 89, 128, 130
Damascus, John of   102, 104
Damietta   140
Daniel Deroda   272
Dante   39, 144
Danube   28
Dark Ages   67, 72, 80, 293, 297
Darkest England   223, 236–237
Darnley   176
Darwin, Charles   240–242, 245, 248–249, 251
Das Kapital   244
Dayton   242
De Revolutionibus   155
de Bure, Idelette   174
de Nobili, Roberto   184
de Rothchild, Lionel   280
de Unamuno, Miguel de   246
deacons   17, 20–21, 28–29, 45, 78, 136, 101, 175
Dead Sea Scrolls   64
Dead Sea   64, 127
death penalty   55, 215
Decian persecution   27–28, 32, 36, 60
Decius   28

Declaration of Rights   205, 218
Decline and Fall of the Roman Empire   33
del Verrocchio, Andrea   154
Demetrius   30, 32
Denmark   141
Der Judenstaat   272
Derbyshire   116, 205, 234
Descartes   208, 246
Descartes, Rene   208
devil   43, 53, 237
Devon   97
Dexter Avenue Baptist Church   295
dialectical materialism   284
Dickens, Charles   228–229
Didache   27
Diego   141
Dio Cassius   11
Diocletian   33–35, 44, 53
disciples   32, 44, 53, 55, 185
discipleship   192, 276
discipline   26, 28, 54, 65, 103, 108, 136, 141, 154, 174–175, 183, 198, 212, 232, 236, 238, 266
Disraeli, Benjamin   225
dissenters   175, 192, 202, 204
dissolution   169, 197
Divine Grace   27, 61
doctrine   22, 47, 73, 102, 143, 149, 159, 161, 175, 255
Dome of the Rock   115, 125
Dominic   141, 144
Dominican   141–143, 148, 153, 160, 173, 181
Donation of Constantine   97
Donatist schism   40, 61
Donatists   40–41, 60–61
Donegal   79
Dorylaeum   124
Dostoevsky   287
Dovey in Flanders   186
Drake, Sir Francis   188, 195
dreams   53, 181, 250, 271, 290
Dreyfus, Alfred   272
Drogheda   199
Druids   78
Druze   120
Dublin   229, 290
Dunbar   199
Dunblane   176
Durham   82, 101, 115
Durham, Simion of   101

East (Church and Empire)   18, 22, 26, 34, 38, 40, 44, 46–47, 54–55, 57, 63–64, 72, 75, 89, 98–100, 104–105, 114, 117, 125, 127, 132, 152, 164, 222, 244, 271, 294
East Anglia   198
East End   115
East Pakistan   290
Easter Day   57, 81
Easter   18, 46, 48, 57, 60, 80–81, 295
Eastern Emperors   75, 99
Eastern Orthodoxy   76, 292
eastern   11–12, 23, 34, 40, 46, 57, 63–64, 72, 75–76, 99, 102, 104, 184, 277, 292
ecclesiastical court   151, 168
ecclesiastical power   105, 177
ecclesiology   180
economics   214
Eddy, Mary Baker   256–257
Edessa   127–128
Edgehill   198
Edict of Nantes   194–195
Edinburgh   199, 233
Edmund   101
Edward VI   170–171, 186, 188
Edwards, Jonathan   209–211, 220
Egypt   10, 30, 35, 44, 47, 65–66, 86, 88–89, 120, 128, 279
Egyptian   30, 36, 44, 46–47, 52, 79
Eichmann, Adolf   277
Eighth Century prophets   243
Einhard   99
Eisenach   164
Eisleben   161

305

El Aqsa Mosque 125
El Cid 120
El Djem 16
elders 175, 191
Elijah 52, 236
Eliot, George 272
Elliot, T.S. 138, 144
Ely 197
emancipation 38, 283
Emperor Alexius 121, 123, 125, 127
Emperor Arcadius 63
Emperor Caracalla 30
Emperor Charles V 164
Emperor Gratian 56
Emperor in Constantinople 72, 99, 126
Emperor Julian 52–53
Emperor Justinian 114–115
Emperor Maximus 70
Emperor Nero 14, 299
Emperor Severus 24, 27–28
Emperor Theodosuis 56
Emperor Titus 10, 71, 205
Emperor Trojan 16–17
Emperor Vespasian 10
emperor 10, 14–22, 24–25, 27–30, 33–36, 38–40, 44–46, 52, 56–57, 63, 70, 72–73, 75, 97, 99, 104–105, 120–121, 123–127, 132, 142, 150, 152, 164–165
Empire 10, 14, 16, 19, 23, 25, 33, 35–36, 38–40, 47, 52, 57, 62, 64, 70, 72, 74–75, 78, 86, 89–90, 96–100, 114, 120–121, 124, 130, 132, 134, 152, 181, 190, 262–263, 289
Empress Eudoxia 63
Empress Theodora 104
Enfide 64
Engels 243–244
England 33, 75, 80–81, 83, 98, 109–110, 116, 128, 130, 136–138, 146, 159–160, 166–174, 176–177, 186–191, 194–196, 198, 200–201, 203, 205, 211, 213, 215, 219, 222–223, 225–226, 232–233, 236–238, 251, 255, 257, 275, 279
English Baptists 194
English language 82, 189, 252
English Plantations 186
English Protestantism 190
English 57–58, 78, 81–83, 102, 125, 131, 137, 146–148, 151–153, 169–170, 172, 176, 188–192, 194–195, 199–202, 268, 285, 293
Ephesus 10, 14, 17, 43, 66, 72–73
episcopate 54
Epistle of Barnabus 27
Epistle to the Romans 213
epistles 159
Epworth 212
Erasmus Desiderius 158–161, 165–167, 173, 180–181
Erfurt 161, 275
Escomb 115
Essay on Man 208
Essenes 52
Essex 230, 267
established church 194, 218
established religion 40
establishment 87, 193, 204, 237, 243, 273
Ethelbert 80
Etheria 49
Etruria 19
Eucharist (see also Communion and Lord's Supper) 17, 23, 40–41, 285
Eugenuis 56
Europe 38, 53, 72, 75, 79, 93, 96–97, 100, 109, 114, 117, 121, 124–128, 133–136, 140, 142, 146, 152, 156, 161, 168, 172, 177, 180–181, 184, 189, 192–193, 199, 204, 209, 244, 248, 269–270, 272–273, 275, 277, 279, 293
evangelical awakening 225–226
evangelical Christians 219
evangelical community 228

evangelical 193, 201, 219, 223, 225–226, 237, 243–245, 282
evangelism 80, 134, 259, 279, 292
evangelist 233, 236, 237–238, 292–293
Eve 23, 60, 254
evolution 96, 241–242, 245, 248, 251
excommunication 44, 65, 105, 136–137, 146, 149, 154, 164, 189
Exeter 97, 229
exile 10, 28, 47, 53, 64, 137, 149–150, 204, 285, 288
existentialism 246, 248, 271
exodus 88
Eyam 116, 205

Fabian 28
Factories Act 226
factories 223, 226, 236, 245, 274
faith 9–11, 14, 16–23, 25–26, 28–29, 31–33, 35–36, 38–43, 46, 48, 52, 60, 62, 64, 73, 79, 82, 88, 90, 101, 109, 113–115, 120, 132, 138, 140, 142, 144, 147–148, 161, 163–164, 168, 170, 172–174, 181–182, 184–186, 190–193, 208, 210, 212–213, 215, 220, 223, 228
fall of Rome 70, 72
Farel, Guillaume 174
Farne Islands 83
fasting 52, 103, 148, 173
Father Almighty 22, 45
Father Gleb 285
Father of the Reformation 160–161
Fatima 92–93
Fawkes, Guy 190
Felicitas 24
fellowship of believers 194
Ferdinand 182, 263
feudalism 165, 175, 242
Fighting Insanity 289
Filoque 73, 105
Fire of London 205
First World War 264, 266–267, 273
Five Mile Act 205
Flanders 186, 263
Flanders, Robert of 121
Florence 144, 153–155, 157–158
Florida 293
Flossenburg 277
Food-for-the-Million 236
Fort William College 221
Fotheringay 189
Fourth Lateran Council 103, 141
Fox, George 202
Foxe, John 190
France 41, 57, 74, 78, 93, 96–98, 121–124, 130, 133, 137, 146, 150–151, 155–156, 176, 182, 188, 194–195, 197, 215, 218, 263, 268, 270, 272, 291
Francis Xavier 184–185
Franciscans 134, 140–141, 146
Franco-Prussian War 248, 268
Frank Buchman 279
Frankfurt University 271
Frankfurt 176, 271
Franklin, Benjamin 209, 211
Franks 74, 78, 80, 98, 127–128
Frederick 164–165
Freiberg 249
French Revolution 209
French 21, 127, 146–147, 153, 174, 189, 208–209, 232, 234, 248–249, 264, 268, 270, 272
Freud, Sigmund 249–252, 257
friars 134, 139–142, 147
Fry, Christopher 138
Fry, Elizabeth 223–224
Fuhrer 273–274
fundamentalism 200, 238, 242
Funk, Robert 47

Gabriel 90
Galapagos 240
Galerius 33
Galilee 9, 14, 48, 89, 129, 279

Galileo 156
Gandhi 290, 295
Garden of Eden 254
Garrick, David 211, 228
Gaul 21, 55, 74
Gaza 35, 127, 130
General Baptists 194
Geneva 174–176, 191
Genghis Khan 133–134
Genoa 125–126, 133
Genseric 70–71
Gentiles 275
Georgia 212–213, 244, 295–296
German crusaders 134
German 96, 98, 134, 152, 164–165, 172–173, 192, 204, 212, 234, 264, 267–268, 270, 272–274, 276, 280–281
Germanic tribes 70
Germany 78, 97–98, 122, 126, 133, 160–161, 166, 169–170, 172–173, 177, 182, 195, 234, 244, 251, 262, 267–268, 271, 274, 276–277, 280, 291, 294
Gestapo 181
Gibbon 33–34, 36, 71
Giotto 144
gladiatorial games 39
Glasgow 221, 233, 294
Glastonbury 82
Gloucester Journal 228
Gnosticism 22–23, 42–43, 57
Goa 185
God in history 48
God of creation 43, 48
God of Trinity 10, 48
God the Father 22, 45, 54
God the Son 54
God 9–10, 16–17, 22–27, 31, 40, 42–48, 52, 54, 56–57, 61–63, 71–75, 78, 82, 87–91, 98–100, 102–103, 108–110, 112, 114, 118, 120–122, 132, 137, 139, 142–144, 148, 151, 158–159, 162–164, 166, 168, 171–172, 174–175, 181–183, 192–193, 195–196, 198–200, 203, 208
Goethe 144
Golan Heights 89, 127
Golden Hind 188
Gonell, William 166
Gonzalez 61
Good Friday 57, 144, 270
Gorbachev, Michail 288
Gospel 17, 27, 31–32, 36, 42–43, 45–46, 58, 82, 97, 149, 159, 163, 180, 211, 213, 218, 220–221, 231, 236–237, 256, 287, 289, 294
Gothic 28
Goths 64, 70, 74
Grace Abounding to the Chief of Sinners 200
Graham, Billy 292–295
Graham, Reverend Stirling 268
Great Awakening 210, 220
Great Bible of Coverdale 169
Great Persecution 33, 35, 53
Great Schism 12, 29, 149
Great War 263
Greater London Crusade 293
Greco-Roman culture 67
Greece 26, 31, 99, 108, 124
Greek culture 10, 26, 32
Greek New Testament 159, 219
Greek 10–12, 19, 23, 26, 30–32, 45, 49, 52, 58–59, 96, 104, 124, 159, 164, 172, 209, 219, 234, 260
Grenada 96, 162
Grey is the Colour of Hope 288
gulags 249, 285
Gunsbach 270
Gutenberg 151–152
Guthrie, Dr Thomas 228
Gwyn, Nell 203
Gwynne, Sally 215

Habakkuk 164
Hadrian 11, 19, 78

Hagia Sophia 39, 101, 104–105, 114, 124
hagiography 53
hajj 89, 91
Hakim 120
Ham, Mordecai Fowler 293
Hamblen, Stuart 293
Hamilton, Patrick 176
Hannibal 70
haram 87
Hardy, T.B. 263
Harnack 62
Harringay Arena 293
Harris, Howell 210–211
Harrison, Eleanor 281
Harrison, Robert 192
Harrow 225
Hartlepool 83
Hasidism 271
Hastings, Selina 211
Hattin, Horns of 129–130
Hawkins, John 195
healing 238, 257
Health and Apprentices Act 226
heaven 11, 22, 46, 62, 101, 121, 139, 144, 154, 162–164, 203, 220, 251, 284
Hebrew language 96, 277, 279
Hebrew Scriptures 27, 31
Hebrew University 271
Hebrew 19–20, 27, 31, 58, 96, 209, 277–279
Hegel 240, 246
Helena 35, 38, 48–49
Heliogabulus 27
Hell 72, 144, 183
Hellenization 11
Heloise 110–114
Helwys, Thomas 194
Henrietta 197
Henry I of England 110
Henry I of France 124
Henry II 136–138
Henry V 34, 189
Henry VIII 167–168, 188–189
Heraclea 124
heresy 10, 22–23, 25–26, 40–41, 44–45, 61, 66, 113, 141, 147, 150, 153, 163, 168, 171, 175–176, 182
heretics 22, 25, 55, 66, 73, 134, 141, 147, 151, 154, 163–164, 180–182, 185, 193
hermit 52–53, 55, 57, 63, 66, 111, 123–124
Herod's Temple 125
Herodias 64
Herzl, Theodor 272–273
Hesse 98
Hexapla 31
hierarchy 88, 238
Hieronymus, Eusebius 57
Hieropolis 21
High Church 188, 197
hijra 88
Hilarianus 24
Hilda 77, 83
Himmler, Heinrich 183, 276
Hindus 290–291
Hippo 41, 60, 62, 73
History of England 219
History of Misfortunes 112
History of the Corruptions of Christianity 209
History of the Jews 182, 272, 279
Hitler Youth Organisations 276
Hitler, Adolf 249, 273–276, 281, 284, 294
Hitlerish 147
Hogarth, William 208
Holland 176–177, 182, 193, 218, 268
Hollywood 250, 282
Holocaust 277–278
Holy Land 38, 49, 121, 124, 126–128, 132–133, 136, 149
Holy Roman Empire 99
Holy Sepulchre 120–121, 125, 130
Holy Spirit 20, 22–23, 27, 46, 48, 54, 73, 105

holy club 210, 212, 215
holy places 121, 125, 130, 132, 180, 183
Holyrood house 176
homeless 196, 223, 229
homoiousion 45, 46
homosexuality 292
Hong Kong 186, 282
honour 24, 103, 122, 137, 151, 189, 228
Hooker, Richard 190
hope 32, 61–62, 66–67, 120, 140, 144, 182, 188–189, 193, 221, 240, 245, 247–248, 266, 275, 280, 288, 291, 297
Horsemen of the Apocalypse 70
hospitality 63, 147
hospitals 54, 67, 126, 130, 175, 212, 214, 223, 234, 267, 291
host 150
Hour of Decision 293
House of Commons 167, 197, 219, 223, 229
House of Lords 197, 229
House of Peers 283
Houses of Parliament 190
Howard, Catherine 169
Hugo, Victor 218
Huguenots 176, 182, 189, 194–195, 204, 232
human rights 220
humanism 159, 166
Hundred Year's war 151
Hungary 123–124, 134, 294
Huntingdon 197, 211
Huntingdon, Countess of 211
Huss, Jan 149–151, 163–164
Huxley, T.H. 241–242
hymns 16, 56, 114, 175, 220, 256

I and Thou 271
Ichud 271
icons 104–105, 173
illegitimacy 156, 168
Illinois 254
Imad-ad-Din 128
imams 92–93
Imitation of Christ 220, 268
immersion 192
incarnation 23, 52, 247
incense 18, 48
Independent churches 204, 230
independent 59, 108, 110, 160, 173, 191–192, 196, 200, 209–210, 238, 249, 257, 278
India 86, 89, 184–186, 189, 221, 235, 262, 290–291, 294–295
Indianapolis 233
Indians 185, 204, 211, 221, 262, 290–291
Indonesia 238
indulgences 103, 149, 160–163, 181
Industrial Revolution 223, 243, 262
industrialisation 225, 243
infidels 122, 185
Inherit the Wind 242
Inkerman, battle of 234
Inn of the Sixth Happiness 282
Inquisition 48, 181–182, 185
Institute of Protestant Deaconesses in Germany 234
Interpretation of Dreams 250
invasion 78, 109, 117, 124, 152
Iona 80–83
iota 44–45
Iran 89, 134, 258
Iraq 86, 88–89, 91, 120, 128
Ireland 78–80, 138, 186, 199, 223, 233, 280, 291
Irenaeus 22–24, 26–27
Irish 78, 80, 103, 186, 199, 224, 263
Isis 36
Islam 11, 41, 88, 90–93, 96–97, 120, 132, 134, 138, 143, 258
Israel 14, 96, 243, 258, 271, 273, 278–279
Istanbul 39, 234
Italy 64, 70, 76, 97, 99, 105, 122, 124, 144, 149, 153, 156–157, 162, 180, 182, 234
Ixelles 267

Jaffa 125, 132
James I of England (VI of Scotland) 176, 177, 194, 190–191, 194–196, 205
James II 205
James, Jesus' brother 10
Janani Luwum 297
Janneken 193
Japan 184, 186, 281, 283, 297
Jarrow 81
Jarvis, Jim 229
Javneh 14
Jehovah 198
Jehovah's Witnesses 259
Jerash 16
Jerome 51, 57–59, 61–62, 67, 70, 75
Jerusalem 10–11, 14, 26, 28, 32, 38, 41, 48–49, 53, 71, 88, 103–104, 115–116, 120, 122–123, 125–131, 183, 273
Jesuit 183–184, 186, 190, 205
Jesus 'Son of God' 44
Jesus College 170
Jesus is Lord 11, 40
Jesus of Nazareth 43, 62, 66
Jesus Seminar 47
Jesus 7, 9–12 14, 17–20, 22–23, 29, 31–33, 36, 38, 40–48, 59, 61–62, 66, 72–73, 87, 90, 99, 102–103, 114, 133, 138–139, 163, 170, 183–185, 209–210, 237, 245, 249, 254, 256, 269, 271, 276–277, 286–287, 291–292
Jesus' tomb 38
Jewish state 271–272
Jewish–Arab 271
Jews 10–11, 14, 18, 20, 23, 26, 30–31, 49, 52, 58, 67, 71, 73, 88, 91, 96, 104, 120, 122–123, 127, 130, 142–143, 167, 181–183, 185, 200, 242–243, 248–249, 251, 268, 270–280, 285, 288, 300
Jezebel 63
Jihad 128
John, Esther 297
John the Apostle 18, 43
John the Baptist 52, 63–64
John's Gospel 17, 31
Johnson, Paul 182, 272
Johnson, Samuel 228
Jordan 16, 49, 89
Josephus 67
Journals 214, 222
Jubilee Pilgrimage 146
Judah 9
Judaism 11, 14, 19, 24, 31, 48, 87, 120, 143, 242–243, 271
Judas 32
Judeo–Christian 251
Judge Bennett 202
Jung, Carl Gustav 251–252, 257, 268
justification by faith 163, 173–174, 210, 213
Justin (martyr) 19–20
Justina 56

Kagawa, Toyohiko 283
Kant, Immanuel 240
Kappel 174
Karnak 66
Kashchenko 289
Kazan Cathedral 287
Kelvedon 230
Kempis, Thomas à 220, 268
Kennedy, Geoffrey Studdert 263–266, 295–296
Kennedy, John F. 295–296
Kent 80–81, 152, 169, 285
Kepler, Johannes 156
Keston College 285
keys of heaven 163–164
KGB 181, 287–289

307

Khadija 86, 88–89, 92–93
Kharijites 92
kibbutz 167, 271, 273, 279
Kierkegaard, Soren 246–248, 268
Kiev 101, 134
Kindertransport 275
King Alfred 102
King James 196
King James' Version 58, 172
King Oswin 83
King Vladimir 101
King, Martin Luther 294–297
Kingdom Halls 259
Kingdom of God movement 283
kingdom of God 62, 283
kingdom of heaven 139, 163
Kipling, Rudyard 116
Knibb, William 221
Knights of St John (or Hospitallers) 126
Knights of the Temple of Jerusalem 126
Knights Templar 113–114, 126, 128, 130
knights 113–114, 121–122, 124–127, 129, 136–138
Knox, John 176–177
Kobe Theological Seminary 283
Kolbe, Maximilian 297
Kristallnacht 274
Krushchev, Nikita 285
Ku Klux Klan 295–296
Kung, Hans 292

La Rochelle 194
Lactantius 35–36
Lady with the Lamp 234
laity 28, 57, 60, 164, 181, 238, 292
Lamborene 270
Lancashire 202, 209
Lancaster, John 215
Lankford, Sarah 238
Large, Robert 152
last judgement 91
Latimer, Hugh 169, 171
Latin 25–26, 49, 57–59, 78, 80, 105, 126–127, 134, 142, 144, 147, 149–150, 159, 169, 184, 188, 201, 209, 234, 238, 292
Latourette, Kenneth 72, 97
Laurentian Library 158
Lausanne 294
Lawrence, D.H. 300
Laws of Motion 208
Lawson, Jeannie 281
lawyers 136, 182
Lay preachers 213
Lazare, Bernard 272
Lazarus, Emma 196
League of Militant Atheists 244
Lecky, W.E.H. 219
Leeds 209, 263
legions 35, 78
legislation 38, 189, 219, 225–226, 285, 295
Leiningen, Count Emich of 122
Lenin 244, 286
Leningrad 244, 286–287
Leo's Tome 73
Leonides 24, 30
lepers 54, 139, 185, 270, 291
Les Miserables 218
Letters and Papers from Prison 276
Libanius 63
libelli 28
liberals 181
Liberation Theology 245
liberty of the press 201
liberty 40, 138, 148, 196, 201
libraries 108, 223
Lichfield 202
Licinius 38
Liguge 55
Lincoln College 212
Lincoln Memorial 296
Lincoln 78, 212, 296
Lincolnshire 81, 190, 195, 212
Lindisfarne 82–83, 100

Lisbon 185
Litany 29, 170
Liverpool Cathedral 224
Liverpool 218, 224, 233, 255
Livingstone, David 221–223
Logos 31
Lollards 147, 213
Lombards 65, 70, 74–75, 97, 99, 105
London City Mission 226, 228
London Missionary Society 221
London 78, 81, 128, 130, 136, 146, 159, 166, 168, 186, 190, 194, 201, 205, 223, 228–231, 233–236, 244, 267–268, 272, 276, 280–282, 293–294
Londonderry 224
Lord Chancellor of England 159, 167
Lord Protector 199
Lord's Prayer 81
Lord's Supper (see also Communion and Eucharist) 18, 102, 174, 256
Loreto 290
Lorraine 127, 133, 268
Los Angeles 238, 293
Louis XII 156
Louis XIV 195
Loyola, Ignatius 183–186
Lucilla 60
Lunokhod 285
Lusignon, Guy of 130
Luther, Martin 45, 153, 160–168, 172–174, 181, 213, 293–297, 299
Lutheran 12, 173, 176, 180–181, 192, 204, 242, 246–248, 276, 279, 294
Lutterworth 147–148
Lynn 257
Lyons 21–22

Machiavelli, Nicolo 156–157, 167
Magdala, Mary 41
magistrates 60
Magna Carta 138
Magnesia 17
Magus, Simon 43
Magyars 100
Maimonides 143
Mainz 98, 122, 152, 160
Malinda 185
Malta 126
Manchester 233, 267
mandarin 184, 281
Manichees 59
Manresa 183
Manual of the Mother Church 257
manuscripts 34, 58, 64, 159
Manzikert 121
Mao Tse-Tung 249, 281, 297
Marks, Simon 280
Marmoutier 55
Marnie 250
marriage 67, 86, 92, 97, 111, 148, 165–170, 197, 215, 256, 274
married clergy 46
Marseilles 133
Marshman, Joshua 221
Marston Moor 198
martyrs 11, 16, 17–26, 28–29, 30, 33, 35–36, 38, 41, 53, 60, 98, 138, 150, 160, 190, 193, 245, 258, 272, 297
Marx, Carl 242–246, 249, 268, 284
Marxism 245, 283
Mary II 205
Mary Stuart 176, 188–189
Mary the mother of Jesus 23, 36, 73, 90, 93
Mary Tudor 170–171, 174, 176, 186
Maryland 211
Masemola, Manche 297
Mass 164, 173, 176, 181, 188, 190, 202, 233, 292, 297
Massachusetts 210, 232
mathematics 31, 79, 99, 184, 208, 234
Matthew's Gospel 58
Maxentius 38

Maximian 33
Maxys 34
Mayflower 195
Mecca 86–91, 96, 175
Medici 153–154, 157–158
medicine 108, 214, 221, 256, 269
medieval Church 141
medieval scholasticism 61
medieval world 74–75, 138, 162
Medina 88–89, 92
Meditations 21, 162
Mediterranean 10–11, 70, 183
Mein Kampf 274
Melanchthon, Philip 153, 172–173
Melun 111
Member of Parliament 197, 219
Memphis 296
Mercia 109
Merton Priory 136
Messiah 10, 271
Methodists 9, 211–215, 218, 230, 236, 238, 255, 281
Methodius 134
Metropolitan Tabernacle 230–231, 233
Mexico 294
Michelangelo 157–158, 160, 249
Middle Ages 19, 97, 108, 113, 117, 142, 151, 153, 160, 171
Middleton, Alice 166
Milan 33, 55–57, 59–60, 72, 155
Mileto 21
Miletus, Isadore of 114
Millennium 7, 110, 118, 120, 292, 297, 300
Miller, Arthur 182, 204
Milner, Isaac 219
Milton, John 144, 199, 201
Milvian Bridge 35, 38
minster 117, 173
misericords 118
Missionaries of Charity 291
missionaries 9–10, 75, 78, 80–81, 97–98, 134, 140, 185, 212, 220–223, 226, 229, 232–233, 236, 256, 259, 270, 281, 283, 290–291, 297
missions 64, 80, 134, 211, 221–222, 233, 282, 293–294
modern world 153, 209, 292, 297
Mompesson, William 205
monarchies 146
monasticism 49, 51–55, 58–60, 62–67, 72–75, 79–80, 82–83, 97–100, 103–104, 108, 112–113, 126, 142, 153, 158, 161, 165–166, 169, 173, 177, 197, 285
Mongol Empire 134
Monica 59–60
monks 29, 47, 49, 52–54, 57, 64–67, 74–75, 79–82, 97–98, 101, 104, 108–110, 114–115, 118, 121, 126, 134, 138, 142, 147, 154, 158, 244, 297
Montanism 26
Monte Cassino 64–65, 142
Montgomery 295–296
Montmartre 183–184
Montserrat 183
Moody, Dwight L. 231–233, 238, 292–294
Moors 93, 96, 182–183
Moral Re-Armament 279–280
morality 20, 40, 42–43, 97, 157, 246, 249, 280
Moravians 212–213
More, Hannah 228
More, Margaret 166
More, Thomas 159, 166–169, 172
Mormon Tabernacle Choir 256
Mormons 254–256
Morning and Evening 230
Morocco 23, 93
Moscow 104, 134, 281, 289, 294
Moses 26, 49, 87, 90, 258
mosque 39, 88, 120, 125, 128
Mother of God 73, 114
Mother Teresa 211, 289, 291
Mount Alverno 140

308

Mount Carmel 258
Mount Hermon 233
Mount Herzl 273
Mount Hira 86
Mount Lebanon 127
Mount Moriah 115
Mount Nebo 49
Mount of Olives 38, 125
Mount Olympus 246
Mount Vernon Church 232
Mozarabs 96
Muggeridge, Malcolm 291
Muhammed 86–93, 96, 258
Mull 80
Muller, George 232
Murder in the Cathedral 138
Murray, Grace 214
Museum of Atheism 244
Muslim world 96, 183
Muslims 39, 87–93, 98, 100, 115, 120–121, 125–129, 132, 140, 142–143, 152, 185, 290–291, 297
mystic 114

Naples 142
Napoleon 183, 249, 262
Naseby 198
natural justice 35, 182
natural selection 241
Navarre 156
nave 54, 115, 117
Nazi anti-Semitism 280
Nazianzus, Gregory of 54, 58
Nazis 248, 251, 271, 274, 276–277, 280, 297
Negev 279
Nelson, Horatio 218
Nero 14–15, 44
Nestorius 66, 73
Netherlands 97, 160, 192
Nettleton, Edith 281
neurosis 252
Nevsky, Alexander 134
New England 196, 257
New Guinnea 297
New Hampshire 256
New Jerusalem 11
New Plymouth 195
New Rochelle 195
New Testament 10, 14, 18, 27, 41, 58, 90, 110, 159, 161, 163–164, 172, 175, 192, 219, 221, 264, 271, 286
New World 167, 184, 193, 195, 203, 218
New York 196, 211, 230, 262, 269–272, 278, 294
New Zealand 262
Newcastle 19, 280
Newgate prison 166, 223
Newman, John Henry 47
Newsweek 293
Newton, John 220, 228
Newton, Sir Isaac 208
Nicaea 27, 44–47, 53, 70, 72–73, 124, 175
Nicene Creed 105
Nicomedia 33–35, 38, 44, 46
Nicomedia, Eusebius of 46
Niemoller, Martin 276
Nietzsche, Friedrich 246, 248–249, 268, 300
Nightingale of the House 219
Nightingale, Florence 234–235
Nile 53, 120
ninety-five theses 161, 163, 294
Nixon, Richard 295
Noah 90
Nobel Peace Prize 270, 291, 296
Nonconformist Conscience 204, 226
Nonconformists 204–205
nonconformity 175, 204, 208
Norfolk 267
Normandy 109, 121, 130–131
Normandy, Robert of 121
Normans 109, 117–118, 136
North Africa 23, 41, 96, 120

North America 176, 254
Northampton 137, 210
Northfield 232–233
Northumbria 81, 83, 109
Northumbria, Edwin of 81, 83
Norwich 192, 223
Notre Dame 108, 111, 117
Nottinghamshire 170, 195, 220
Novatian schism 29–30
Nun of Kent 169
nuns 81, 83, 101, 111, 165, 169, 173, 188, 244, 289–290, 292
Nur-ad-Din 128–129
Nuremberg 277
Nursia, Benedict of 51, 64–65, 75, 113, 300
Nyssa, Gregory of 10

Oates, Captain 299
Oates, Titus 205
Octavius 14
Oedipus Complex 250
Old Testament prophet 87
Old Testament 14, 20, 23, 26, 31, 42, 52, 58–59, 87, 198
oligarchy 90
Omar Khayyám 299
Omar 89
omnipotent 174
On the Papacy in Rome 164
One Day in the Life of Ivan Denisovich 285
ontological argument 109
Orange, William of 205
Orange, Prince of 189
ordinances 175
ordination of women 292
organisation 28, 90, 108, 111, 174, 229
Oriental 91, 115
Origen 24, 26, 28, 30–32, 54
Original sin 61
Orleans 74, 150–151, 174
orphanage 224, 231–232, 282
orphans 28, 282
Orthodox Christianity 30, 60, 101, 133–134, 152
Orthodox Church 104, 130, 244, 285, 289
Orthodox worship 101
orthodox belief 41, 45, 53
orthodox position 46, 56
orthodox 12, 23, 30, 40–41, 45–47, 53, 55–56, 60, 101, 104, 130, 133–134, 152, 208, 241, 244, 254–255, 259, 285, 287, 289
orthodoxy 26, 43, 47, 76, 134, 181, 292
Orvieto 143
Osma Cathedral 141
Oswald 81–83
Othman 90, 92
Owen, Robert 225
Oxford University 190
Oxford 96, 108, 146–147, 171–172, 190, 210, 212, 233, 242

Pachomius 51, 53
Padua 108
pagan priests 33, 52
pagan temples 39, 66
paganism 19, 26, 31–33, 36, 38–39, 46, 52, 55–56, 60, 62–63, 66, 71, 74, 98, 100, 104
Palagius 61
Pale Galilean 101
Palencia University 141
Palestine 19, 32, 38, 49, 65, 89, 271–274, 278
Palmer, Phoebe 238
papacy 30, 56, 86, 97–99, 105, 113–114, 128, 142, 146, 149, 153–157, 156, 164, 169–170, 180–181, 188–189, 276
Papua 297
Paraclete 112–113
Paradise Lost 201–202
Paradise Regained 201

Paris communists 244
Paris Missionary Society 270
Paris 74, 98, 108, 111, 117, 127, 136, 142, 174, 183–184, 189, 194, 214, 244, 266, 269–270, 272, 294
parish priest 173
parish 160, 173, 180, 189
Parks, Rosa 295
Parliament 164, 190–191, 196–199, 204–205, 219, 225–226
Parr, Catherine 169
parson 205, 208, 214
Particular Baptists 194
Pascal, Blaise 240
passive resistance 295–296
pastors 54, 141, 174–175, 176, 202, 210, 220, 230–231, 251, 276, 297
paters 161
Patriarch John 75
Patriarch Michael Cerularius 105
Patrick 78–79
Paul the Apostle 10, 16–18, 30, 35, 38, 43, 45, 59, 61, 71, 97, 159, 163–164, 186, 213
Paulinus 57, 81, 83
peasant unions 283
Peasants' Revolt 147
Peasants' Crusade 123
peasants 79, 81, 104, 122–123, 157, 272, 281
Peasants' War 165
Peking 134
Pembroke College 210
penance 66, 103, 122, 138, 162–163
Pendle Hill 202
Penn 203–204
Pennsylvania 203–204, 259, 279
penny pamphlets 228
Pentecost 48
Pentecostal 238
Pentecostalists 238, 245
people of the book 91
Pepin III 97–98
Pepys, Samuel 203
perestroika 288–289
Perpetua 24
persecution 13–14, 16, 18–19, 21–22, 26–29, 30, 32–36, 38, 40–41, 44, 48, 53, 55, 60, 147–148, 171, 182, 185, 192, 245, 258, 273, 284–285
Persia 120
Persian Empire 86, 89
Persians 52, 89, 257
Person of Christ 73
Perugia 143
Peter the Apostle 30, 32, 71, 99, 157, 160–161, 163–164, 174
Peter the Hermit 123–124
Peters, Sarah 215
Petition of Rights 197
Pharisees 14
Philadelphia 17, 204
Philip II 130–131
Philip IV 146
Philip the Arabian 28
Philippi 18
Philo 31
Philology 248
philosopher 20–21, 31, 35, 208–209, 269–270, 273
Philotheus 134
Phrygia 21, 26
Picts 80
Pied Piper of Hamlin 133
Pieta 157
Pietists 177
Pilgrim Fathers 176, 195
pilgrim 49, 88, 176, 195, 200–201, 247
Pilgrim's Progress 200–201
pilgrimage 48–49, 55, 80, 87, 89, 91, 121, 123, 138–139, 144, 146, 149, 183, 200–201, 295
Pitt, William 219
Pittsburgh 259
Pius, Antoninus 19, 21
Plague of London 205

309

plague 29, 75, 104, 116, 146, 154, 182–183, 205
Plato 19, 21, 26, 166
Pliny 16
Plonsk 278
Plymouth Brethren 229
Plymouth 189, 195
poet 79, 83, 144, 157, 287
pogroms 49
Poitiers 93
Poland 134, 183, 277, 294
political 10, 52, 72, 74–75, 80, 88, 99–100, 113, 148, 156, 177, 188, 199, 219, 238, 271, 273, 288, 290, 295
politicians 63, 184, 199, 226
politics 92, 97–98, 136, 219, 276
poll-tax 147
Polycarp 17–18, 21–22
polygamy 254–256
Ponticus 21
Pontifex Maximus 71
Poor Law 189
Pope Alexander IV 142
Pope Alexander VI 155
Pope Celestine I 73
Pope Celestine V 146
Pope Damascus 58
Pope Gregory I (Gregory the Great) 64–65, 69, 74–76, 80, 86, 97, 102, 104–105, 111, 130, 146, 149, 181
Pope Gregory II 102, 104–105
Pope Gregory VIII 130
Pope Gregory IX 181
Pope Gregory XI 75, 146, 149
Pope Innocent I 64
Pope Innocent II 114
Pope Innocent III 139, 141
Pope John Paul II 292, 294
Pope John XXIII 292
Pope Julius II 156–157, 160
Pope Leo I 70–71, 73
Pope Leo III 104–105
Pope Leo IX 105
Pope Leo X 159–160, 163
Pope Martin V 150
Pope Paul III 180
Pope Paul VI 291
Pope Urban II 103, 121–122, 125
Pope Urban VI 149
pope 29, 47, 99, 109–110, 123, 147, 161, 165, 169–170, 179, 183, 188–189,
Pope, Alexander 208
Popish Plot 205
Portiuncula 139
Portugal 182, 218
Pothinus 21–22
Pounds, John 228
poverty 113, 126, 141, 150, 183, 251, 280, 283, 290
Prague 149–150
Praise–God Barbon 199
Pravda 294
prayer 11, 14, 20, 24, 52–53, 58, 65, 74, 81–82, 88, 91, 96, 102–103, 113, 123, 128, 141, 147, 162, 170–171, 174, 184, 191, 197, 200, 204, 211, 232, 245, 256, 270, 277, 280, 286, 291, 295
preachers 9, 44, 60, 63, 72, 75, 114, 123, 133, 141, 147, 161, 171, 173, 176, 182, 200, 203, 210–211, 213, 221, 229–231, 236, 276, 293–297
Precisians 177
Predestination 61
predestined 175, 192, 220
presbyter 17–18, 25, 32, 44
Presbyterianism of Scotland 176–177
Presbyterians 191, 196, 283
President Carter 284
President Truman 278
pride 58, 144, 296
priesthood of all believers 164, 173, 191, 202
Priestley, J.B. 262
Priestley, Joseph 209

priests 10, 16, 27–29, 33, 35, 41, 52, 58, 60, 63, 65, 71, 78, 81, 86, 100–101, 103, 116, 118, 122, 137, 147, 149–150, 163–164, 173, 175, 180–181, 185–186, 188, 190, 194, 202, 220, 228, 244–245, 266, 272, 285, 288, 290, 292
Prince of Peace 125
prince 98, 127, 129, 156, 164, 167, 173, 199, 231
Princeton College 211
Printing 151–153, 164, 172
Pripet Marshes 264
prisoners 160, 166, 185, 212, 215, 223, 276, 288
prisons 28, 204, 212, 223, 272, 295
proletarians 244
Promised Land 49, 195, 296
proofs for the existence of God 109, 208, 240
prophetess 89
prophets 19, 22, 87–93, 164, 193, 243, 285
proselytising 120
Protestant ethic 175
Protestant Reformation 193, 294
Protestantism 12, 61–62, 76, 154, 164, 167, 169, 174–177, 180–181, 183, 188, 190–192, 193, 199, 205, 229, 234, 259, 268, 276, 294
Prouille 141
Psalms 58, 62, 102, 160, 212
Psalter 80
Psychiatric Hospital 287, 289
psychiatry 249, 251
pulpit 64, 150, 202, 208, 213, 230, 276, 294
Punic Wars 23
Purgatory 144, 149, 161–162, 181
Puritanism 29, 92, 176–177, 188, 190–191, 194–197, 200–202, 204, 212
Pyranees 98

Quakers 203–204, 223
Quarry Hill 263
Queen Elizabeth I 176, 186, 188–191, 223–224, 297
Queen Isabella 182
Queen Mary 170, 174
Queen Victoria 223, 235, 262, 297
Quimby, Phineas 257
Quintus 18
Qumran 52, 64
Quo Vardis 15
Qur'an 90–91
Quraish 87–88

Rabbi Akiva 10–11
Rabbi Jonathan Sacks 280
Rabbi Lord Jacobovits 275
rabbis 20, 96, 243, 277
Ragged School 228–229
Raikes, Robert 228
Raleigh, Sir Walter 189, 195
Ramadan 91
Ratushinskaya, Irina 285, 287–288
Ravenna 71, 75, 97, 105
razzia 88
reconciliation 137, 271
Red Indians 211, 262
Red Sea 129
Reformation 12, 23, 31, 36, 148, 150, 160–161, 165–166, 169–170, 172–177, 180, 182, 193, 200–201, 254, 294
Reformed Church of Amsterdam 192
Reformers 109, 146, 153–154, 160, 165, 169–174, 176, 180, 182, 188–191
refugees 54, 126, 130, 244, 275, 280, 290
Reich Church 276
relics 36, 58, 82, 123
religionless Christianity 276
Religions of the Book 96

religions 16, 87, 91, 96, 120, 127, 251–252, 254, 257, 262, 271
religious freedom 204
religious leaders 87, 226
Remigius 74
Remus 71
Renaissance 144, 153–154, 157, 262
repentance 163, 180, 200, 230, 211
Republic 153, 258, 280–281
Republican Commonwealth 199
Restoration 199–201, 204, 254
Resue, Vera 293–294
resurrection 22, 27, 42
Revelation 14, 96
revolution 101, 156, 209, 215, 223, 243–244, 258, 262
revolutionary 200, 218, 295
Reynolds, Sir Joshua 228
Rheims 74, 151
rhetoric 59, 108
Rhine 74, 98, 127
Rhineland 133, 242, 267
Rhodes 126
Rhone 22
Ricci, Matteo 184, 186
Richard I 130
Richard II 147
Richelieu 194
Richmond 146
Ridley, Nicholas 171
Rio de Janeiro 240, 294
Ripon 197
Ritz 65
River Glen 81
River Swift 148
Robespierre 183
Robinson, Haddon 230
Rochester 81
Rodriguez, Simon 185
Rogers, David 288
Roman Catholic Church 75, 177, 276, 292
Roman Catholicism 62, 174, 204
Roman Catholics 173, 181, 191, 205, 229
Roman Empire 10, 14, 23, 33, 35–36, 39, 62, 70, 74, 78, 99, 120
Roman imperialism 41
Roman law 67
Roman soldiers 70, 78
Roman 10–12, 14, 16, 18, 20–21, 23–25, 28, 30, 32–33, 35–36, 39, 41, 55, 59, 61–62, 67, 70–71, 74–75, 81–83, 96, 99, 104–105, 115, 120, 144, 173–174, 177, 181, 191, 204–205, 213, 229, 238, 276, 292
Romania 16
Rome 10, 14–19, 23–25, 27–30, 33, 35, 38, 54, 56–59, 61–62, 64–65, 70–75, 80, 96–99, 104–105, 109, 113, 120, 132–134, 137, 139, 142–143, 146–147, 149, 153–155, 157, 160, 162, 164, 168, 170, 180, 182, 188, 205, 294
Romero, Oscar 297
Romulus 71
Ross, Reverend J.J. 260
Rouen 151, 264
Roundheads 197
Rousseau, Jean–Jacques 218
Rubiev, Andrei 104
Rugby 263
Rule of Faith 22
Rump Parliament 199
Runcie, Archbishop Robert 275
Russell, Charles Taze 259–260
Russellites 259
Russia 101, 133–134, 238, 244, 262, 278, 284, 287, 297
Russia, Cyril of 134
Russia, Grand Duchess Elizabeth of 297
Russian 12, 39, 104, 157, 264, 272, 281, 284–288, 297
Russian communism 39, 284
Russian Orthodox Church 104, 285
Rusticus 20

310

Sabbath 205
sackcloth 57, 183
sacraments 40–41, 102, 133, 154, 164, 175, 180–181
sacrifice of Christ 164
sacrilege 71, 169
Sadducees 10
saint's days 118
Saint–Argenteuil 111
Saint–Geneviève 74
Saint–Gildas–des–Rhuis 112
saints 27, 29, 36, 58, 61, 111, 144, 163, 183, 254, 267, 290, 297
Sajda 89
Sakharov, Andrei 288
Saladin 128–132
Saladin's Tithe 130
Salem 204
Salisbury cathedral 190
Salona 34
Salt Lake City 255
Salvation Army 236–237
salvation 22–23, 42, 46, 59, 110, 129, 158–159, 175, 177, 192–193, 213, 225, 259, 283
San Salvador 297
Sancion 186
Sanctus 21
Sangster, William 9
Sankey, Ira 233, 293
Saracens 132, 140
Sardis 21
Sarejevo 263
sari 91
Satan 202, 237
sati 221
Sattler, Michael 192
Savannah 212
Saviour 18, 20, 44, 47, 122, 237
Savonarola 153–154, 157
Saxon 101–102, 116, 161
Saxony 164, 294
Scandinavia 100, 182, 238
schism 12, 29–30, 40–41, 61, 92, 105, 149
Schleirmacher, Friedrich 240
Schnoudi 66
scholars 14, 19, 24, 28, 30–31, 47, 54, 58, 79, 87, 99, 108–109, 111, 113–114, 142, 146, 158, 174
scholarship 64, 99, 108–109, 260
Scholastica 64–65
Scholasticism 61, 108, 191
schools 19, 21, 30–32, 59, 75, 80, 83, 96, 99, 108, 153, 159, 166, 175, 197, 204, 209, 212, 220–221, 225–226, 228–229, 231–232, 235, 243, 247, 249, 251–252, 271, 275–276, 280, 290
Schopenhauer, Arthur 248
Schweitzer, Albert 268–271
Science and Health 256
science 31, 96, 208–209, 249, 256–257, 297
scientific 155, 209, 242
Scilla 24
Scooby 195
Scopes monkey trial 242
Scotland 19, 80, 169, 176–177, 188–190, 196–197, 199, 211, 221, 225, 233
Scots 19, 78, 82, 197–199
Scott, Captain Robert 299
Scott, Coretta 295
Scott, Orange 238
scribe 79
Scripture 22–23, 25, 27, 31–33, 45, 60, 65, 134, 149–150, 159, 164–165, 172–173, 177, 181, 191, 203, 254, 286, 292
Scythians 64
Sea of Galilee 89, 129
Sebaste 38
Second Crusade 128
Second Vatican Council 292
second coming 259
sects 10, 14, 26, 59, 219, 254, 257, 259

secular 67, 118, 151, 175, 182, 277, 284
Secularisation 90
Segregation 295–296
Seljuk Turks 121
Selma 296
Senate 20, 296
senators 29, 70
Separatists 194
Sephardic Jews 96
Septuagint 31, 58
sepulchre 120–121, 125, 130, 157
Serampore College 221
Serbia 289
Sergius 104
sermons 56, 60, 63–64, 87, 120–121, 139, 142, 147, 150, 162, 171, 175–176, 191, 208, 210, 213–214, 220–221, 230, 256, 270, 286, 289, 296
Servetus, Michael 175
Seven Wonders of the Ancient World 30
Severus, Alexander 27
Seville 96
sexual love 114
sexuality 62, 250, 252
Seymour, Jane 169
Seymour, William J. 238
Shaftesbury, Anthony Ashley Cooper 224–226, 228–229, 231
Shakespeare, William 144, 189, 201, 249
Sharon 254
Sheffield 229, 233
Shepherd of Hermas 27
Shiites 92–93
Shintoism 283
Shirkuh 128
shizo 288
shrines 36, 86, 101, 138–139, 183, 202, 258
Siam 282
Sicca 35
Siena, Catherine of 148, 150
Sierra Leone 223
sin 18, 23, 61–62, 103, 110–111, 162–163
Singapore 186
sinners 56, 60–61, 200, 236
Sircius 56
Sister Teresa 290
Sisters of Loreto 290
Sistine Chapel 157–158
Skopje 289
slavery 82, 109, 204, 214, 219–222, 225, 238
slaves 11, 21, 38, 75, 78, 101, 185, 211, 218–220, 296
Slavia 12
Slavs 134
Small Zone 288
Smith, Joseph 254–255
Smyrna 17–18, 22
Smyth, John 194
social justice 243
socialism 245
Society of Friends 203
Society of Jesus 183
Socrates 20, 26, 249
Soissons 113
Solomon 115, 125–126
Solzhentsyn, Alexander 284–285
Something Beautiful for God 291
Son of God 10, 20–22, 24–25, 44–46, 48, 54, 56, 104–105
Sorbonne 269
South Africa 221–222, 294, 297
Southern Baptist 293
Southern France 96, 98, 121, 146
Southwark 138, 230
sovereign 169, 189, 272
sovereignty of God 175
Soviet Union 287, 289
Spain 93, 96, 120, 156, 181–182, 189, 218
Spanish Armada 189, 201
Spanish Inquisition 182

Spanish 56, 96, 182–184, 189, 201, 290
Spanish–Arabic culture 96
Speaker of the House of Commons 167, 199, 232, 282
speaking in tongues 26, 238
Spencer, Herbert 241
Spirit 20, 22–23, 25, 27, 46, 48, 54, 56–57, 73, 82, 105, 108, 139, 147–148, 159, 188–189, 196, 203, 208–210, 238, 271, 277, 280
spiritual exercises 184–185
spirituals 211
Spitalfields 194
Spurgeon's Homes 231
Spurgeon, Charles Haddon 229–231, 233, 254
St Albans 33
St Andrew's Castle 176
St Chad 202
St Damian 139
St Denise 98, 111
St Denise, Abbey of in Paris 111
St John's Ambulance Service 126
St Martin's Place 268
St Mary's Church in Leeds 263
St Paul's Church 159, 201, 205, 263
St Paul's School 159
St Peter's Church 99, 157, 160, 163
St Petersburg 244
St Thomas 185, 235
St Vincent's 229
Stalin, Joseph 249, 284–285, 288
Stanley, Henry Morton 222
statements of belief 40
Statue of Liberty 196
stigmata 140
Stock, Thomas 228
Stott, John 254
Strasbourg 152, 173–174, 269
Stratus Quadratus 18
Stribo, Jakoibek of 150
Studd, C.T. 233
Studd, Edward 233
Students' Christian Movement 233
Stylite, Simon 66
Suffolk 101, 209
Sufis 92
Sunday Schools 226, 228, 232
Sunday 38, 46, 48, 212, 230–231, 245
Sunna 90
Sunnis 89–90, 92
suns 42, 123
Superman 249, 300
superstitions 71, 147, 160
Supreme God 42–43
suras 90
Sussex College at Cambridge 197
Swansea 281
Sweden 291
Swiss 173, 192, 251
Switzerland 173, 195, 272, 276, 280, 291
Syagrius 74
symbols 40, 252
synagogues 49, 57, 274–275, 277
synods 109, 191
synthesis 108, 143
Syria 57, 65–66, 86, 88–89, 140
Syriac 49
Syrian Christians 130

Tabard Inn in Southwark 138
Tabernacle 205, 230–231, 233, 256
Tacitus 14–15
Tagaste 59
Taiwan 282
Takrit 128
Talmudic academies 277
Tangier 70
Tapiedi, Lucian 297
Tarragona 29
Taurus Mountains 64, 124–125, 127
Tax reforms 153
Taylor, Hudson 221
tea 186, 256, 265
teachers 82, 175, 228

311

Tearfund 280
Tel Aviv 273
Temperance and Clothing Societies 231
Temple Mount 128
Temple 10, 71, 87, 104, 115, 125–126, 128, 190
Ten Articles of Faith 170
Terminalia 33
Tertullian 16, 24–27, 29, 36, 96, 245, 299
Tetzel 160–161
The Book of Common Prayer 171, 173, 200
The Book of Mormon 254
The Crucible 182, 204
The Descent of Man 242
The Divine Comedy 144
The First Blast of the Trumpet against the Monstrous Regiment of Women 176
The Freethinker 31
The Grand Failure 284
The Hallelujah Army 237
The History of King Richard III 166
The Imitation of Christ 220
The Institutes 174
The Last Supper 155
The Martyr's Mirror 193
The Mine's Act 226
The Origin of Species 241
The Place of the Pure Heart 291
The Praise of Folly 159
The Prince 125, 156, 164, 167, 189, 199
The Quest of the Historical Jesus 269
The Recuyell of the Historyes of Troy 152
The Small Woman 282
The Trumpet Call 286–287
The War Cry 236
the priesthood of all believers 164, 173, 191, 202
Thebes 53
theologian 45, 54, 60, 62, 75, 102, 113, 175, 194, 230, 269
theological 40, 44, 47–48, 55, 61–62, 66, 99, 102, 105, 111–112, 163, 165, 173, 175, 190–191, 208–209, 214, 240–242, 269, 283
theology 23, 31–32, 61, 73, 79, 83, 99, 102, 108, 142, 150, 154, 156, 174–176, 191, 194, 220, 245, 269, 276, 292
Theophanes 104
Theotokos 73
Therese 290
Thessalonica 57
Third Reich 277
Thirty–nine Articles 191
Thomas Ball Barratt 238
Thor and Odin 101
Thor 98, 101
Through the Bible in Eighty Days 11, 64
Thruis 35
Tiber 70
Tiberius 129–130
Tienstin 281
tithe 91, 130
tithing 193
Toc H 266
Tocco, William of 143
Toledo 96, 120
Tolstoy, Count Leo 287
tombs of martyrs 36
torture 28, 32, 35, 71, 121, 181
Toulouse, Raymond of 121
Tours 49, 51, 55, 74, 102, 124, 215
Tours, Berengar of 102
Tours, Gregory of 74
Tours, Martin of 51, 55
Tower of London 117, 136, 168, 171
trade–unions 283

traditions 7, 11, 23, 55, 78–79, 81–83, 87, 90, 93, 108–110, 147, 181, 191, 244, 254, 267
traditors 34, 41, 60, 78
Trafalgar Square 268
Tralles, Anthemius of 114
translations 159, 172, 221
transubstantiation 102–103, 149, 169, 175, 181
Travers, Walter 190
treason 137, 168, 171, 182, 255, 277
Tridentine Index 181
Trier 242
Trinity 10, 27, 47–48, 54, 56, 78–79, 91, 113, 209, 255
Tripoli 70, 127
True Word 31
Trypho 20
Tubingen 276
Tunisia 16, 23, 59
Turkey 44, 127, 234
Turkish Ottoman Empire 289
Turkish 120, 124, 152, 289
Turks 120–121, 123, 125–127, 152, 183, 278
Tuscany 153
Tyndale, William 167–168, 171–172
tyrannical 109, 170
Tyre 130, 132

Uganda 297
Ukraine 134, 286
Umayyad dynasty 93
Unitarianism 204, 209
United States 183, 255–256, 262, 291, 295
Universal faith 46
University of Basle 248
University of Berlin 269
University of Naples 142
University of Wittenberg 162, 172
university 59, 108, 111, 141, 147, 149, 159, 161, 166, 170, 175, 190, 205, 219, 243, 256, 271, 291, 296
US Congress 255
Uskudar 234–235
Utah 255
Utopia 167

Valencia 120
Valens 18
Valentinian 56
Valentinois, Duke of 156
Valerian 29
Vandals 62, 70–71, 96
Vans, Jim 293
Vatican Hill 160
Vatican 146, 160, 292
Vazeille, Mary 214
vendetta 122, 149
Venice 126, 185
Vermont 254–255
Versailles 266
Vespers 138
vestments 104, 150, 202
Vicars, George 205
Victoria Falls 221
Victorian 201, 229–230, 236
Vienna 173, 249–250, 272
Vienne 21–22
Vietnam 290
Vigilantius 58
Vikings 100–102, 109, 126
Vins, Georgi 285
Virgil 144
Virginia 189, 211
Visigoths 70
Viterbo 143
Vladivostok 281
Voltaire, Francois 208
von Liechtenstein, Leonhand 192
von Westphalen, Baroness 243
Vulgate 58, 181

Waddell, Helen 111
Wagner, Richard 248
Wales 198, 211
Wang Zhiming 297
Waraqa 86
Ward, William 221
Warrington Academy 209
Wartburg Castle 172
Washington 295–296
Watchtower 259
Wembley 293–294
Wesley, Charles 212–213
Wesley, John 212, 214–215, 219–220, 293–294
Wesley, Samuel 212
Wesley, Susannah 212, 215
Wessex 102, 109
West Indies 219, 221, 262
Western church 23, 46, 54–55, 58, 75, 156
Western Empire 96
Western Europe 72, 79, 114, 123, 140
Western philosophy 142
western monasticism 53, 64
western world 100, 108, 137, 153
Westminster Abbey 220, 222, 235, 268, 297
Westminster 137, 152, 203
Whitby 83, 237
Whitechapel 236
Whitefield, George 210, 212, 220
Wilberforce, Samuel 242
Wilberforce, William 218–219, 228, 242
Wilkinson, Kitty 224
William II (Rufus) 109–110
William the Conqueror 109, 124
Williams, George 232
Willibrord 98
witches 202–204
Wittenberg 161–162, 164–165, 172, 294
Wolsey, Cardinal Thomas 167–169
Woodforde, James 214
Wooller 81
Worcester 169, 171, 263–264, 281
World War I 278
World War II 279, 283
Worms 123, 164–165, 172
worship 19–20, 24, 28, 34, 36, 38, 40, 48, 52, 54, 57, 71, 87–89, 91, 101–102, 104–105, 117–118, 147, 149, 169, 171, 203–205, 208, 238, 256, 276, 281, 285
Wren, Christopher 205
Wyclif, John 146, 149, 151, 161, 171–172, 213

Xavier, Francis 184–186
Xystus 29

Yajiro 186
Yale 209
Yangcheng 281–282
Yarmuk 89
Yes and No 113
YMCA 226, 232–233
York 35, 78, 81, 99, 110, 117, 137, 196, 211, 230, 233, 262, 269–272, 278, 294
Yorkshire 7, 81, 195, 281, 290
Young, Brigham 255–256
Youth for Christ 293
Ypres 264
Yugoslavian 290

Zagorsk 104
Zambezi 222
Zamparini, Louis 293
zealots 92, 208
Zionism 271–273, 278–279
Zoroaster 258
Zurich 173, 192
Zwingli, Ulrich 165, 173–175

312